EDWIN MUIR: MAN AND POET

P. H. BUTTER

EDWIN MUIR:
MAN AND POET

GREENWOOD PRESS, PUBLISHERS
WESTPORT, CONNECTICUT

Library of Congress Cataloging in Publication Data

Butter, Peter H
    Edwin Muir, man and poet.

    Reprint of the ed. published by Oliver & Boyd,
Edinburgh which was issued as no. 7 in Biography
and criticism.
    Bibliography: p.
    Includes index.
    1. Muir, Edwin, 1887-1959. I. Title.
PR6025.U6Z58 1976   828'.9'12 [B]   76-11018
ISBN 0-8371-8169-0

Copyright © P. H. Butter 1966

First published in 1966 by Oliver & Boyd, Edinburgh

Reprinted with the permission of Peter Butter

Reprinted in 1976 by Greenwood Press,
a division of Williamhouse-Regency Inc.

Library of Congress Catalog Card Number 76-11018

ISBN 0-8371-8169-0

Printed in the United States of America

Foreword

A biography of Edwin Muir can be no more than a footnote to his own *Autobiography* and to his *Collected Poems*. Nevertheless I thought it would be worth while to collect his letters and the memories, while they were still available, of those who knew him, and to try to relate his life and his work. I am very much indebted to all the many people who have helped me—by providing letters and information, by giving permission to quote copyright material, and in other ways. Most of the more important of these debts are acknowledged in the course of the book and in the bibliography; but I am grateful to all who have written to me or talked with me about Muir or have helped me in other ways. I would still be glad to hear from any one who has letters or other relevant material which I have not seen.

My chief debt, of course, is to Mrs Muir—for her unfailing kindness and generosity to me, added to the debt which I, in common with all those who love Muir's work, owe to her for her part in making its production possible.

P. H. B.

Bridge of Weir
May 1966

v

Acknowledgments

For permission to quote from Edwin Muir's writings, thanks are due to Mrs Willa Muir, and to the publishers of the following works: *Collected Poems 1921-1958* and *The Narrow Place* (Faber & Faber, Ltd, and the Oxford University Press, New York); *Chorus of the Newly Dead, An Autobiography,* and *First Poems* (Hogarth Press); and *Poor Tom* (J. M. Dent & Sons, Ltd).

Acknowledgments are also due to Mrs T. S. Eliot for permission to quote from T. S. Eliot's letters and to A. P. Watt & Son and Victor Gollancz, Ltd for *Autobiography of David,* ed. Ernest Raymond.

Grateful thanks are finally due to the B.B.C. who have proved as generous to his biographer as they were to Muir himself.

Contents

Abbreviated Titles

A.	=	*An Autobiography.*
C.N.D.	=	*Chorus of the Newly Dead.*
C.P.	=	*Collected Poems: 1921-58* (2nd edition).
E.L.S.	=	*Essays on Literature and Society*
E.P.	=	*The Estate of Poetry.*
L.	=	*Latitudes.*
M.	=	*The Marionette*
P.A.	=	*The Present Age.*
P.T.	=	*Poor Tom.*
S.F.	=	*The Story and the Fable.*
S.J.	=	*Scottish Journey.*
S.N.	=	*The Structure of the Novel.*
S.S.	=	*Scott and Scotland.*
T.	=	*Transition.*
T.B.	=	*The Three Brothers.*
V.T.T.	=	*Variations on a Time Theme.*
W.M.	=	*We Moderns.*

I

Orkney

I

THE island of Wyre in the Orkneys is about two miles long and one mile across at its broadest. The ground rises gently from the sea to no more than about a hundred feet high in the middle. From a pier opposite the much larger and hillier island of Rousay to the North a road runs through the centre of the island, connecting up its eight farms. There is a Post Office, a shop, a ruined twelfth-century chapel and, on a green mound, the remains of a twelfth-century castle. Just below this mound lies the farmhouse of the Bu, a long, low, one-storied house with farm buildings behind pleasantly harmonising with its surroundings. The farm, of ninety-five acres, is the largest on the island. To it in 1889 James Muir brought his wife Elizabeth, their four sons and two daughters, his sister Maggie, and the children's cousin, Sutherland. Like the other farmers on the island he rented the land from General Burroughs, whose large castellated mansion, Trumland House, could be seen across the narrow sound on Rousay. Edwin, the youngest child, had been born two years before on 15 May 1887 at their previous farm, the Folly in Deerness on the west of the Orkney mainland. In middle life he remembered his experiences during the next six years on Wyre with unusual vividness, and these memories were of great importance to him both as man and poet.

Some one like myself who remembers comparatively little of his early childhood approaches childhood memories with some suspicion, but Muir's account of his life on Wyre in the first chapter of his *Autobiography* soon sweeps away all doubts. He writes plainly, quietly, without inflation, sentimentality or whimsy, and creates for us a world which is solid and real as well as wonderful. He heard, from his father and others, stories of fairies, of a mermaid and of other supernatural happenings; but it is not of such things that he himself tells us, but of ordinary things and events seen with a child's freshness and intensity of vision. When there is splendour in the grass, in the earth and every common sight, there is no need to retreat into a world of fantasy.

He was fortunate in his parents. His father came originally from Sanday, an island some twelve miles to the north-east of Wyre, to which Muirs had come over from Caithness in the sixteenth century in the time of the Stewart Earls, when the Scots were consolidating their rule over the previously Norse Orkneys. He was "a little, slight man with the soft brown beard of one who had never used a razor", a narrowish face, long delicate nose and large, fastidious lips; his head inclined sideways owing to a contracted neck muscle. He was slightly deaf and very embarrassed by it, and fond of talking to himself. He was a good story-teller; a man of gentle and meditative character; religious, "but not strict or ostentatiously pious". One of his favourite sayings was: "Never lift your hand to a bairn in anger. Wait, and you may change your mind." The worst punishment the children knew was an occasional clip across the ears from their father's soft cap. "Afterwards he would sit back looking ashamed."[1] Mr Magnus Flaws, who was a child on Wyre with Muir, remembers James Muir as "a fine gentleman"—a phrase which shows the pleasant lack of class-consciousness in Orkney. A fine gentleman is simply some one of fine and gentle character; the phrase can be used without any sense of paradox of a person in any walk of life. James Muir, I was told, had in youth been fond of the bottle, but gave it up after one of the children who was sleeping with him said: "I don't like the smell of that coo's milk you've been drinking, father." He was not a very efficient farmer. The singing at the Bu was famous, Magnus Flaws told me; and "when James of the Bu came round to our house in the evening, we children never got our home-work done", but sat up listening to the stories and the singing. Not only the neighbouring children's home-work, but the work on the farm also was sometimes behindhand. One day the landlord came over

[1] *A.*, pp. 25-7.

from Rousay, and pointing in his military way with a short cane at muck which had not been removed from byre or stable for several days said: "Muck, muck; muck means money—if it's in the right place." Writing to Kathleen Raine near the end of his life Muir admitted that he "would have been a bad farmer, as my father was—and I'm thankful for that too; he had all the good qualities of the Orkney peasantry, without the bad acquisitive ones that narrow life down".[2]

His mother, Muir says, had greater practical sense than his father, but was just as gentle. Her stories were of the actual past, whereas his father's were mainly of the supernatural. She had a greater regard for appearances and a deeper family sense; her children were always in the right to her, and she wanted them to "get on". She had a deep respect for religion, but not the spontaneous piety of her husband. She was fond of singing—hymns and traditional ballads. Muir could not remember ever hearing his parents exchanging a discourteous word or raising their voices to each other.

Though themselves by nature gentle and tolerant Muir's parents had been affected by something life-denying in the religious tradition they had grown up in. They regarded "profane" literature as sinful and thought poetry a vanity (in spite of their own enjoyment of ballads). They gave Muir a childhood in which he could see his vision of Eden, but also perhaps contributed, though blamelessly, to his difficulties and inner divisions in the Glasgow years, and to his lateness in finding his true vocation as a poet.

The family lived within the larger, but still small, community of Wyre. "The farmers did not know ambition, nor the petty torments of ambition", but helped each other when help was needed. In summer the doors stood open, and neighbours (and later on the mainland beggars) were welcomed. The arts of singing and story-telling were a natural part of life. In the Bu there were few books, but these included the *Bible*, *The Pilgrim's Progress* and the poems of Burns. Burns was their only poetry book, but poetry was not for them something which existed only, or even primarily, in books; for they knew hundreds of ballads and songs which had been handed

[2] E. M. to Kathleen Raine, 6 Dec. 1954.

down from generation to generation. "They were part of our life, all the more because we knew them by heart, and had not acquired but inherited them. They were not contemporary in any sense, but entered our present from the past."[3] Poetry of a high order was the communal possession of the whole people. They "had a culture made up of legend, folk-song, and the poetry and prose of the Bible; they had customs which sanctioned their instinctive feelings for the earth; their life was an order, and a good order".[4] They made their own entertainment, filling the long winter evenings with singing, playing on the violin and the melodeon, story-telling and games. And not only their own entertainment; for every man needed to be a craftsman in many crafts on land and in boats. The arts, and various crafts, were a natural part of life—and so was religion. Every Sunday night James Muir gathered his family together to read a chapter and kneel down in prayer. These nights were among Muir's happiest memories. "There was a feeling of complete security and union among us as we sat reading about David or Elijah. My father's prayer, delivered in a sort of mild chant while we knelt on the floor, generally ran on the same lines; at one point there always came the words, for which I waited, 'an house not made with hands eternal in the heavens'."[5] The particular family was thus related to the whole of God's creatures, the particular house to the house in which all are at home.

From his memories of Orkney Muir constructed an image of the good life. He knew well that this was an image, which even in Orkney was broken. Nevertheless the materials out of which the image was constructed were really there. Even now one is conscious there of a greater sense of community than in most other places in Great Britain; and it is easy to believe that it was greater still in the past when communications were less good and there was greater need for mutual help. Now the farmer at the Bu has a land-rover, a tractor and a television set. He told me that the farmers still help each other, but that there is not often need to do so. With a tractor the work of the farm can be done quickly, and people do not often get behindhand. The television keeps the families at home, and

[3] *E. P.*, pp. 9-10.   [4] *A.*, p. 63.   [5] *A.*, p. 26.

there is less making of their own entertainment; the pull of the outer world is more keenly felt. Yet most people there still think theirs a good life—in some ways better than in the past —and do not want to leave. It is a mistake to think of the Orcadians as a quaint, dreamy, poetic people. They are, on the contrary, shrewd, practical and hard-headed. Artists, such as Muir and Stanley Cursiter, have been just as rare there as anywhere else. Dr Hugh Marwick, in his book on Orkney, notes that the islands have produced a large number of professors, especially of science and medicine; and that in general Orcadians have been marked by "rationality and good sense . . . manifestations of reason rather than of imagination or aesthetic taste".[6] Recently they have made the islands prosperous by intensive and skilful farming.

First the home; then the human community of which the family was part; then the animals and the natural surroundings —all seemed to the child Muir to be alive and to fit together. "The sky fitted the earth then."[7] Something of the ancient comradeship between men and animals still existed on the small farms. In the traditional farmhouse the human living quarters, the byre, the stable, the threshing-floor and barn had all been under one long roof, and one could walk through them all through gaps in the internal walls. The Bu is more modern in plan, with the farm buildings seperate from the house, but still very close. Animal life was all around—horses, cows, pigs, insects—and inspired the child with intense and mixed feelings. The horses seemed enormous and filled him with terror and delight. Some insects inspired disgust, even hatred, though he was fascinated by them; but even they were all characters to him, interesting though squalid, "with thoughts that could never be penetrated, inconceivable aims, perverse activities". Flying insects, however, delighted him, for "at that stage the novelty of seeing a creature fly outweighed everything else".[8] Animal pain and death were close as well as fertility and birth. He vividly remembered the ringing of a bull, the animal's bellowing filling the island, and afterwards drops that looked like tears rolling from his eyes and the neat shining ring in his

---

[6] Marwick, *Orkney* (London 1951), p. 244.   [7] *S. F.*, p. 245.
[8] *A.*, pp. 21-2.

nose; and he remembered the killing of a pig which broke loose after its throat had been cut and ran screaming round the yard.

Going out of the back of his home into the farm-yard and then turning to the left the young Muir would have only some two hundred yards to go to get to the round grassy knoll which was even then known as the castle, though at that time no castle could be seen on it but only some large stones sticking out of the ground. From the top of the mound he could see most of the island—a little world small enough to be known intimately, but full of various life and of wonder. This gave a sense of security and peace, but not of isolation or confinement. For most families, including the Muirs, had their own boat, and could voyage out where they would among the islands. The landscape entered deep into his mind. Later, when he began to read of the heroes and heroines of antiquity, it was Wyre, though he had by then left it, that became a sort of universal landscape across which all the characters passed; and the mound came to be associated with Troy. But now he would just play in the ruined chapel with a girl from a neighbouring farm or lie through the long summer afternoons on the mound and watch people passing along the road and boats going slowly through the sound. Over the narrow sound to the north he could see Rousay, the General's house and the high hill behind; and to the north-east Egilsay with the high round tower of St Magnus church—the most beautiful man-made object in view—on the site where the saint had been treacherously killed in the twelfth century. Farther away to the east are Eday, Sanday, Stronsay, and other islands, low lying and difficult to distinguish from one another. One knows that there are straits between, but cannot see them; so one's imagination is led on to picture the unseen shores. Nearer, to the south, is Gairsay rising quite high out of the sea, and to the south and west the Orkney mainland can be seen, in parts quite high. It is a landscape which combines many things in a harmonious way—the human present and the past; the life of men, of animals and of the earth; land, sea, and sky.

One element in the normal landscape that is not present is trees. One might think that this would give an impression of bleakness. In one of Muir's dreams connected with the Bu the scene is transformed by the addition of great trees standing round the house, "their foliage darker and thicker than any I had ever seen, the leaves hanging like dark green tongues one over the other in a motionless security which no wind could reach".[9] His subconscious has added a suggestion of fullness of life and of a southern luxuriance of fertility to the bare simplicity of the Orkney landscape. But the treelessness imparts a special beauty. One sees the shape of the land, and objects stand out clear against the horizon. After his last visit to Orkney in 1956 Muir wrote for a B.B.C. programme: "If you are an Orkneyman, you feel the real shape of the world can lie before you only when you are not fussed by these pretty decorations, the trees. I remember that when I went south to Glasgow at the age of fourteen, and got out of that chaotic city on Sundays for a walk in what was called the country, I wanted to push the woods away so that I might see the land; the trees stifled me, and it took a long time to become reconciled to them and to grow fond of them."

Another distinctive thing is the special quality of the light. In summer the days are very long; indeed at midsummer it is never completely dark, sunset merges into sunrise. This helps to give a sense of leisure; farm work can be done at any time, and there is no need to let life be ruled by the clock. In the child's day the sun is always in the sky; one day merges into another to become one "motionless blue summer . . . in which nothing happened".[10] Nearly everywhere one is near water; light is reflected upwards as well as pouring down from above so that one has almost the sense of the islands floating suspended between heaven and earth. Revisiting Orkney after a long interval Muir found that "the beauty of the light showered from the wide sky and reflected from the spreading waters, and diffused, a double radiance, over the wide fields, was the same beauty [he] had known as a child; and the loneliness of every shape rising from the treeless land, the farm houses and the moving outlines of men and women against the sky, had, as then, the simplicity of an early world".[11]

Muir's childhood world was not a dream world, but a

[9] *A.*, p. 64.　　[10] *A.*, p. 32.　　[11] *A.*, pp. 241-2.

perfectly real and solid one, containing ordinary objects and happenings seen with a freshness which few adults are able to recover even in memory. It contained things which inspired disgust and terror—insects, killings, the dirty red, rag-like stuff left on the ground after the birth of the first two lambs that he saw—as well as things, like his christening suit, which glowed with splendour. But all were accepted as part of a natural order, and all seemed magically close "as if they were magnets drawing me with a palpable power".[12]

The vividness with which he recalled such experiences, in themselves not unusual in a child, contributed to give him in later life his special sense at once of order and disorder. Most people, I suppose, have some image in the mind of a good life, of a good society in which all men live in harmony, an image which contrasts painfully with the disorder within and around them. Those with any religious faith must believe that there is a larger order also, in which earthly life is contained. For most the ideal social order is a perhaps rather sentimental dream, and the supernatural order something believed in rather than perceived. Muir was conscious both of the order and the disorder in a much more direct, physical and visual way than is common. He *saw* dislocation between earth and sky, which had once seemed to fit; he *saw* people and things as twisted from their true natures. This way of looking at things is consonant with the Christian belief in a divinely created, but fallen, world. But he did not see things like this because of any belief. The seeing came first.

Similarly immortality was to be to him a state of being, something experienced rather than just believed in; and here too childhood memories contributed. Trying to recapture his first mental impression of his parents, he could not do so because it was

> overlaid by later memories in which I saw them as a man and a woman, like, or almost like, other men and women. I am certain that I did not see them like this at first; I never thought that they were like other men and women; to me they were fixed allegorical figures in a timeless landscape. Their allegorical changelessness made them more, not less, solid, as

---

[12] *A.*, p. 20.

if they were condensed into something more real than humanity; as if the image 'mother' meant more than 'woman', and the image 'father' more than 'man'. . . . Men and women, and mankind in general, are secondary images, for we know them first as strangers; but our father and mother were never strangers to us, nor our brothers and sisters if we were the last born, as I was. When I was a child I must have felt that they had always been there, and I with them, since I could not account for myself; and now I can see them only as a stationary pattern, changing, yet always the same, not as a number of separate people all following the laws of their different natures.

This experience had a great effect on his poetry in which the people are seldom strongly individualised. They are "fixed allegorical figures in a timeless landscape". They are not abstractions, but solid and real, seen with the intensity of childhood vision, not evolved by the intellect by a process of generalisation. "My brothers and sisters," he goes on, "were new creatures like myself, not in time (for time still sat on the wrist of each day with its wings folded), but in a vast, boundless calm. I could not have put all this into words then, but this is what I felt and what we all feel before we become conscious that time moves and that all things change. That world was a perfectly solid world, for the days did not undermine it but merely rounded it, or rather repeated it, as if there were only one day endlessly rising and setting. Our first childhood is the only time in our lives when we exist within immortality, and perhaps all our ideas of immortality are influenced by it."[13]

This is the strangest thing that he says about childhood. Is it really true that the child experiences the days as if they were only one day endlessly rising and setting, or is it rather that in memory childhood days merge into one, and so give—to the man—the feeling of timelessness? Memory is certainly one means of experiencing this feeling. Proust is the prime explorer here. "But let a sound, a scent already heard and breathed in the past be heard and breathed anew, simultaneously in the present and in the past, real without being actual, ideal without being abstract, then instantly the permanent and characteristic essence hidden in things is freed and our true being which has

[13] *A.*, pp. 24-5.

for long seemed dead but was not so in other ways wakes and revives, thanks to this celestial nourishment. An instant liberated from the order of time has recreated in us man liberated from the same order, so that he should be conscious of it."[14] This is what happened in Muir, as he himself says, when his childhood memories came back to him. Was he then projecting back into childhood an experience which really belonged to the moment when something from the past was recovered rather than to the past itself? I do not think so entirely. For the feeling of timelessness can be entered not only through the door of memory, but also through an unusually intense experience of the present moment. Children live more in the present than adults, and so perhaps are constantly near that way of seeing which comes only occasionally to most older people, when consciousness of time and of self drop away, and things seem to shine, more solid and real than usual, in the light of an eternal present.

When Edwin was seven the family moved to the neighbouring, and not so good, farm of Helzigartha. At about this time he took his first step out of Eden with the onset of a consciousness of change, of death, and of guilt. He had been aware of death and of pain before, of course, but had accepted them, unreflectingly, as part of a natural order. Now a neighbour who had been kind to him died after sufferings described in detail and perhaps with relish by Sutherland as "diabolical". This terrified him and gave him a new, indefinable, sense of wrongness in the outside world, breaking his vision of harmony. More important was a new sense of division and guilt within himself—guilt which he could not understand and so could not cleanse himself of. This phase came after a bad attack of influenza, and was associated with a sack of poisonous sheep dip which his father had left in a field with strict orders that it was not to be touched. He kept away from it; but after the sack had been destroyed he went about in terror because he could not be sure that he had not touched it.

My fear was beyond any argument, so I washed my hands many times a day, until they had a wasted, transparent look,

---

[14] Proust, *Remembrance of Things Past*, trans. Stephen Hudson (London 1931), XII. p. 218.

and pored upon them afterwards in a sort of agony . . . I had gone away into a world where every object was touched with fear, yet a world of the same size as the ordinary world and corresponding to it in every detail: a sort of parallel world divided by an endless, unbreakable sheet of glass from the actual world. For though my world was exactly the same in appearance as that world, I knew that I could not break through my fear to it, that I was invisibly cut off, and this terrified and bewildered me. . . . My sister playing in the sun a few feet away, was in that other world; my brothers cut and gathered hay in it, the ships passed, the days followed one another in it. I could not reach it by getting close to it, though I often tried; for when my mother took me in her arms and laid my head on her shoulder she, so close to me, was in that world, and yet I was outside. How long this lasted I cannot tell, but at last the actual world appeared again in twisted gleams, as through running glass, and the fear and the frenzied longing to cleanse myself went away.[15]

I suppose that something of this kind is not unusual, though to experience it with such intensity is. It was his personal Fall, the eating of the apple which gave knowledge of good and evil. In Eden, in early childhood, there is neither good nor evil; there is innocence. The Fall gives consciousness of evil, but also brings the possibility of the choice of positive good; it is therefore necessary. The road through experience curving back to a higher kind of innocence is one which man must take. Such understanding, of course, was only reached much later. At the time the first consciousness of guilt was merely bewildering and terrifying. It is a sign of his extraordinary sensitivity that he should have reacted so strongly, especially in view of the comparatively favourable circumstances in which he was living. One might expect gloomily moralistic or Calvinistic parents to produce a neurotic feeling of guilt in a child; but his parents were, by all accounts, gentle and tolerant people, whose religion was not of a fanatical kind. The extremity of the child's reaction was the product more of his own fineness of nature than of his environment, though something life-denying in the Scottish religious tradition probably contributed.

I believe that children usually become capable of feeling a

[15] *A.*, pp. 34-5.

sense of guilt by about the age of three, whereas Muir places this experience a good deal later. It may be that the gentleness of his parents, his being the youngest and a rather delicate child, and perhaps rather spoiled by his mother, and his being kept away from school combined to keep him in that state which he calls Eden longer than most children, and that this contributed to make this state more available to him later in memory than it is to most people. If the feeling of guilt came to him later and more suddenly than to most that would also help to explain the intensity of his reaction. He suggests in the *Autobiography* that this consciousness of guilt may have arisen from "the obsession which all young children have with sex . . ., natural in itself, but coloured with guilt by the thoughts of their elders".[16] The way in which a similar stage in the life of Mansie Manson in his novel, *Poor Tom,* is treated suggests that his obscure sense of guilt about sex may have been projected retrospectively on to his friendship with the little girl with whom he had played through the long summer days in the roofless chapel. Their friendship had taken place in Eden and had been quite innocent, but the later consciousness of sex and of the feelings of guilt associated with it by adults may have cast a destructive light backwards upon it.

It is important to remember that the shades of the prison-house began to fall around the growing boy on Wyre itself. The vision splendid was seen there, and faded there; its fading was inevitable, and was nothing to do with the later departure to Glasgow. It would be sentimental, and reactionary, to identify Eden with a remote pastoral community and the fallen world with the modern world of industrialism. At times he was tempted to do so, to let Orkney stand for innocence and Glasgow for experience; but he was always aware that this was a simplification, and that innocence and experience are universal and have little to do with particular places. Eden may be, and is, experienced anywhere, though some environments are more favourable than others; it must be left, wherever one lives; and the journey back is a spiritual, not a physical, one.

It was at the time when his first world was crumbling that

[16] *A.,* p. 35.

he first went to the small school on the island, one of some fifteen children. Because of his illness he was late in going there; was backward at his work and shy of the other boys. Though Miss Angus the schoolmistress was kind, the school seemed to him a prison; through the high windows of the small, hot room nothing could be seen but the sky. As a young child he had been normally pugnacious, but now he was timid. The older boys used to tease him and play tricks on him; so, as soon as lessons were over, he would seize his cap and run home as fast as he could—once, out of habit, dashing left off the road to the Bu instead of right to his new home at Helzigartha. It was at about this time that the two encounters with another boy, Freddie Sinclair, took place, which later loomed large in his imagination. On the first occasion he fought with Freddie for the possession of a knife, and knocked him down so that he lay crying on the grass. On the second Freddie wanted to fight again, but Edwin was afraid and ran home in terror. "What I was afraid of I did not know; it was not Freddie, but something else."[17] I think the something else was the aggressiveness in himself displayed in the first fight. As a young child he could accept his own pugnacity as part of the natural order; but in his new state of guilt he was obscurely afraid of it. Again it is not the rather trivial events themselves which are remarkable, but the extremity of the child's reactions and the way the man is foreshadowed. He was never to be a fighter, could never enjoy being a victor; though stubborn would always prefer to avoid a contest. The conqueror he thought, is to be pitied equally with the vanquished:

> The conqueror before his fallen foe
> (Fingering his useless sword he cannot go,
> But stands in doltish silence, unappeased)[18]

The story fits well into the fable; for after Eden and the Fall came Cain and Abel. His extreme reaction against his own pugnacity and perhaps against his dawning consciousness of sex foreshadows his later neurosis, which was caused in part by his wish to thrust out of sight things, in himself as well as in his surroundings, that he did not want to see.

[17] *A.*, p. 42.   [18] *V. T. T.* IX, in *C. P.*, p. 51.

Pain and guilt were present on Wyre, and also the ordinary necessity to make a living. Rents were high in relation to the prices that could be got for farm produce. A subsistence for a family could be won, but no capital could be accumlated for improvements; and in bad years the stock had to be depleted to pay the rent. One year the Flaws at Russness sold four cattle, and were still thirty shillings short of the £25 needed, the balance being made up by collecting whelks from the shore. The Bu was more than twice as big as Russness; so James Muir must have had to pay £50 or £60 a year for it. He found it too much, and was driven, as his son puts it, out of that farm and then out of Helzigartha by the landlord's exactions. From his own point of view no doubt the General was just charging the usual rent; and if a farmer who did not make proper use of his dung got into difficulties, who was to blame for that? General (later Sir) Frederick Burroughs had been a distinguished soldier, but did not understand the people. Mr Flaws put it charitably to me: "He did not know how to be a good landlord." He had not been brought up to it, and was badly advised. He expected everything to be as in the army. However that may be, the Muir family moved, when Edwin was eight, to another farm of about a hundred acres, Garth, some three miles from Kirkwall on the Orkney mainland.

II

Muir's memories of Garth were coloured by the misfortunes of his family there and by the fact that their failure there led to the greater disasters they suffered in Glasgow. The land was poor, he says; the house damp. His mother was always ill; his brothers and sisters left, one by one, for jobs in Kirkwall, Glasgow, and Edinburgh; his father grew discouraged, strained his heart, and had to give up the farm. After reading his account the visitor to Garth is surprised to find a prosperous-looking farmhouse and to learn from the owner and from his neighbours that it is now considered to be a very good farm, one of the best in the area. But one need not doubt the substantial truth of what Muir says. The farm-house is new, and money has been spent on the land, for manuring, drainage, etc., which in the old days the tenants could not afford. Since those days scientific knowledge and capital have made many improvements in Orkney, in the quality of the pasture and of the animals. Edwin used to say that in his day there were only two kinds of cow—those that wandered away (which they frequently did under his absent-minded care) and those that stayed put. Rents here, as on Wyre, were too high in relation to the value of what was produced. One need not think James Muir much, if at all, to blame for the failure at Garth. He strained his heart trying to keep the place going, and this must have contributed to his early death.

From Garth, some 250 feet above sea level, one looks down a slope to Inganess Bay about a mile away to the north. Beyond the large semi-circular bight of the bay the island of Shapinsay can be seen. From this height one can see further than from the Castle on Wyre; the view is in some ways grander, but lacks the intimacy and variety of one's immediate surroundings in Wyre; it is bleaker. In the same way Edwin's horizons were in some ways to expand during his five years here, but his first clear vision of the world had been lost. At the Bu he had lived his own life "separately and in peace, but now I felt that need to become at once like grown-up people which tortures growing boys: it was as if time had suddenly spoken loud within me".[19] He could no longer see with his own eyes, but tried to see as adults saw and to construct, like others, a protective mask to enable him to live at ease in the adult world.

Garth is only three miles or so from Kirkwall, and from there ships could be seen setting out for Aberdeen and Edinburgh. The pull of possibly greater opportunities in another life was felt; and the family began to break up. At the Bu the family had been for him "a stationary indivisible pattern", but now he became aware of the people around him as individuals. Jimmie, the eldest brother, was working in Kirkwall, had a life of his own there separate from the family, and yet when he came home was still the brother Edwin had worshipped as a child. This paradox of unity and separateness worried Edwin. Jimmie, he thought, was the one of the children that most resembled their father, having the same

[19] *A.*, p. 66.

sensitive, gentle nature and the same sense of fun. The difference of their ages, eleven years, was too great for there to have been any close friendship between them when Edwin was a boy, and later their interests were very different. Jimmie lived on into the second world war—solid, dependable, rather conservative-minded, a buyer in a Glasgow store. When he came to see Edwin and Willa in Edinburgh the people they were living with were struck by the fact that they, though the hosts, gave the head of the table at meals to Jimmie as head of the family. Willie, the second boy, went into a lawyer's office in Kirkwall and later to Edinburgh. He seemed to those who knew them at the time the ablest of the brothers, and was expected to go far. He was very intelligent as well as an expert musician, but sardonic and subject to deep fits of despondency. Johnnie was a wild, adventurous boy; witty, able to make friends easily; he chafed against the restrictions of life on the farm and later in the shop in Kirkwall where he worked, and wanted to go to sea. Elizabeth, six years older than Edwin, was a spirited, intelligent girl who "scorned stupidity and easy sentiments and shouldered responsibilities far beyond her years". Later, in Glasgow, she married a house-painter, George Thorburn, who was frequently out of work in the depressed years in the 20s and 30s; she had to go into domestic service to keep the household going. Clara, Edwin's closest companion as a child, was "kind, patient, and unexacting, and grew up into an easy, comfortable woman".[20] Also in the household were Aunt Maggie and cousin Sutherland. She was a bitter, disappointed woman, and talked much of the lovers she had rejected as a young girl. Later, living alone in Kirkwall she found release from her disappointments in a gentle piety, which embarrassed Edwin when he last went to see her, he then being in his anti-religious phase. Sutherland was a small, stocky, coarse-grained man. He was lecherous, and used to go out in a boat on calm summer nights from Wyre with other young men to try his fortune with women on neighbouring islands; he had a number of illegitimate children. His language was very free, and when drunk he would invent words. Edwin's parents, though religious and moral in their own lives,

[20] *A.*, p. 81.

seem to have accepted him easily and tolerantly.   Illegitimacy
was indulgently regarded.   His mother used to talk of a woman
in Deerness who had had seven illegitimate children, and though
speaking of her refusal to marry with disapproval would always
add, "she was a fine lass".

To the growing boy the family now appeared not as a
single harmonious whole but as a number of differing, no doubt
sometimes discordant, personalities developing in different
directions.   Shy, sensitive, delicate in health and often allowed
to stay away from school, the youngest and perhaps spoiled by
his mother, he may well have been regarded with some
irritation by his brothers at times.   No longer were things in
their place;   there was a consciousness of discontent and of
division both within and between people.   One can say that he
was growing up and coming to grips with the real world;   and,
also with truth, that he was losing his vision of the larger
realities he had been conscious of as a child.

From Garth, looking north towards the bay, one sees below
the main road winding away to the right to Deerness and to
the left over the hill to Kirkwall.   On this road Muir saw for
the first time gigs, brakes, bicycles and cars;   for there had been
no such vehicles on Wyre.   Behind the house a smaller road
goes up past the large farm of Wideford to join the main road;
once over the crest Kirkwall in its bay with the great red
Cathedral of St Magnus comes into view.   Going down past
the substantial houses of Dundas Crescent one reaches Kirkwall
Grammar School, to which Muir used to go, rather irregularly,
during his time at Garth.   Sometimes he was ill, sometimes
his help was needed on the farm, and on the short midwinter
days he had to leave early to get home before dark.   School
was a bigger (in a sense) world than he had known before,
with its large staff and several hundred pupils.   He was
beginning to grow up, to adapt himself to life and to people.
He did not hate this school, as he had the one on Wyre;   for
with part of his mind he accepted what it stood for.   And yet
for most of the time he dreaded it.   The irregularity of his
attendance meant that he was often behindhand with his work.
At first it was a shock to be flung in the midst of so many new
faces;   but he presently found that he could make friends.

Mr James Groundwater, who still lives in Kirkwall, remembers him at school as a shy, remote boy, not especially good at work—he was somewhere in the middle of the class; but says that even in those days he felt the presence of a special quality in him, difficult to define, a purity. Stanley Cursiter, the artist, was also at the school, and became a friend. "I first remember Edwin Muir", he writes, "when he came to Kirkwall School, a fair-haired, pale boy, in a light-coloured suit with a Norfolk jacket neatly buttoned and the belt fastened. This impression of his being snugly buttoned up in shy self-protection continued, but we in his class quickly found that this seemingly colourless boy knew all the answers. When examination time came he was always top—or near the top—and we knew that Edwin was 'different'."[21] (This was probably during Edwin's final year at school, when he was able to attend more regularly. By then he had read more than the others, and was especially good at general knowledge.) Cursiter used to bicycle over from his home on the other side of the town on Saturdays and meet Edwin at the bridge over the Wideford burn; then they would fish in the burn and play on the beach. Others who remember him then are Miss Marian McNeill, the writer, and her sister, Margaret, who were daughters of a well-known minister and doctor. There was less sense of class divisions in Orkney than elsewhere at that time. Every one went to the Grammar School, and mixed together naturally. The McNeill sisters remember him as a quiet, studious boy, very tidily dressed, with an air of "difference", of distinction about him even then. Margaret McNeill especially felt that he would do something remarkable, and used to wonder what had happened to him during the long time during which they lost touch with him.

Mr Cursiter's memory of Edwin's wide reading confirms his own account of his avid devouring of print from the age of nine onwards. He read largely and without plan everything that he could lay hands on—the books that happened to be in the farm, his school books and later books from the Borough library. Much that he read was beyond him and much was rubbish; but he began to have an appreciation of good poetry

[21] *The Orcadian*, 8 Jan. 1959.

—of Keats and *As You Like It*, for example. What delighted him most was a volume which contained a condensed version of Morris's *The Earthly Paradise*. "The little book did not, of course, contain all of Morris's huge poem; but it told the stories in simple language, with occasional extracts from the poetry; the story of Atalanta and the apples, of Perseus and Andromeda, of Ogier the Dane and all the Northern heroes and heroines; and it seemed to me that I was watching a new race in my familiar countryside: a race of goddesses, beautiful women, and great warriors, all under the low Northern sky, for even the Greek stories unfolded for me in a landscape very like Orkney."[22]   It was at this time that he decided himself to be a writer, and, to meet his parents' objections to profane literature, that he would write a life of Christ. His imagination was vivid; while herding cows after reading adventure stories in *Chums*, he would glance over his shoulder in case a tiger might be creeping up behind. This was imagination of a more commonplace and lesser kind than he had had as a child. On Wyre his imaginative vision was a perception of splendour in natural things around him, a contact with reality not an escape into fantasy. That this higher type of imagination was still sometimes with him during his time at Garth is suggested by a story in his novel, *Poor Tom*. Mansie Manson, the central character to whom many of Muir's own experiences are demonstrably attributed, remembers a strange experience he had at the age of twelve:

> It took up only a few minutes, but afterwards it seemed to have filled the whole of that summer afternoon, and to have coloured not only the hours which followed, but the preceding hour as well, which became a mysterious time of preparation whose warnings he had not heeded.
> "That strange afternoon" was how he thought of it, and the strangeness had begun with the class being dismissed after the dinner hour. Some state event had just been published, an important event, for it had to do with the royal family, yet human and touching, for it might have happened in any ordinary household; and this was what had made the teacher's voice, for all its reverence, sound almost confidential when he

asked the class to give three cheers. Yet there had been something unreal in the teacher's elation, and although the class were glad to get an unlooked-for holiday, and felt grateful to the royal family, the cheers had a hypocritical ring. Afterwards Mansie's companions had decided to spend the afternoon in town, and he had taken the road alone. In the bright afternoon sun the road looked unusually deserted; on the fields the men and women seemed more active than usual, as though they had just begun the day's work, a day in which time had been displaced in some curious way, making everything both too early and too late. So even the wild flowers along the roadside were unfamiliar, as though they had sprung up that moment, supplanting the ones that should have been there. Still this was the road he had always taken, and so he went on.

It was in the little sunken field sloping down to the burn that it happened. There were generally several horses in this field, and he had always passed them without thinking. This day, however—it may have been because of the displacement of everything, for the shifting of time had subtly redistributed the objects scattered over space as well—there was only one horse, a young dark chestnut with a white star on its brow. Mansie had almost reached the footbridge over the burn before he saw it, for it was standing half-hidden in a clump of bushes. They caught sight of each other at the same moment, and Mansie stopped as though a hand had been laid on his forehead: into his mind came instantaneously, as a final statement of something, the words: "A boy and a horse". For out of the bushes the horse looked at him with a scrutiny so devouring and yet remote that it seemed to isolate him, to enclose him completely in the moment and in himself, making him a boy without a name standing in a field; yet this instantaneous act of recognition came from a creature so strange to him that he felt some unimaginable disaster must break in if he did not tear his eyes away. This feeling was so strong that his body seemed to grow hollow. Then slowly the stone dyke by which he had stopped grew up, wavered, and steadied itself; he put out his hand to it, the stones were rough and warm, and this gave him courage to stand his ground a little longer. But now as he gazed on at the horse, which still stared steadily and fiercely at him, he seemed on the point of falling into another abyss, not of terror this time, but of pure strangeness. For unimaginable things radiated from the horse's eyes; it seemed to be looking at him from another world which lay like a hidden kingdom round it, and in that world it might be anything; and a phrase from a school book, "the kingly judge", came into his mind. And how could he tell what it might do to him? It might trample him to death or lift him up by its teeth and bear him away to that other world. He took to his heels and did not feel safe until he was at the other side of the footbridge, with the burn behind him.[23]

One must emphasize that this is a passage from a novel, and that Mansie is not intended as a self-portrait. But Muir does not often in his novels write with this vividness except out of direct personal experience. So I think the incident must be from life.

III

When Edwin was thirteen the farm had to be given up. Aunt Maggie went to stay with a sister, Sutherland to join cousins in Leith. The elder children had all gone, and only his parents, his sister Clara and Edwin were left; they went to live in a small house in Kirkwall. The advantage for Edwin was that he was able to go to school regularly, and he began to do well there. He was inspired by the excellent teacher of English, Miss Annan. If he could have stayed on a bit longer he would have got into the top form under the Headmaster Mr McEwan, who is said also to have been a remarkable teacher and very good at getting bursaries to university for bright boys. In that case the path to a comparatively easy future might have opened before him.

In spite of his voracious reading and his improved work at school his year in Kirkwall was on the whole an unhappy one. Needing to identify himself with the boys of his own age he turned against his family, and made friends with rough boys of the town, with whom he played savage games of football in a little field called the Craftie near the slaughter-house. "To us in our raw and unhappy state the slaughter-house had an abominable attraction, and the strong stench and sordid colours of blood and intestines seemed to follow us in our play. Our language and manners grew rough; even our friendship had an acrid flavour. There were savage fights in the Craftie, and

[23] *P. T.*, pp. 170-3.

the boys, crying with rage, would have killed each other if they could; yet behind their rage was a sort of sad shame and frustration."[24] In reaction against this he experienced, at the age of fourteen, a rather superficial "conversion" when a revivalist preacher called Macpherson came to the islands. The experience had real, but not lasting, effects; for a time coarse words and thoughts became unendurable to him. It was not a genuine religious conversion; he had no clear knowledge of sin, nor of the need for salvation. Neither the coarse, rough boy in the Craftie nor the "saved" boy giving himself to Christ was the true Edwin. His inner integrity and wholeness were lost—not through his fault, but as part of the process of growing up; and he went to opposite extremes in the effort to be at one with others and to incorporate different elements of the lost wholeness in his life.

Before we leave Orkney there is one other feature of the place that may be mentioned—the sense of a living past that one feels there. Muir does not speak of this much in connection with his childhood, and probably he was not then much conscious of it. The mound near the Bu was just a mound, though it was called the Castle, and the ruined church just a convenient place to play in; the sight of Kirkwall Cathedral was, perhaps, more oppressive than inspiring, for it meant that school was not far off. Nevertheless the Orkney past was to become important to him later, and probably began to mean something even during his boyhood.

It may be said that a child anywhere in Europe is likely to grow up near monuments of the past. Yet one does experience in Orkney an especially vivid sense of a living past. Many of the houses in which people still live are built with the same big flat stones with which the ancient monuments are made. The standing stones set up at the corners of fields and acting as supports for wire are reminiscent in miniature of the great standing stones of the ceremonial rings. Most of the place-names are Norse, and the language retains some traces of Norse in diction and intonation. Muir wrote of "the soft sing-song lilt of the islands, which has remained unchanged for over a thousand years",[25] and claimed that the inflection of Orkney

[24] *A.*, pp. 83-4.   [25] *A.*, p. 62.

voices is still the same as that of the present inhabitants of the Norwegian valley from which the Norsemen came. Stanley Cursiter claims to find in his Stromness neighbours the same subtle biting humour as in the sagas. He finds other Viking characteristics in the seamen he knows there, and thinks of Muir's cousin Sutherland as a Viking.

To Orkneymen, though most of them are at least partly Scottish by descent, Scottish rule is a comparatively recent and in many ways unfortunate thing. In the fourteenth century the Scots began to infiltrate into Orkney, but it was not until 1468 that the islands came under Scottish rule, being pledged for 50,000 florins in connection with the marriage of James III to Margaret of Denmark. The pledge was never redeemed, so Orkney remained permanently part of Scotland. In the sixteenth century came a period of pillage and oppression under the Stewart Earls—Earl Robert Stewart, an illegitimate half-brother of Mary Queen of Scots, and Earl Patrick Stewart. Even after the more savage tyranny was ended by the hanging of Earl Patrick in Edinburgh in 1615, the growth of landlordism subjected the peasantry to the exactions of people who often did not understand them nor contribute much in return for the rents. So Orkneymen will tell you, only half in jest, that they are not Scots, that the Scots have brought to the islands nothing but oppression and the landlords. They are a shrewd and realistic people, however, and having built up a new prosperity in this century have no wish to sever the ties with Scotland. But for the golden age of their history they still look back through the Scottish period to the eleventh and twelfth centuries—the high point of Norse civilisation there. In the eleventh century Thorfinn ruled from Orkney a large realm including the Hebrides, the Isle of Man and parts of the Scottish mainland and of Ireland. After a turbulent youth he visited Rome and thereafter ruled quietly, founding a Bishopric and a fine church at Birsay. In the twelfth century came the rule of the saintly Earl Magnus, killed treacherously on Egilsay in 1117, and of Earl Rognald, his nephew, who built the great Romanesque Cathedral in Kirkwall in honour of him, and went to Jerusalem. In the mid twelfth century Kolbein Hruga imitated the general plan of the new Cathedral, begun in 1137, in miniature in the chapel next to his Castle on Wyre. Muir writes of Kolbein Hruga as "a freebooter", but he must have been more than merely that. His son, Bjarni, became a Bishop and poet and may have been the founder of Kirkwall Grammar School. So Muir was not the first poet to play around the green knoll in Wyre. The Norsemen were great fighters, seamen and travellers, but at home they were farmers and builders and no mean artists.

At fourteen Muir must have been conscious at least of the Scottish and the Norse past of Orkney. On his many later visits he must have come to know something of the more distant past, whose relics are to be found everywhere. The "Papa" island names (Papa Westray, Papa Stronsay) take us back to the Celtic missionaries who brought Christianity to the islands in the sixth century or earlier. Symbol stones remain from those days, and ruined chapels—one in Deerness consecrated to Cormack the Sailor and one on Damsay named after Adamnan, the biographer of St Columba. The brochs, circular stone forts of which there are over a hundred in Orkney, belong to the first few centuries before Christ. Some thousand years or more earlier is the Ring of Brogar, great standing stones some fifteen feet high in a wide circle on a bare moor between two lochs. Earlier still is the great chambered burial cairn of Maeshowe; when Earl Rognald and his followers on their way to the Crusades broke in and carved their names on the finely-fashioned stones it was already older than the time of Christ is to us. The remnants of some four thousand years of history are scattered thickly over a small area, and seem to blend quite naturally with each other and with the landscape. They give a sense both of familiarity and of strangeness. Orkney makes one think at once of great stretches of time going back into the past and of different times existing together in an eternal present. All this must have contributed to Muir's obsession with time, and the way he thought of it— as also did his move at the age of fourteen from the pastoral community of Orkney to the great industrial city of Glasgow. As he wrote long afterwards: "I was born before the Industrial Revolution, and am now about two hundred years old. But I have skipped a hundred and fifty years of them. I was really born in 1737, and till I was fourteen no time-accidents happened to me. [Not quite true. It was in his first childhood only that he lived in immortality.] Then in 1751 I set out from Orkney for Glasgow. When I arrived I found that it was not 1751, but 1901, and that a hundred and fifty years had been burned up in my two days' journey. But I myself was still in 1751, and remained there for a long time. All my life since I have been trying to overhaul this invisible leeway. No wonder I am obsessed with Time."[26]

Edwin and his parents and Clara set out from Stromness in the middle of the winter of 1901-2; stayed a night in Edinburgh, where Willie was working in a lawyer's office; and went on to Glasgow where Jimmie and Johnnie were working and where Jimmie had taken for them a flat in the respectable Crosshill district in the south of the city near the Queen's Park. Perhaps the parents wanted to reunite the family; but it was soon to be disrupted again by death.

[26] *S. F.*, p. 263.

C

II

Glasgow

I

O N their first night in Glasgow James Muir went for a dander through the streets, stopped, as a countryman might, to relieve himself in some open space, was arrested and spent the night in gaol. It was a sad augury of the difficulties the family were to find in adapting to the new life. James Muir was interested in everything, and got into long conversations with strangers, but found it difficult to accustom himself to such things as the need to shut the door of the flat and to turn away beggars. Edwin wandered about the streets quite friendless. People seemed abrupt, ill-mannered and thrustful after the slow, courteous ways of the islanders. This crowded, ruthlessly competitive city, containing with its suburbs about a million people, could hardly have been a greater contrast to what he had known. It was a place of great wealth, vitality and enterprise; a city of rich merchants, of the craftsmen who had made the Clyde famous throughout the world, of the great scientist Lord Kelvin, of Charles Rennie Mackintosh, an architect ahead of his time in devising a modern and distinctively Scottish style, of the Glasgow school of painters, of "Wee Macgreegor". In the most widely read of all Glasgow books J. J. Bell collected sketches of the life of a small boy and his family which appeared in an evening paper from 1902 onwards. It presents a charming and humorous, and within limits authentic, picture of the life of the prosperous working class; but its success was dependent on what it excludes as well as on what it includes, on its exclusion of anything that might seriously distress readers. For Glasgow was the most overcrowded, the most slum-infested of all Britain's great cities. All through the nineteenth century people had poured in from the Highlands and Islands, from Ireland and elsewhere to man the expanding industries. To house them grim tenements, "backlands", were built in the gardens and other vacant spaces behind the original streets. In these people lived in the most appalling conditions, whole families in a single room without proper sanitation, sunlight or fresh air. About a quarter of the population lived in one-room apartments; the death rate among children in these was over twice that in four-room houses. There were great opportunities of wealth for the thrustful; for the unskilled worker there was little prospect of ever being able to afford a decent house. On this base of human misery the prosperity of the Clyde was built.

In these surroundings a sensitive person could live contentedly only by shutting his eyes, and Edwin's eyes were at first distressingly open. Like David Blackadder in his novel *The Three Brothers* he returned from his walks "deafened by the noise and nauseated by the stench. In those first weeks he fell into a strange state. The crowds seemed incomprehensible and frightening to him, yet every incident printed itself on his mind as if he were an empty and shrinkingly sensitive mirror. Having no companion he was defenceless, and he seemed gradually to be losing his identity."[1] He got a job as an office boy in a legal office at 4s. 2d. a week. It was boring work; he was shy, and the clerks chaffed him because of his Orkney accent. To save money he walked to and from work, going from his respectable suburb along Crown Street or Eglinton Street through the Gorbals to the central business area. Neither of these streets was among the worst slums, but the squalor and violence he saw were enough to appal him: "These journeys filled me with a sense of degradation: the crumbling houses, the twisted faces, the obscene words casually heard in passing, the ancient, haunting stench of pollution and decay, the arrogant women, the mean men, the terrible children daunted me, and at last filled me with an immense, blind dejection."[2] The people among whom he lived in Crosshill were "a respectable church-going lot intent on making money and rising, as the saying goes, in the world",[3] and he could not understand how they could live surrounded by such sights

---

[1] *T. B.*, p. 195.   [2] *A.*, pp. 91-2.   [3] *S. J.*, p. 107.

without feeling ashamed. In time he too had to train himself, never quite successfully, not to see. This partial shutting of himself off from experience was the reason why his start as a poet was so long delayed.

A year after their arrival in Glasgow his father died suddenly of a heart attack. The next summer, 1903, when Edwin was sixteen, Willie came home from Edinburgh dying of consumption. He and Edwin had become friends during week-ends when Willie had come home. Now they went together on a holiday to Millport; but Willie was too ill to enjoy it, hating everything that had the glow of health. They went home early, and after that he never left the house. Near the end he told his mother that he had the assurance of acceptance by Christ, which he had prayed for night after night years before and which now came spontaneously; and he died reconciled to God. He was the one friend with whom Edwin was able in some degree to share his developing intellectual interests. He was closer to Edwin than the other brothers in intelligence, but in other ways dissimilar. "He had a far clearer picture of the world—a somewhat Swiftian picture—than the rest of us, and knew what he wanted to do and how to set about it."[4] He tried to explain to Edwin the law of the new society they had come to, which consisted in looking after yourself. Probably he did not get on easily with people. It looks as though he was deliberately making himself hard in order to cope with the world and succeed in it. Something of his character and of his relationship to Edwin are reflected in Sandy Blackadder and his relationship to his younger brother David in *The Three Brothers*, though most of the incidents are imaginary. David is shown as sensitive, compassionate, wanting to believe in a God of love and in human goodness; he suffers a series of shocks, which open his eyes to the reality of evil, and shake, without entirely destroying, his faith. Sandy says to him: "Man, I wish I was your age again, and believed that everybody was good, in spite of the evidence. . . . When you come to see that folk arena good but evil, that's when you begin to know them; but the bit comfort you had is gone then. For when you once see the evil in folk, then you see it everywhere, you canna help

[4] *A.*, p. 80.

seeing it. . . . And in the end you take pleasure in seeing it, and in seeing nothing else; the sight of goodness fills ye with a scunner, for you ken it's no what it seems—it canna be; but the pleasure's a gey queer kind of pleasure too, you would be better without it. Folk are no better than beasts, Davie, when you see them in their right colours."[5] Sandy's perception of human depravity led him (though not, as far as I know, Willie) to a narrow Calvinistic religion; and he, like Willie, died peacefully with the assurance of Christ's acceptance. Edwin himself, soon after Willie's death, experienced another dubious conversion of a superficial kind, this time at a Baptist chapel. He was seeking a faith which would give meaning to life, the life around him in Glasgow seeming to him a chaos after the order of Orkney. Perhaps also he was trying to get closer to his dead brother by sharing in his final confidence of salvation. He read a lot, but now mainly thinkers rather than poetry. Poetry, fully experienced, opens the senses, whereas one can escape into a world of ideas.

After Willie's death Edwin was often ill—partly due to his inner conflicts and unhappiness. He seems to have had no close friend with whom to share his thoughts, and the brand of religion he had adopted was not natural to him. He was playing a part as one of the saved, going about "with the forgiving smile of a martyr about to be swallowed at any moment by a lion."[6] The people he came in contact with at this time he described in *Scottish Journey*,[7] and contrasted with those he met later in the Labour movement. They were clerks and others in the lower ranges of the business world, but above, in their own view, the working class from whom they wanted rigidly to distinguish themselves. They were pushful young men, in whom the wish to get on was not only a natural desire, but was exalted to a kind of mystical faith. "Inherited Calvinism was at the bottom of their contemptuous reprobation of any one who, out of weakness or amiability or scruple, refrained from striving to his utmost to make money." This attitude was supported both by an economic theory which taught that ruthless competition was necessary to increase the general wealth and by a moral belief in the pursuit of wealth

[5] *T. B.*, pp. 202-3.   [6] *A.*, p. 98.   [7] *S. J.*, pp. 108-12, 144-51.

as a means of strengthening the character. Every success was a tangible proof that the strengthening process was going on. The striver in his climb "would have been false to his cause if he had foregone an advantage, even though he knew it injured somebody else; his whole ethic would have been imperilled." After the co-operative life of Orkney this was an ethic quite new and shocking to Muir. Most of the strivers were professing Christians, but their Christianity was connected with the part of their lives which they spent at work only in so far as the mad logic of Calvinism corresponds to the equally mad and inhuman logic of unrestrained Capitalism. Loss of wholeness and order does not produce freedom, but enslavement to partial systems, each having a dreadful logic of its own. It may be that for a time Muir tried to persuade himself to accept both the hollow piety and the business ethic, but one cannot imagine that he was successful.

He had office jobs in an engineering firm in Renfrew and then in a publishing office; but lost them after a short time because of his ill health. Eventually he was advised to look for outdoor work, and took a job as apprentice chauffeur at Kirkmichael House in Ayrshire. He hated the work, and did not have much in common with the people he met there, but was happier than he had been in Glasgow. His health improved; he learned dancing in the village hall; and had his first flirtations with girls. His contemporaries were rough, realistic, Rabelaisian—hide-bound intellectually, but in their actual contact with life less puritanical than he was. After the initial shocks he was able to make friends. He was getting over his priggish religiosity and adapting himself to ordinary people, but his deeper self was in abeyance.

He went back to Glasgow in 1905 and got a job as a clerk at fourteen shillings a week in the office of a beer-bottling factory. This was—or perhaps just seemed to him to be because of his greater maturity—a more cheerful and friendly place than the other offices he had worked in, and he had more responsibility. But ill-luck still dogged the family. Johnnie had fallen on his head from a tramcar, and was suffering from headaches; he had a tumour on the brain, which soon began to affect his control of his limbs. His pain increased through that summer and autumn until the family knew there was no hope. Edwin prayed night after night for his recovery. If he had to die what point could there be, he asked himself, in his pain—pain which achieved no purgation, but which wrecked not only his body, but his mind and spirit as well. He could find no answer to that question except that life was ruled by an iron law. Outside he saw the operation of economic laws condemning thousands to live in degradation in the slums, and of the laws of eternal justice, as understood by Calvinists, consigning millions to inescapable damnation in hell. Now nearer at hand he saw natural law working without pity and without any apparent purpose or meaning in his brother's body. A few months after Johnnie's death his mother died too, of an internal disease she had concealed while nursing him. Edwin's prayers for her seemed to have been equally in vain, and his religious faith, never securely based, was further weakened.

Muir's novel, *Poor Tom*, written some twenty-five years later, deals with a death in some ways similar to that of Johnnie. In it the Manson family have come from a farm on a northern island; the father has died of a heart attack, and the two brothers, Tom and Mansie, are living with their mother and a girl cousin in a flat in Glasgow. Tom, the younger of the brothers, is reckless, had wanted to go to sea when sixteen, has had sexual adventures with girls in the country. Mansie is more sensitive and intelligent, is successful in business as a commercial traveller, is well-dressed and rather priggish; has been converted to the Baptist Church. There is silent enmity between the brothers, partly because of rivalry over a girl and partly because of their differing characters. Mansie seems to Tom smooth, a "creeper". Tom falls off a tram when drunk; gets a tumour on the brain; loses control over his limbs and becomes self-absorbed; dies after great agony. When sending the novel to his sister Elizabeth, Muir warned her not to "look for any living model (or dead one either) for any of the characters; that would be completely wrong, for they are all synthetic, made up of scraps taken from all sorts of nooks and corners, and mostly from imagination, like the main situation."[8] What he means by the main situation is presumably the triangular relationship between Tom, Mansie and a girl, Helen

[8] E. M. to Thorburn, 29 Sep. 1932.

Williamson; and one accepts that this is wholly fictional—it is not at all adequately presented. One must accept also that Tom is not intended as an exact portrait of Johnnie, and still less is Mansie intended as a portrait of the young Muir. Nevertheless it seems probable that he was compelled to return in *The Three Brothers* and *Poor Tom* to the relationship of brothers by some psychological need. At the time he was "merely stunned" by the successive deaths in his family; he was "too young for so much death".[9] Later he needed to go back, to experience these deaths in a way he had not been able to at the time, to try to see meaning in a world in which such apparently wasteful and purposeless suffering was possible, and to face and free himself from any sense of guilt he may have felt, especially with regard to Johnnie. The very fact of staying alive while people close to him die may make a sensitive person feel guilty, even if his relationship to them has been good. But it is probable that there were tensions in Edwin's relations with his brothers which after their deaths could not be resolved in life, but only in imagination. With Willie he had been on friendly terms, but he may have asked himself whether he might not have done more for him during their last holiday together. Willie's internal struggle had been a solitary one, confided to no one until after it was over; and in the end it was his mother whom he had told that he had at last found peace. In *The Three Brothers* it is David who is Sandy's confidant, the one person whom Sandy wants to have with him at the end; so vicariously perhaps Muir sought to get closer to his dead brother. We know little of his actual relationship with Johnnie, but it seems not unlikely that, newly converted to a rather self-conscious religion after the death of Willie, he may have been shocked by Johnnie's wildness and recklessness, and that Johnnie may have thought his young brother a prig. The later Muir may therefore have been taking an unconscious revenge upon himself by making Mansie more smooth and priggish than he himself had ever been, and by making him in part responsible for the incident that led to Tom's death. The real life situation is, of course, much altered in the novel by Mansie being older than Tom. In so far as the

[9] *A.*, p. 104.

novel is autobiographical it tells us more about the older Muir's thoughts and feelings about Johnnie's death than about his actual experience of that event at eighteen. In thinking about the past, recreating it and trying to transform it into fiction, he was seeking to release himself from it. But the final transformation of this part of the past came, characteristically, much later in a dream, which formed the basis of the poem "The Brothers", written in 1957.

At the time of his mother's death he was numbed, and unable to realise, or to express, his feelings. Again it was in a dream, and much later, that release came. In Germany seventeen years afterwards he dreamed that he was summoned to a great, high room where his sister (he thought that the dream made a substitution here) lay dead. He passed by the silent mourners, and began to cry; he let the tears flow unchecked for a long time, then went to sit beside the dead girl. He saw a faint glow tinging her cheeks; it deepened, her eyes fluttered, and she held out her hand. "The glow appeared to come from within her; but I knew that it flowed from a warm, limpid, and healing point in my own breast." He turned to the others, "crying 'Look! I have brought her to life!' But at these words a terrible fear came over me, and I hastily added, as if to blot them out and destroy them, 'Look! God has brought her to life!' " His memory of her "which had once been unendurable, could be borne again, and she actually came to life in my mind. In the dream I wept for her the tears which I could not weep at her death, when life seemed to be ruled by an iron law, the only response to which was a stupefied calm."[10] Later still, in 1938, he wrote in his diary of walking past the house of an old lady in St Andrews who had a great number of stalwart sons, and he wondered if any of her sons and their families were staying with her; and he suddenly realised how he would have liked to have a mother still to go to with his wife and son. "A deep yearning that surprised me; and I guessed how much I must have lost in losing my mother at 18—How bare and hard it made the world! so that I still see it as bare and hard."

These first five years in Glasgow were the worst time in

[10] *A.*, p. 109.

his life, except perhaps the last few months in Prague in 1948. He had lost his first vision of the world, and then his rather superficial religious faith, and was now at a loss to find any meaning in the life he saw round him with its squalor and violence and lack of order and in the deaths in his family. Much of what he had seen was etched deep in his memory, and some of the scenes he reproduced vividly in his novels and in the *Autobiography*. It may seem surprising that he did not make more direct use of the experiences of these years in his poetry. If he had he might have given the poetry the grittiness which some find lacking in it. This was not to be his way. But the experiences do enter into the poetry. "The tall and echoing passages" of the labyrinth in his poem "The Labyrinth" are on one level the slums of Glasgow. In order to become the poet of inclusive vision that he was to be he needed to experience with equal intensity both the vision of freedom and union and the anti-vision of a world which seemed to be either a chaos or, if ruled by law, by an iron, pitiless law. In his first six years he had experienced the one without any consciousness of the other; between fourteen and nineteen he had experienced the other, and the first was lost. Later he needed to recover the first, not in a merely nostalgic way rejecting experience, but at a higher level where innocence and experience could be reconciled. The Glasgow years, however painful to the man, contributed to his achievement as a poet by deepening his experience of suffering. For a long time, however, they made him prone to the temptation to identify innocence with Orkney and the past, and experience with industrialism and the modern world.

II

Early in 1906, at the time of his mother's death, the world certainly looked bare and hard to him. The surviving four members of the family went their own ways, Edwin going to live in lodgings by himself—though later he lived at times with both Jimmie and Elizabeth after their marriages. He was suffering from a nervous illness of the stomach, which caused perpetual faint sickness and dizziness, and a succession of doctors had been unable to do anything for him. However, things took a turn for the better. A doctor in the slums cured his illness—perhaps as much by courtesy and kindness as by physical treatment. He began to make friends at the office, and daily contact with the lorry-men and boys, some from the slums, who worked for the firm helped him to lose his fear of the rough characters met in the streets. He was earning sixteen shillings a week. He turned away from death and, for a time, from all thought of serious things; made friends, went out with girls and began to enjoy his leisure in the evenings.

But he could not live for long merely for the day and without some positive faith. The chief clerk in his office was a socialist; having resisted his arguments for a long time Muir at last accepted his advice to read about Socialism, "got Blatchford's *Britain for the British*, and surrendered at once, crying over his statistics as I sat in the tramcar".[11] His Socialism was not really a matter of statistics; it arose out of his compassion for the suffering he saw around him and out of his need for a new imaginative vision to replace the religious one he had lost. He dreamed of a future in which everything would be transformed. He experienced a new conversion, similar to that which he had known at Kirkwall. For a time his sense of human potentiality was so strong that he saw the people around him not as they were, but as they might be in a new society where all should be free and equal. He felt this most strongly during his first May Day demonstration when he was twenty-one. In the procession he walked beside a pot-bellied, unhealthy man; there were middle-aged working-class women with shapeless bodies as well as a handsome man in a brown velvet jacket; well-to-do and slum children were all mixed together. But now he felt that "all distinction had fallen away like a burden carried in some other place, and that all substance had been transmuted".[12] He no longer felt repugnance for ugliness or disease, but a spontaneous attraction to every human being. It was a genuine imaginative vision of life, falsified, he later realised, by being attached to a purely secular faith. Mansie in *Poor Tom*, to whom at least some of Muir's own experiences on that day are transferred, is shown as soon reacting strongly against his initial enthusiasm. "As he sat on the top of the tram he reviewed again his feelings on May Day, and they

[11] *A.*, p. 111.   [12] *A.*, p. 114.

filled him with alarm. Something far wrong with the whole business; something soft and sticky, almost indecent." The memory comes back to him (one cannot be sure that this part is autobiographical, but it is possible) of his childhood friendship with a young girl—originally innocent, but now covered with guilt because of puritanical feelings about sex. "This episode seemed to him, grotesquely enough, the most shameful in all his life." So what might have been the beginning of an imaginative wakening had to be suppressed because of this association with guilt. He was filled with apprehension, "evoked by things born irrevocably before their time, or made of too soft and perishable substance".[13] It may be that Muir too was troubled by a similar complex of feelings until his marriage released him and enabled him to recover fruitful contact with his childhood. In any case the May Day experience was before its time because it could not be fitted within the system of ideas in which he was coming to believe. It was a religious experience which he had to try to force into a secular framework.

His Socialism led him to place heaven in the future—in some distant future; but such a dreamed-of future could not redeem the present or the past. So Mansie, in *Poor Tom*, while Tom is dying, realises that death is difficult to reconcile with the socialist scheme. He wishes to restore heaven to a place outside time, "for so long as it was in Time, Time would sunder him from it. And with his sense of separation his old dread of chaos returned, for chaos is universal separation; and at the uttermost end of the blind longing to lift heaven from the distant future where it stood so implacably, there must have been the hope that if it could be raised high enough, uplifted to an inconceivable height, Time would once more become whole and perfect, and a meaning be given not only to present death, but to all the countless dead lying under their green mounds, so that the living and the dead and the unborn might no longer be separated by Time, but gathered together in Time by an everlasting compact beyond Time."[14] A hoped for socialist heaven in the future could not give meaning to the deaths of Muir's parents and brothers, nor bring him closer to

<hr/>

[13] *P. T.*, pp. 109, 111, 116-17.   [4] *P. T.*, pp. 235-6.

them. A heaven beyond time may seem more remote than a heaven on earth in the future; but really it is, in a sense, nearer, and can give meaning to present and past as well as future. But at twenty-one, and for many years afterwards, his revulsion against his past was too great for him to be able to realise this. So he remained inwardly divided, attaining moments of peace and exaltation only on a few such occasions as the May Day parade, and afterwards not being able to relate these experiences to the rest of his life. The May Day experience of a transfigured humanity could only be properly understood in the light of the Transfiguration.

For the time being, however, he was happier than he had been before. He joined the Clarion Scouts and later the I.L.P., went to socialist demonstrations, street-corner meetings, and dances; attended a speakers' class. These activities took him out of himself, and helped him to find friends. Since the death of Willie his mental life had been quite solitary; he had read and thought a lot, but had had no one with whom to share his interests. After some time in the Clarion Scouts, he gravitated towards a group within it known as "the intellectuals". They talked eagerly about everything, followed the literary and intellectual developments of the time, and were filled with faith in the future. Looking back in *Scottish Journey* he contrasts the new friends he made in the Labour Movement very much to their advantage with the pious "business mystics" he had known earlier. These people were working for the good of everybody, not just for themselves. Their moral principles, though they were not solemn about them, were seriously held and were put into practice—in their working lives. One of his first surprises after joining the I.L.P. and coming into contact with trade unionists was "the discovery that moral theories were not necessarily mere words, but could be taken quite seriously and a real attempt be made to put them into practice."[15] A large proportion of them were agnostics, whereas the business mystics professed a Christianity which had no effect on their conduct at work. The contrast justifiably increased his revulsion against religion as he had known it. His new interests and new friendships made him happier for the time

[15] *S. J.*, p. 148.

being, but they did not lead him towards his true vocation as a poet nor towards the rediscovery of his true self. His new friends were interested in politics and in ideas—a great improvement on being interested solely in "getting on"; but they did not call out nor speak to what was deepest in him. He was still lonely.

Membership of the Clarion Scouts put him in touch with a forward-looking group of young intellectuals in Glasgow. *The New Age*, which he began to take soon after A. R. Orage became sole editor in 1909, put him in touch with the movement of ideas on a larger stage. This was a weekly periodical, dealing with politics, economics and philosophy as well as with literature and the other arts. It had been failing in 1907, when it was bought by Orage and Holbrook Jackson; the latter withdrew in 1909, and from then until 1922 it was entirely under Orage's control. Born in 1873 he had worked as a teacher in Leeds before coming to London as a journalist in 1906. He made *The New Age* a forum for new ideas. He was a man of great charm and persuasiveness, able to get some of the best-known writers of the day—Shaw, Wells, Belloc, Chesterton, Galsworthy, Bennett—to contribute for little pay, as well as to encourage new ones—Pound, Katherine Mansfield, Middleton Murry, etc. *The New Age* was a stimulus to Muir's mind, but, like his friends in the Clarion Scouts, did little to help him rediscover the source of his special power within himself. It released over him a flood of exciting ideas, but he could not at that time distinguish those which were in accordance with his deepest intuitions from those which were not. In consequence we find him in the next few years adopting a series of opinions and attitudes which were not native to him.

Increasingly he found his faith in the future more difficult to sustain, but having nothing to replace it with he needed to cling to it. Heine helped him to do so for a time. During his summer holiday in Orkney after his conversion to Socialism he read a selection of Heine's prose in translation. Tears came into his eyes as he read: "Yes I know that there shall come a day when all men and women will be free and beautiful and live on this earth in joy". Heine's lyrical faith in the future was combined with wit and irreverence and an ironical paganism attractive to the young refugee from Scottish puritanism. The example of Heine gave him an excuse to laugh at his hopes with one part of himself and at the same time to cling to them; but the contradiction remained. After about three years of this Heine period he wrote for advice to Orage, who answered in a kind and long letter describing his own intellectual struggles and saying that he had been much helped by studying the whole works of some writer and so getting to know the working of a great mind. Orage recommended the *Mahabharata*, but Muir chose Nietzsche. He bought a complete English edition of Nietzsche and began to read him carefully in the evenings. It was an unfortunate choice.

Soon afterwards, in the summer of 1912, the beer-bottling firm for which he had worked for about seven years, was taken over by a new proprietor. Fearing that he would soon lose his job he looked round for another, and rather hastily took one which was to lead him into a new period of squalor.

III

The place where Muir worked for the next two years and which in his *Autobiography* he calls "Fairport" was Greenock, a town on the south bank of the Clyde some twenty miles from Glasgow. His suppression of the true name suggests that he knew that his unhappiness there had made him give an unfair impression of it. Much of it is ugly, and the housing in its industrial east end was very bad, but there are splendid views from it over the firth to the highland hills. Nearby Gourock (the "Faldside" of the *Autobiography*), where he lodged, is a pleasant seaside resort. There are sights as beautiful as anything in Orkney, but his inner conflicts and his need to protect himself against his environment made him incapable of responding to them. Over twenty years later he went for a sail down the Clyde, and only then realised the loveliness of the area where he had lived for so long.

The factory, where he worked for Poynter, Sons and MacDonald, was every bit as bad as he said. To it bones, covered with fat yellow maggots, were brought from all over Scotland to be shovelled into furnaces and reduced to charcoal.

Those who worked there lived constantly in a nauseating stench. (There is a pretty bad smell there still.) Mr Edward Scouller, who worked afterwards in the Refuse Destructor nearby, says that even the stokers and firemen in that insalubrious abyss used to complain of the still worse odours that drifted down from "Poynter's broth pot". He says that Dante himself could not have devised a more inappropriate place for a sensitive person to work in.

Added to the physical squalor of the surroundings was the moral squalor in the office itself. At first Muir tried to do his work with strict accuracy, "maintaining in it a cleanliness which did not exist in the bone-yard". But this proved impossible. The office had been badly conducted in the past; the foreman was unreliable. Daily complaints in an insulting style came from the clean and methodical head office in Glasgow. "We lived in a state of chronic reprobation, always in the wrong, among the filth and stench, grinding out the profits. The errors were not made by me, but I had to find an excuse for them and drearily lie them away every day, year in, year out. I ended by acquiring a habitual bad conscience, a constant expectation of being accused."[16]

Underneath these distresses was the unhappiness caused by his intellectual and spiritual conflicts. In the evenings he was reading Nietzsche and discussing Socialism. He says that he refused to recognise the incompatibility between the two, but he must have been at least partly aware of it. And there must have been a strain, again not fully acknowledged to himself, in maintaining his allegiance to a philosophy parts of which were so alien to his nature as the Nietzschean. Mr Scouller says that Muir "quite literally drove himself ill trying to reconcile the intellectual appeal of Nietzsche with his latent Christian idealism".

So much for the dark side of these years. To concentrate attention too much on this, as he does himself in his *Autobiography*, might lead us to under-rate his strength and resilience. He was able to present a cheerful face to the world, to help some more unfortunate than himself, and to join in, indeed to initiate, constructive activities. Edward Scouller, who knew

---

[16] *A.*, p. 133.

him well, never realised how unhappy he had been until reading the *Autobiography*. He and his brother Bob were active socialists, and formed a branch of the National Union of Clerks. Edwin became Treasurer. They had cheerful, rather bibulous meetings at a member's house ("Edwin had no head for liquor, at least for the 'glasses and pints' sacred to Clydeside."), and discussed how a new society might be brought into being. Edwin was not an orthodox socialist and had little understanding of economics, but he was a rebel against convention and hated Capitalism as he knew it for its cruelty. The Scouller brothers loved him for his gentleness and kindness; but saw also "beneath the gentleness a core of steel. . . . He attracted people with a mothering instinct, but we never mothered him, for we knew that at bottom he had more strength than either of us—and probably more masculinity too despite his air of delicacy. . . . He was vastly attractive to women".

Another activity was the debating society which he founded at Gourock. He put a notice in the local paper suggesting the formation of a discussion club. Fifty people turned up to the opening meeting, and insisted that the club should be a parliamentary debating society. Edwin was deputy leader of the small Labour group. They debated such subjects as women's suffrage and unemployment insurance. This enterprise brought him a new friend, referred to in the *Autobiography* as David P. This was David Peat, then a journalist on the Greenock Telegraph. Though born in more prosperous circumstances than Muir (he was the son of an intensely religious Glasgow business man), he had had even greater difficulties to contend with. From childhood he had suffered from acute agoraphobia, sometimes being unable to go even a few yards over open ground without being overcome by terror. More recently he had suffered from the even more distressing compulsion to self-exposure, which had led to his being arrested and confined in a mental hospital. Now he was courageously trying to work himself back into normal life. Though his mental balance was never secure, he later achieved some success as a journalist, and in the 1920s organised the Arbitrate First Bureau. Muir wrote of him: "David was filled with a love of

D

humanity which I could not feel at that time. He would stop
beside beggars and street-hawkers and have long talks with
them; he could be perfectly natural with anyone; it was as if
to him the class divisions did not exist, and he saw people
simply as human beings. For this reason he was liked by all
except the rigidly-respectable, who were suspicious of a man
who showed no sign of severity to poverty and vice. . . . I do
not know what I should have done without him during those
two years."[17] Muir here stresses his debt to Peat, but in Peat's
own account of these years in *The Autobiography of David* the
emphasis is all the other way:

> I secured cheap lodgings in a tenement attic; where I met the
> best man friend I have ever had. For many years his friendship
> was a wonderful thing. He was wiser than I, widely read, with
> something more than culture, for he had a great and original
> mind, and though at that time he was unknown, one felt he
> was destined for noble and outstanding work. I had seen him
> at the local Parliamentary Debating Association of which I was
> a member, and his first speech on the Insurance Act, unusual
> in form and matter, made me want to know him. Walking
> home I felt I had met some one to whom I might one day tell
> everything. He was a clerk then and, our combined weekly
> income being something like £2. 10. we were glad to secure full
> board and lodging in the attic for 15s. each per week. He had
> a small but very fine collection of books, in which Nietzsche
> and the Russians had, I thought, rather more than their fair
> share. One evening, sitting in the little window which looked
> out over the restless water of the Clyde, backed by silent hills,
> I told him many things; and since then, in times of stress, the
> thought of that friendship has been a source of strength. I had
> not his intellect, nor his fineness, but I felt *that he respected me for
> something at the very core of my being*, which enabled me at times
> to see beauty beyond my rather feckless struggles. I was a
> broken-winged bird, and could not follow him on all his flights,
> but enjoyed watching him. How it cut me to know that he was
> fond of walking and I could not be his companion! When we
> reached the end of the line of houses, I had to wave farewell as
> he went off into the open country. I looked out over the green
> fields and the waving corn, the woods and white road in a

perfect frenzy; longing to feel the green grass beneath my feet, to run down freely to the seashore, to climb the hills and follow my friend. But the storm broke over me, and I turned bitterly back to the town, eager for something to make me forget.

I was often driven to 'pick up' some girl and to indulge in a more or less passionate flirtation, sometimes sordid. . . . There was then the gloomy, sickly return, the disgust and self-reproach, the cerebral excitement, and the physical exhaustion. In some such state I would stumble home to the attic, to find Edwin, his muddy boots beside him, calm and comfortable, toasting his toes by the fire, reading his *New Age*. . . . I knew that he guessed how things were, and there was always kindness in his silence. . . .

The guild idea was then making its way into favour, and this subject, the works of William James, and long discussions on war and peace provided most of our intellectual fare.

Peat wrote an article on Women's Suffrage which was accepted by an important Scottish newspaper. "My first thought was to let Edwin know of my success. I caught him at the station going to lunch: 'It's in', I exclaimed. 'Look at this' and flourished the paper in his face. There was another surprise in store for us a week later, for when the *New Age* was opened, an article appeared in the Pastiche page—Edwin's first contribution."[18]

Muir had contacts also with the more respectable and conformist elements in Gourock society by being lecture secretary of the St John's Church Literary and Debating Society. This ended when he invited Ned Scouller to give a lecture. Scouller, by his own account a brash young man at that time, gave an unsuitably anti-religious talk. After some particularly outrageous remark, a motion was put and carried that the speaker be no more heard. In loyalty to his friend Muir resigned.

His first publication, referred to by Peat, was in the *New Age* on 29 May 1913, and was a short dialogue, "The Epigram", on the decay of wit. It is not a very distinguished piece, but characteristic in its plea for intellectual honesty, its denunciation of mere surface brilliance. "How bored one gets with this monstrous cleverness! . . . The epigram is a mark of an hysterical

[18] *Autobiography of David*, ed. Ernest Raymond (London 1946), pp. 73-5.

age. It denotes lack of mastery." It is not a weapon which modern writers have mastered, "but an obsession which has mastered them." Thus was an obscure clerk living in a Gourock attic launched as an author. It was to be a long time before he himself was to be the master of a style combining true wit and intellectual honesty. Unhappily, under the influence of Nietzsche, he too was to surrender to the obsession of the epigram.

Peat mentions Guild Socialism, which Muir, following Orage and other *New Age* writers, was beginning to believe in at this time. Those who hoped for a new society realised the danger that State Socialism might merely substitute a centralised bureaucracy for control by employers without giving any greater freedom or dignity to the individual worker. Under Guild Socialism the different branches of industry would belong to the nation, but would be controlled by Guilds, made up of the workmen employed in them. The machinery for this already existed in embryo in the Trade Unions—and, Muir thought, the men to work it. Looking back twenty years later in *Scottish Journey* he still thought that the labour leaders he had known and their Unions could have been made the basis of a new society; they were incorruptible, with a sincere desire for the general good, and had a discipline which they themselves had created. The Guild movement grew during the war, especially on the Clyde, and Muir worked for it.

In spite of these friendships and interests he was physically and spiritually in a bad way by the end of his time at Greenock. His stomach trouble returned, and he suffered from a persistent cough. His dreams were filled with images of stagnation and decay, and with maggots with blind writhing heads melting in the furnace. He escaped into occasional shabby affairs with girls, which probably made matters worse. The dreams suggest a perhaps not consciously acknowledged self-disgust, a revulsion from the physical side of his own nature which was finding no satisfactory expression, as well as disgust with the external world of the bone-yard. One night walking by the Clyde with David Mason—a friend he had met through his Union and who later became an important figure in the Co-operative movement—he said, hardly knowing what he was saying, "If

I don't get out of this place I expect I'll jump in there soon."
Mason got him a job in the office of the shipbuilding firm of
Lobnitz at Renfrew, and he returned shortly after the outbreak
of war to lodgings in Glasgow, travelling out to his work by
tram. It is characteristic that the move was organised for him.
He had great tenacity of purpose, but not the ability to push
for himself. He was rescued from the bone factory by Mason,
and later from Glasgow by his wife.

IV

The move improved the external circumstances of his life. His
health improved, and he had better chances of making a wide
circle of friends and of meeting intelligent people. But the
removal of some of his external distresses made him even more
conscious of his internal conflicts and of his sense of dissociation.
His imagination was dormant, and he was not a whole man.
Most of his activities seemed to him later to have been means of
escape from himself, actions in which only parts of himself
were engaged.

During the first winter of the war he offered himself for
the Army, but was rejected as physically unfit. He says little
about the war, but it would be wrong to assume that he was
insensitive to what was going on. Some verses by him in the
New Age in October 1914 state an honourable enough attitude,
though in deplorably pedestrian verse. He castigates the war
poets for their bluster, and says that if one cannot treat the
subject with sincerity, due reticence and dignity it is better to
remain silent:

> Forbear! Forbear! If that you cannot sing
> From your full heart in numbers consecrate,
> Then silent be. It is a shameful thing
> To feign the bully's rage, the coward's hate.

Conditions at Lobnitz were much better than at Poynter's, but
he could take no interest in his work. It was a pleasant office
to work in, as he recalled when revisiting it in 1934 on a tour
round Scotland recorded in *Scottish Journey:* "The cashier, an
old gentleman now dead, had for fifty years or so resisted the
importunities of travellers for newfangled devices such as

adding-machines and filing systems, and had stuck to the methods he had found in operation when he entered the office as a junior clerk. . . . We were all proud of him, and grateful for the way in which he left us to ourselves: I have never been in a little community where such an idyllic and quietistic atmosphere reigned."[19] Under this benevolent regime he was able to write a good part of his first book, *We Moderns,* in the office. But though his intellectual interests were thus brought into the office there was no real relationship between the two. Speaking much later in a B.B.C. broadcast about his start as a poet he said that while he was a clerk his intellectual life was kept quite apart from his workaday routine; a thing which very often happens among young working men interested in things of the mind. "On the one hand was the intellectual world with all its possibilities; on the other was the setting down and adding and balancing figures for a certain number of hours each day. It was quite easy to keep them apart. The point I am coming to is that this was bad for the writing of poetry. If I had spent my time on Shakespeare or Wordsworth instead of on Nietzsche, I could not have separated my life so neatly in two; for once the imagination is awakened it cannot stop until it tries to unite all experience, past and present, serious and trivial." His fellow-clerks, remarking that he was constantly asking the time so as to know how long it was to the next break, thought a watch the appropriate present to give him when he married. His pay, by the end of his time there, was £3. 17s. 6d. a week, which wasn't bad for a clerk in those days.

Much of his spare time was taken up by work for the Guild Socialist movement. A branch of the National Guild League was set up in Glasgow in 1915. They had meetings, at which he sometimes spoke, and from December 1916 brought out a periodical, *The Guildsman.* This was a monthly, sold at first for 1d, later for 2d; in 1919 it was taken over by the central Executive in London and was afterwards edited by G. D. H. and Margaret Cole. So he was a member of one of the most enterprising branches of what at one time looked like becoming an influential movement. Mr W. D. Ritchie, an associate of

[19] *S. J.,* pp. 139-40.

his in the branch, describes him in those days as "an angry young man", a bitter opponent of the established order, a voluble talker when roused. But it was clear to his associates even then that politics was not to be his vocation, that his genius lay elsewhere. The one contribution of his to *The Guildsman* that I have come across is a slight fantasy called "Caliban" in the March 1918 number. Three elves return at dusk of a spring evening to a wood near a large town where long ago men used to dance. Now the labourers who come are insensible to the beauty of the scene, and do nothing but talk bitterly of their poverty and tell coarse jokes. After the men have gone the elves reflect:

> 3rd Elf: I mourn for them, for I think they must be dead! They are dead things walking about making a noise.
> 2nd Elf: They love nothing, they rejoice in nothing, they create nothing but hatred and ugliness. They have become inaccessible and blind, like a dead tree that is hollow within.

It is not a very effective piece, but is enough to show the direction in which his interests naturally led him even in the political phase of his life—to dealing in an imaginative way with man's dissociation from nature and with the inner impoverishment produced by industrialism rather then towards a consideration of specific measures to remedy the situation. The one account of a speech of his that I have found is in *The Guildsman* in January 1917: "Instead of sketching a Guildsman's Utopia . . . the speaker devoted his time to arguments against that practice, holding that all Utopias are substantially the same Utopia, a picture of a state in which all men are happy. He did not claim that any such condition would necessarily follow the establishment of the Guilds; the most he could say was that he believed society must be reconstructed roughly on the lines indicated in the Guild idea if there is to be any advance at all." It sounds reasonable enough, but hardly a clarion call. His political activities and his large reading of political literature were misdirections, albeit honourable ones, of his energies.

More effectual than either his Socialism or his Nietzscheanism as means of escape from himself, he says, were the series of absent-minded affairs with one woman after another, none carried very far and none lasting very long, in which he engaged at this time. He was a good dancer, a witty talker and a gay companion. When his future wife got to know him in 1918 his nick-name was "king of the flappers". He writes of these affairs as escapes, but what was really escapist was not that he should engage in them but that he should be so keen to disengage himself before they had gone far. He was too uncertain of himself to be willing to take on responsibility. These deliberately incomplete affairs must have been unsatisfying. In *Poor Tom* he writes of couples who enter the ante-room of love, who seem to be happy there, but who in secret "are thinking of those other chambers whose existence they never admit to each other, and which have become a subterranean domain through which their thoughts can licentiously roam. . . . In time their embraces become merely a device to gain them admittance to that place, where they can wander in solitary thought, and where, if they once met, they could not greet each other. So as they stand pressed so closely they are as far apart as secret drinkers indulging their craving in shameful privacy." They are not really giving to each other; there is no real communication; they are "filching from each other something they are ashamed of and wish to hide. . . . Such secret pleasures are exciting, but they leave a sense of guilt towards the object that was employed to produce them."[20] A little later in *Poor Tom* there is an account of Mansie's encounter with a superior-looking, well-dressed girl, whom he takes for a walk one evening. She is outwardly correct and careful of the proprieties; but when he kisses her in a park she responds with an alarming passionateness which is essentially cold and ungiving. When she has got from him the sensual thrill she wanted she casts him off. One should not say that these passages are directly autobiographical, but it was his experience in Glasgow that enabled him to write them. Outward propriety combined with secret, sterile and guilt-ridden sex he regarded as especially characteristic of urban puritan communities.

Many of his encounters with girls were no doubt quite

[20] *P. T.*, pp. 24-5.

happy flirtations, and some were genuine friendships, though his diffidence made him cut them short. Mrs McIntyre, then Jessie Roberton, eldest daughter of Sir Hugh Roberton, conductor of the Orpheus Choir, remembers a happy companionship with him in 1917-18 after her father, who regarded him as the outstanding member of the Guild Socialist group, had invited him with other Guildsmen to their house.

> In retrospect, forty-five years ago I was probably a mature twenty-one year old while Edwin in many ways was younger than his thirty years . . . a rural man in an urban setting . . . an urban setting where he had no inclination to settle or take root. . . . He was delightful company. He took me to hear for the first time the London String Quartet, then at the zenith of its art. I was a chorister in the Orpheus Choir; Edwin also sang and was familiar with light opera, Gilbert and Sullivan, etc. He was a very good dancer, fleet of foot and completely happy in folk dances especially Scottish reels. . . . The width and variety of his knowledge of literature enhanced his conversational gifts. He was pessimistic regarding his prospects as a writer, a state of mind probably conditioned by his frailty of health at that time. He was ruminative and quiet on occasions but never moody.
>
> When we parted in the springtime of 1918 Edwin was in despondent mood. He found the ways of women difficult to understand and had an idea that he would never marry. With the precocity of youth I ventured three predictions . . . he would find a girl who would understand his level of thought and be a helpmate to him in his work . . . that he would become a writer of outstanding distinction and that he would probably marry before I did. All of which happened. . . .

Though inwardly divided and unhappy, he was able to present a brave face to the world. When his future wife first met him she was attracted at once by the "blue flash in his eye whenever he laughed. His eye flashed with an extraordinary blue flash which is very endearing."

Touching him, perhaps, at a deeper level than any of these activities were his friendships with Denis Saurat, then lecturing in French at Glasgow University, and with Francis George Scott, the composer. These friends opened up to him the worlds of intuitive speculation and of music—in the latter of

which he for a time took greater pleasure than in poetry. He
wrote long afterwards to F. G. Scott: "I often think of those
wonderful days when you and Saurat and I met each week and
discussed everything under the sun. It meant a great deal to
me at the time; I think that was when I began to have some
understanding of music, a little, a very little, and it is nothing
more than a very little still. But it gave me immense enjoyment, which I would not have missed."[21]

The happiest times of all, and those which came nearest to
enabling him to rediscover his deepest self, were his summer
holidays in Orkney. After writing in his 1937-39 diary of
having travelled a hundred and fifty years in his two days
journey to Glasgow, he goes on: "Every summer, during my
two weeks' holiday, I travelled back that hundred and fifty
years again. What a relief it was to get back to the pre-
industrial world, and how much better everything was arranged
there! And even in Glasgow I could make little excursions
into it on Saturday afternoon and Sunday by taking a walk in
the country. On these walks I often met other Glasgow people
doing the same thing. They thought they were 'nature-lovers',
but what really drew them into the country was a personal or
racial memory of a protective order which had existed before
the modern chaos came upon us."[22] I think he overstates the
case in saying that he was able to acomplish the journey back
during these holidays. If he had done so his imagination
would have woken, and he would have started to write poetry
earlier. This journey cannot be accomplished simply by change
of place. He was too inwardly divided and too wrapped up in
himself to be able to see and respond to what lay around him.
The squalor and degradation he had seen in his early years in
Glasgow had forced him to erect a protective shield. In
training himself not to see the squalor—not at any rate with
the first freshness—he had made himself incapable of seeing
the beauty also. He felt separated from things, as he had
during his phase of acute childish guilt. "Standing before a
shop-window, or taking a country walk, I would waken with
a start, conscious that for some time I had been staring at some
chance object, a ring in a jeweller's shop, or a hill in the distance,

[21] E. M. to Scott, 20 May 1957.   [22] *S. F.*, p. 263.

with a dry, defeated longing. It was as if I could grasp what was before my eyes only by an enormous effort, and even then an invisible barrier, a wall of distance, separated me from it. I moved in a crystalline globe or bubble, insulated from the life around me, yet filled with desire to reach it, to be at the very heart of it and lose myself there."[23]

The philosophy in which he was trying to believe was at odds with his nature. In some moods men, himself included, seemed to be no more than animals. He wrote in his diary in 1939: "Once long ago when I was sitting in a crowded tram-car in Glasgow, I was overcome by the feeling that all the people there were animals: a collection of animals all being borne along in a curious contrivance in a huge city where, far and wide, there was not an immortal soul. I did not believe in immortality at the time, and I thought I was happy in my unbelief. That realisation of being among animals was a deep shock to me; I put it out of my mind as quickly as I could; I was troubled by my own morbidity of mind. But now I know that if you deny people immortality, you deny them humanity." He could not believe in immortality which alone for him made sense of human life, nor could he accept the animal side of his own nature. David Blackadder's fearful dreams and speculations towards the end of *The Three Brothers* probably reflect Muir's own experience at this time. "One night he dreamt that he was lying in warm mud and gazing at his hand, which was strangely wasted. Presently he could see all the bones hard and keen beneath the pulpy flesh, and then the wavering veins pulsing softly; but as he looked the veins paled to a loathsome whiteness, and the blood was like milk flowing languidly, and in the midst of his hand appeared a great black worm writhing and coiling and sucking, and he awoke sick and drenched with sweat."[24] If others were merely animals, so was he; and he could not accept himself as merely an animal. In the dream a deeper self was speaking than that which tried to affirm merely natural life in *We Moderns*. Beneath the surface his unhappiness and sense of dissociation were increasing, and he was not far from nervous breakdown.

Fortunately help of just the right kind was at hand. In the

[23] *A.*, pp. 149-50.　　　[24] *T. B.*, p. 270.

autumn of 1918 he met Willa Anderson. She was then twenty-eight. Her parents had come originally from Shetland, and though she had never lived there she shared with Muir a feeling for the northern islands and their way of life. To the end they would sometimes use Orkney and Shetland words to each other. She had been brought up in Montrose, Angus, where her father was a draper. Her reaction against the narrowness of small-town life in Scotland can be seen in her two novels, *Imagined Corners* and *Mrs. Ritchie* (the second a book of considerable power). She had had a brilliant academic career, getting first class honours in classics at St Andrews' University and then teaching in a school, at her old University and at Mansfield University Settlement in Canning Town, London; in 1918 she was Vice-Principal of Gipsy Hill Training College in London. Her skill as a linguist was to be of the greatest help in keeping the two of them afloat in later years. But above all she was a person of great courage and gaiety—not fundamentally stronger than he, but having at that time greater self-confidence. During the winter he wrote to her for advice about getting literary work in London. In the spring they met again at a dance in Glasgow, and fell in love. He tried his usual evasive tactics when feeling his personality in danger of being intruded upon. They went with others for a week-end at St Andrews. On the beach he suddenly looked at her and said. "This is not going to do"; but by then she knew that it was going to do perfectly well, and just laughed. They were married at a registry office in London on 7 June 1919. His marriage was, as he says, the most fortunate event in his life. She gave him courage to leave Glasgow and launch himself in London; enabled him to rediscover his hidden self, and to become a whole man again; and created the conditions in which his genius could flower. After the honeymoon they returned to their separate jobs, but gave them up in September and set up house at 13 Guildford Street in London.

Interesting impressions of Muir at the time of his marriage were recorded by two new friends—"Hugh Kingsmill" (Hugh Lunn, son of Sir Henry Lunn) and John Holms. These two were younger than he—in their early twenties—and had come from more prosperous backgrounds. They had become friends in a prison camp in Germany, and now in early 1919 were waiting to be demobilised from the Army. Hugh Kingsmill had been interested by Muir's writings in *The New Age* and by his first book, *We Moderns*. When at Bridge of Allan near Glasgow he took the opportunity to call on Muir, and wrote to Holms on 26 March:

> I called on Edward Moore [the name under which Muir wrote in *The New Age*] . . . E. M. seemed surprised to see me—he is a quiet reserved Scotchman. It was not quite as bad as bearding Oxo [his name for Holms] in the character of a complete stranger, but for a few minutes a little trying! However we set off for dinner, and had a great evening. You would like him immensely. He has really remarkable intelligence, and is absolutely unaffected, and his laugh bursts through the intervening obstacles like, in a more subdued key, your own. . . . He was as reserved as yourself, but these details came out one by one. He has never been able to learn languages, except French to read. Not even German, though he worships Goethe, and of course not Greek or Latin. He goes to work at 8.15 and returns at 6.30 with hardly any vitality to spare. He takes no interest in his work, and this for seventeen years—just think of it. His book *We Moderns* was completed last April. It's only about 45,000 words, but the strain led to a nervous breakdown. He can't . . . get a more or less easy teaching job, because he's never been able to get a degree. His book has sold 460 copies, and he doesn't see a cent until it gets above 500. . . .
>
> He is trying to get to London as a journalist. Orage of the *New Age* is helping him. I wish you could meet him, I have seldom liked any one so much, and he is really first rate critically. I think if he can free himself he will write great criticism.

In April he met him again, and wrote to Holms:

> I have had another long talk with E. Moore. He is a charming fellow, but as I told you his views are certainly artificial. He has some theory of a creative force which is *not* the absolute (he won't have an absolute at all . . .). I must leave his metaphysics to you, when you meet him. He seems to derive a ghastly joy from denying the absolute, and he won't have it that one has a reasonable ground for complaint if one believes,

as he tries to, that this life is as good as any other form of existence extant. I told him he was biting an aching tooth, and that whatever satisfaction the process gave him, it could not be accounted a very high form of joy. Still he really is delightful, and I feel a private income would dissipate his intellectual freakishness.

Holms took Kingsmill's advice to read *We Moderns*, but did not much like it. He had a formidable critical intelligence, and was to stimulate Muir both by his sympathy and admiration and by his trenchant dismissal of nonsense. In July he was in barracks near Glasgow, was taken by Kingsmill to see Muir and went for a long walk with him in the country. His account to Kingsmill of that day is quoted nearly in full in the *Autobiography*;[25] so I will not repeat it here, though it contains powerful insights into Muir's condition at the time, as Muir himself later recognised. "Holms saw, as I was incapable of seeing then, that my belief in the ideas of Nietzsche was a willed belief, and that in my struggle to maintain myself against fantastic odds personality had become my last desperate defence." In his struggle for survival since the age of fourteen he had needed to assert his individual personality. Any self-surrender seemed "an ignominious acceptance of a world where all I could become was an ageing, round-backed clerk". In fighting against unfavourable circumstances he had got himself into a position where he was in fact, without knowing it, fighting also against what was deepest in himself, his imagination, his genius. In reaction against his religious "conversions" any resigning of the will to Christ now seemed to him to be, as Holms says, "a denial of his own individuality, and of any responsibility"; but he had not during these conversions experienced religion in any profound sense, and so did not know what he was denying. His genuine childhood experience of union was buried under subsequent impressions. Holms too had experienced this sense of union as a child, and for him the longing for it was still his profoundest emotion when moved by beauty. That day, walking with Muir through beautiful country, he caught his emotions as a child more vividly and more often than for a long time; but, he says, Muir would have

[25] *A.*, pp. 167-9.

little of it. "He wanted a roaring gale to inspire him and to fight with physically. So obviously to that type of mind the idea of the absolute as rest, as union with beauty, or whatever you call it, is merely boring."

Holms for a time became Muir's chief friend. He re-kindled his love of poetry, and contributed to bring back, or rather to modify, his belief in immortality, to incline him to think of it as a state of union rather than as the eternal recurrence of personality.

III

Early Writing and Nietzsche

SEVENTEEN verse contributions by Muir appeared in *The New Age* between 1913 and 1916; they do not invalidate his statement that it was not until the age of thirty-five that he began to write poetry. Some are versified propaganda on current politics, much what any clever young angry man might write. Some, more original, are satirical observations on contemporary writers; he was soon afterwards much ashamed of the conceit displayed in these, and thought of them as the product merely of his own unhappiness. A few, written in imitation of Heine, attempt to combine irony with sentiment. None are the expression of an authentic personal vision.

At this stage he was more effective in prose. In October 1916 he began to send aphorisms to *The New Age*. These came thick and fast during the next two years, and were collected and arranged in book form as *We Moderns* in 1918. Later he was anxious that this book should be forgotten, and went too far in pouring scorn on everything he had done in his Neitzschean phase. He looked back on his Nietzscheanism as a compensation, an escape from unhappiness into the fantasy of a superman. So, no doubt, it was, but there must have been more to it than that. When he began to read him in about 1912 Nietzsche was enjoying quite a vogue among progressive thinkers and perplexed young men. Fashion may explain why he took him up, but not why some seven years later when first visiting his future wife he was still carrying in each side pocket of his thin and battered suit a volume of the same master's work.

It is not difficult to see some of the reasons why Nietzsche caught and held his attention. First, Nietzsche was a poet and prophet as well as a thinker, expressing himself in myth and parable and metaphor rather than by logical argument. Second, he had a special appeal for those who had lost faith in Christianity, and yet felt the need for something more than a merely materialistic creed to put in its place. In the famous parable in *The Joyful Wisdom* Nietzsche's madman comes running to the market place crying "I seek God! I seek God!" The people laugh and jeer, and the madman cries "God is dead! ... And we have killed him! ... The most holy and powerful that the world has yet owned, it has bled to death under our knives—who will wipe this blood off us?" The madman sees the tremendous importance and the possibly disastrous consequences of this event. "Whither do we move now? Away from all suns? Do we not fall incessantly? Backward, sideward, forward, in all directions? Is there yet any up and down? Do we not err as through an infinite nought? Do we not feel the breath of empty space? Has it not become colder? Is not night, and more night, coming on all the while?" The madman is appalled at the insensitivity of the people to what has happened. "This tremendous event is still on its way ... it has not yet reached the ears of man. ... This deed is still farther from them than the farthest stars—*and yet they have done it themselves.*"[1] Men have killed God in that they, many of them, no longer have any real belief in Him. Whether or not one agrees with Nietzsche's philosophy one can recognise this as at least a partially true perception of the actual state of things in Europe. Though a declared enemy of Christianity Nietzsche was a true prophet in that he felt and expressed with intensity the agony of a godless world at a time when most others were blind. For Muir too God had died—at the time of his unsuccessful prayers during Johnnie's illness. This may not at the time have seemed a loss; to throw off the conception of God presented by Calvinist revivalists was a liberation. But he had a desperate need for faith—and for faith in something more than the material improvement of man's condition by Socialism. Like Nietzsche he was aware of the enormous gap left by the death of God, and of the need to fill it. Thirdly, Nietzsche's special combination of pessimism and optimism was attractive to one who could not find comfort in more complacent philosophers. He was a subtle psychologist, who anticipated many of the insights of more recent and systematic enquirers;

[1] Nietzsche, *The Joyful Wisdom* (London 1910), § 125.

E

he had a deep understanding of the pride, the egoism, the hypocrisy of men; and he was a penetrating critic of modern society. He experienced deeply all that might tempt a man to despair, and yet at the end of the day he affirmed life, he said "yes". His vision is at once tragic and, in intention at least, joyous.

Among the key ideas which enabled him to include his tragic vision within a joyous affirmation of life were the Will to Power, the Superman and the Eternal Recurrence. The Will to Power might be better described as the will to self-mastery, to self-overcoming. The Superman will be he who shall achieve this self-overcoming, and who will be able to contemplate Eternal Recurrence with joy. To accept the idea that our lives, just as they are and have been, are to recur eternally is presented as the supreme affirmation. "How well disposed towards yourself and life would you have to become to crave nothing more fervently than this eternal confirmation?"[2] Nietzsche advances no convincing reason for believing the theory of Recurrence to be true; what he was interested in was the consequences of believing it to be so. It enabled him to assert immortality in a new form, not making any supernatural assumption; it enabled him to provide a new basis for morals —"so live that you must wish to live again"; and to assert the tremendous significance of each moment, since no moment will pass away.

In an article in *The New Age* in January 1924 the influence of Nietzsche on his followers was said to consist mainly in two things: "the joyous affirmation of life even at moments when everything threatens to go to pieces, and an enormous strengthening of will-power." Nietzsche gave his followers a faith to put in the place of faith in the God whom they could no longer believe in, a faith in their own capacity to raise themselves to, or at least towards, the Superman.

> God is a supposition; but I want your supposing to reach no further than your creating will.
> Could you *create* a god?—So be silent about all gods! But you could surely create the Superman.

---

[2] *Op. cit.*, § 341.

Perhaps not yourselves, my brothers! But you could transform yourselves into forefathers and ancestors of the Superman:
and let this be your finest creating!

One is to make oneself into the Superman by an act of will.

Willing liberates: this is the true doctrine of will and
freedom—thus Zarathustra teaches you. . . .
This will lured me away from God and gods; for what
would there be to create if gods—existed!
But again and again it drives me to mankind, my ardent,
creative will; thus it drives the hammer to the stone. . . .
The beauty of the Superman came to me as a shadow. Ah,
my brothers! What are the gods to me now! [3]

This later seemed to Muir to be arrogant; but if one does
not believe in grace one must believe in oneself if one is not
to despair. If there is no possibility of forgiveness one must
try to believe that there is no sin to forgive. But the declamatory style suggests that there is something wrong, something
false; and Muir later puts his finger on what it was. Nietzsche
"rarely reached past a will-to-acceptance to acceptance itself".[4]
Nietzsche had to shout to convince himself, and some of his
beliefs were willed rather than the outcome of genuine insight.
Similarly, in much that he wrote under Nietzsche's influence,
Muir had to declaim to still his own doubts; and much, though
not all, of his Nietzscheanism was willed.

We Moderns is our most direct means of making contact
with Muir as he was in his twenties. Though like many other
young men he was experimenting with borrowed ideas and
attitudes in the effort to find himself, the true man can be seen
behind the masks. He borrows from Nietzsche and others, but
he does so selectively, and the most important things he has to
say come from his own experience, not just from books. His
opinions are not quite what one would expect to find in a
young socialist in his circumstances. He reacts strongly against
some of the most fashionable leaders of opinion (Shaw, Wells,
Chesterton) and writers (Bennett, Galsworthy) of the time; and
this not merely destructively, but in defence of positive, though

---

[3] Neitzsche, *Thus Spoke Zarathustra*, R. J. Hollingdale; Part II "Of the Blissful
Islands", (London 1961).
[4] *T.*, p. 198.

as yet dimly realised, ideals. There is much that is true and wise in the book and a genuine expression of his experience as well as much that is borrowed and much that is expressed in an exaggerated, deliberately provocative and shocking way. The book is difficult to get; so I shall summarize and quote from it at greater length than its literary merit warrants. Some of the 209 aphorisms of which it consists extend to two or three pages and are really short essays in a pithy, jerky style. They were not written in any logical order, but were poured out into *The New Age* as they came to him, and were then arranged in a rough sequence in the book. He would have made a more easily readable book if he had taken time to digest his thoughts into a continuous argument, but some of the freshness, as well as some of the extravagancies, might then have been lost. His choice of the aphorism was suggested by the example of Nietzsche, but also suited his circumstances; he had only scraps of time in which to write.

The most effective parts are those in which he satirises contemporary attitudes rather than those in which he tries to express his own values. He finds in modern life a shallowness, a lack of conviction and of ideals adequate to the dignity of man. Intellectual coquetry, he thinks, is one of the worst vices of the age. It arises from fear of a decision rather than from a genuine love of freedom. For "to abstain from a choice is not freedom, but irresponsibility. . . . It is responsibility that the intellectual coquettes fear; rather than admit that one burden they will bear all the others of scepticism, pessimism and impotence. To accept a new gospel, to live it out in all its ramifications, is too troublesome, too dangerous." In the end "their coquetry destroys not only the power but the will to choose. To flirt with dangerous ideas in a graceful manner—that becomes their destiny".[5] Another characteristic vice of our time is the crude and shallow "realism" of much modern art. Modern realists attempt no more than to copy the surface of life. This is not the proper aim of art, as it has been understood by the great artists of the past. "The Greeks did not aim at the reproduction but the interpretation of life, for which they would accept no symbol less noble than

those *ideal* figures which move in the world of classic tragedy."[6]
Modern "problem" dramas and novels are no better than the
shallowly "realistic", for they oversimplify for the sake of
appealing to the average man. Some writers want to appear
to deal with profound themes, but they have not the power
which Shakespeare and the classical dramatists had to give
significance and nobility to the inevitable calamities of human
existence. "This absence of meaning, however, is itself, in
the long run, made to appear the last word of an un-
fathomably ironical wisdom. And in this light, how much
modern wisdom is understood! The superficiality which can
see only the surface here parades as the profundity which has
dived into every abyss and found it empty."[7]

The triviality of modern realism is seen especially in the
treatment of love. Love is equated with sex, and sex, instead
of, as in the past, being treated within the limits of a well understood convention which enables writers to ennoble it and place
it in its proper context, is presented in a crude and shallow way.
"No matter how 'unreal' [the older writers] might be in writing
about Love, the physiological contingencies of Love were un-
mistakably implied in their works, but only, it is true, implied.
The moderns, however, saw in this treatment of Love nothing
but a convention, a 'lie'; and they became impatient of the
artificiality, as if art could be anything but artificial!"[8] This
decline has been due to a failure among readers as well as
writers. "So incapable have readers become, so resourceless
writers, that whatever is said now must be said right out; sex
must be called sex; and no one has sufficient subtlety to suggest
or to follow a suggestion."[9] This debasement in art corresponds
to a similar debasement in life. "The ceremonious in manners
arose from the recognition that between the sexes there must
be distance—respect as well as intimacy—understanding. The
old gallantry enabled men and women to be intimate and
distant at the same time; it was the perfection of the art of
manners. . . . But now distance and understanding have alike
disappeared."[10]

This decadence he connects with materialism and with

[6] *W. M.*, pp. 15-16.   [7] *W. M.*, p. 18.   [8] *W. M.*, p. 27.
[9] *W. M.*, p. 21.   [10] *W. M.*, p. 20.

industrialism. Men, artists included, have succumbed to the environment, have lost their sense of power and their sense of the possible greatness of man. In a time when man appears as the helpless appendage of a machine too mighty for him, it is natural that theories of Determinism should flourish. Confronted with the vast machine of modern society the artist feels the sense of power dying within him; and "along with the sense of power, power itself dies".[11] So we must work for economic emancipation so as to give all men a sense of freedom and of power over the industrial machine which they have created. In the mean time artists, even within the present system, must take the lead by recovering their own sense of power and of human possibilities, and so help others to do so. Modern art which merely copies life has forgotten the origin, meaning and end of art. But art would be rejuvenated if artists had faith: "Against this aimless Realism we must oppose idealization, and especially that which is its highest expression, Myth."[12] The emphasis here on the Will to Power may be said to be Nietzschean; but what he says came out of his own experience, not merely from books, and much of it interestingly anticipates what he was later to say in a more balanced and mature way.

His emphasis on the importance of art should not lead one to associate him with the aesthetes, whom he condemns as roundly as the shallow realists. "By escaping from industrialism instead of fighting it, Pater and his followers made its persistence . . . more secure. . . . Art as forgetfulness, art as Lethe, the seduction of that cry was strong! But to yield to it was none the less unforgiveable: it was an act traitorous not only to society but to art itself. . . . Art as something exclusive, fragile and a little odd, the occupation of a few aesthetic eccentrics—this is the most pitiable caricature!"[13]

In his final two chapters, "Creative Love" and "The Tragic View", Muir tries to define the positive values to which the earlier satire had been related. Even here, underneath the posturing, the real man can be seen, seeking a way to include his perception of the suffering within and around him in a vision of human life which would give it meaning and greatness.

[11] *W. M.*, p. 23. [12] *W. M.*, p. 173. [13] *W. M.*, pp. 50-1.

It is not surprising to find a thinker following his diagnosis of the ills of society by prescribing Love; but Muir's creative Love has special features, mostly derived from Nietzsche. Creative Love is opposed to that lesser Love which in various forms is known as Liberalism or Humanitarianism or the greatest happiness of the greatest number, and whose central dogma is sympathy. Sympathetic Love cries: "Life is suffering, suffering must be alleviated, and, therefore, Life must be abated, weakened and lamed! . . . This Love is barren. But creative Love does not bring enjoyment, but rapture and pain. It is the will to suffer gladly; it finds relief from the pains of existence, not in alleviation, but in creation."[14] Secondly, creative Love is opposed to all static values, to all moral imperatives thought to be absolute, to any conception of an ultimate goal in some static perfection. "When Jesus said, 'God is Love,' He defined a religion of Becoming. Was it not necessarily so? For Love is not something which may *choose* to create; it *must* create, it is fundamentally the will and the power to create. And Eternal Love, or God, is, therefore, eternal creation, eternal change, eternal Becoming. Consequently there is no ultimate goal, no Perfection, except that which is realized at every moment in the self-expression of Love."[15] Creation and suffering are seen as necessarily going together; and that is why sympathy is condemned as a force opposed to life. Static Heavens or Utopias suggest a state in which man no longer creates, but enjoys. Creation involves "the dissolution of the outworn, the birth of the new; a continuous fury in which the throes of death and of life are mingled."[16]

The repudiation of sympathy was part of the system of ideas taken over from Nietzsche, but the real reason for Muir's temporary acceptance of something so alien to his nature was perhaps his need to maintain himself against disintegration in his unhappy circumstances. Pity for others might bring in pity for himself and an inner breakdown. He felt the need to fortify himself with Nietzsche's command, "be hard". Humility and sympathy were banished—in theory, at least. Actually, as his relations with Peat and others show, he never was able to

[14] *W. M.*, p. 178.   [15] *W. M.*, p. 184.   [16] *W. M.*, p. 197.

turn himself into a Nietzschean man. The Superman was only a dream, and had little effect on his conduct.

In a penetrating criticism of *We Moderns*[17] Muir's own mentor, A. R. Orage, though praising the book highly, complained of his romantic rejection of fixed truths. The romantic, Orage says, "assumes the absence from the world of reality of anything inherent and outside of man's power", affirms the infinite alterability of the world. The classic view on the other hand says that the world is alterable only within fixed limits. There are fixed truths; intellect is our organ for discovering them, morality our method of using them. Morality is "not the will to power or the will to create new values; it is simply working within fixed limits for the perfection of what is". In 1918 Muir had a special need to believe in the alterability of the world and in man's power to change it; but there was something deeper and more permanent than this psychological need behind his early rejection of fixed truths. In 1918 he proudly asserts man's power to create new values; later he humbly asserts man's inability to arrive at the final truth.

In the final chapter of *We Moderns* he discourses on the Tragic View, which accepts and affirms the whole of life, suffering as well as joy. In the last two centuries men have set up happiness as their goal; and altruism has been preached as a means of universalising happiness. The failure to attain constant happiness and to be continuously altruistic have led to cynicism and despair, to nihilism. The answer is to renounce a false and impossible ideal, and to restore the conception of life in which happiness is regarded only as an accident, a tragic conception of life. The Dionysian or Nietzschean man who has this conception says to himself: "Even if pain and necessity be the truths of Life! There is something within me which can turn these, also, to account! I can transfigure them. Pain, Struggle, Change—these will no longer enslave me; for these shall be my slaves!"[18] The same thought is expressed in a more personal and moving way in the next section:

> To feel happy at this moment—is not that to approve of your
> whole life, of its suffering, conflict, envies and scepticism no less

[17] A. R. Orage, *Selected Essays and Critical Writings*, pp. 165-71.
[18] *W. M.*, p. 228.

than its victories and festivals? This moment is what it is by virtue of these experiences; justify it and you justify them. The physical agony which left its mark upon you; the anguish of bereavement and of disillusionment; the cynicism with which you consoled yourself; the years when you lived altogether bereft of hope; your most profound and most petty thoughts and actions; your meanest, bitterest and noblest experiences: all these are unconsciously affirmed in your affirmation of this moment. Let them be affirmed consciously! Or is your soul afraid to go as far as your will? Looking back now with new eyes over your life, you find that precisely what you cannot do is to repent—least of all of your sins and griefs! For to repent is to will Life to be other than Life, and essentially not to affirm.

He who contemplates his life thus, perhaps understands for the first time what is the meaning of Tragedy.[19]

There is still something declamatory here, for he is aspiring after a state of acceptance which he has not really attained. When he really attained it many years later he expressed it humbly and quietly in such poems as "A Birthday". In writing *We Moderns* he was trying to persuade himself into it by shouting—of course, unsuccessfully. The attempt buoyed him up for a time, and helped to disguise from himself his own unhappiness. The completion of the book removed the artificial support, and he was left more consciously unhappy than before.

He made no money out of *We Moderns;* but its publication was of some material as well as psychological use to him. The aphorisms had already brought him to the attention of Orage and the readers of *The New Age*. The book got a laudatory review in the American periodical *The Freeman*. It was the support of these two periodicals which was to enable him to live as a man of letters. The opportunity of escape from clerking and Glasgow had been created. The courage to take it was supplied by his wife.

[19] *W. M.*, pp. 229-30.

IV

Marriage

I

WILLA MUIR believed in Edwin before he believed in himself. It was her courage and faith that enabled him to take the risk of leaving a secure, though unsatisfying, job for the uncertainties of the literary life. At the same time she sacrificed her own far better job as Vice-Principal of a Teachers Training College. She had contacts with many interesting people in the educational world in London, and had considerable ambition either to take a lead in the development of continuation education or to help in the reform of the Training Colleges. Now all this had to be given up; for married women were not allowed in her College. They set up house in a flat she had taken at 13 Guildford Street in the Holborn area of London not far from the British Museum. It was the first real home he had had since his parents died.

They could not afford to wait long for suitable openings, and soon had to take less interesting work than before—she in a crammer, he in an office making up little parcels all day long. She soon found that in marrying him she had taken on a more difficult job than she had realised. Before he could be a whole man again he needed straightening out, physically (years of clerking had left one shoulder higher than the other) and mentally. The vastness and impersonality of London oppressed him. Going about the streets he was afraid at times that the houses would fall on him, and he was not far from nervous breakdown. Her hope sustained him, however, and in memory those days seemed to him to have been happy ones. Faith was soon justified; for after a few months he was taken on part-time as assistant to Orage on *The New Age* at a salary of £3 per week, and got work as dramatic critic for *The Scotsman* and as a reviewer. Literary journalism was an improvement on the clerking he had been confined to from nine to six for the past eighteen years, though it still did not give him the leisure to discover his creative powers. She got a well-paid job as head of a continuation school for the work girls at a group of West End stores. They got to know a lot of people, and London lost its impersonal strangeness. It may well be that these changes and, especially, his marriage would have enabled him to resolve his inner conflicts without any other help. But already Orage, seeing that he was in bad shape, had introduced him to a well-known psycho-analyst, Maurice Nicoll, who offered to analyse him free for the mere interest of the thing. He was unwilling to admit that he was a neurotic needing help, but was interested in psycho-analysis, which had been discussed a lot in *The New Age*, and so agreed to the experiment. Nicoll was only five years older than Muir, but had already gained a great reputation as an analyst and a minor one as a man of letters under the pseudonym of "Martin Swayne". He was the son of Sir William Robertson Nicoll—formerly a minister in the Free Church of Scotland, at this time a well-known editor and critic—and a man of wide culture. He had studied under both Freud and Jung, preferring the teaching of the latter, who became his friend and came to stay with him. He had done much work on shell-shock cases in the war, and was now in practice in Harley Street. His book *Dream Psychology* is an unusually sensible, humane, and undogmatic work; he does not try to interpret dreams in accordance with any narrow, preconceived notions. Shortly after this time he gave up his lucrative practice to join Gurdjieff's "Institute for the harmonious development of man" near Fontainebleau.

Muir's analysis started a few months after he came to London, and was broken off when he left for the Continent in 1921. Maurice Nicoll took him himself for a time, and then handed him over to another doctor with whom he felt less in sympathy. The analysis was very painful, especially at first. Material gushed up from the unconscious in dreams and day-dreams, which he recorded for the analyst. The resulting self-knowledge was hard to accept. As Nicoll says, "no one must expect to live in contact with the unconscious without being constantly humiliated".[1] When the analyst began to interpret his dreams he at first refused to accept their disreputable meanings, but afterwards was shaken with disgust and dread of himself. In Glasgow he had suffered from double blindness —inner and outer. To have continued to see the Gorbals and the bone-yard with his first freshness would have been intolerable; so his outer senses were protectively dulled, and he was driven in on himself. To have responded vividly to the four deaths in his family would have been too much for a sensitive boy left alone at eighteen; so his inner senses had been numbed at that time. To see the slums and the bone-yard in oneself is also intolerable unless one has some more satisfactory way of dealing with them than the Nietzschean; so unpleasant things were shovelled out of sight, or were affirmed with the false confidence of a would-be superman. Now the psycho-analysis helped him at least to begin to look steadily into himself. He came to realise that every one, like himself, is troubled by sensual desires and thoughts, by failures and frustrations and by memories of shame and grief; and that by confronting these things one can win a certain liberation from them. "It was really a conviction of sin, but even more a realisation of Original Sin."[2]

Nietzsche's hold on him was released after a dream in which he found himself in a crowd watching the Crucifixion; expecting to see Christ upon the Cross he instead saw Nietzsche staring round him "with an air of defiant possession . . . he was like a man who had violently seized a position which belonged to some one else".[3] Nietzsche arrogated to himself the position of redeemer which belonged to some one else. The Nietzschean expects to raise himself to the position of superman by his own efforts, by proud self-assertion. Having faced the worst about himself, and about humanity in general, Muir could no longer be content with such a hope. Obscurely, though he would not have put it in that way at the time, he became aware not only of Original Sin, but also of the need for Grace.

The object of analysis, as understood by Nicoll, is not only to help the patient to rid himself of conflicts, but also, having

---

[1] Nicoll, *Dream Psychology*, (London 1917), p. 187.
[2] *A.*, p. 158.   [3] *A.*, p. 128.

removed blockages, to put his conscious mind in fruitful contact with the unconscious, which is a source of energy. It was one of his objections to Freud that "the Freudian conception of the unconscious seems to concern itself only with repressed material. The Freudian method of psycho-analysis seeks to liberate this repressed material,"[4] which it interprets solely in sexual terms. But according to the Zurich school, "when the repressed material psychic surrounding consciousness is liberated and properly assimilated into the conscious life, there remains the unconscious. It is now freed from the encumbrances that the person has put upon it during his life. The nascent material travelling towards consciousness will now, without confusion, form the material of the dream, and so we may expect that a fore-shadowing element will enter into the dream life."[5] The patient will then be able to use material from the unconscious creatively, to realise himself and to express himself more fully. Something of this sort was happening in Muir at the time of and after the analysis, though to what extent it was due to the analysis rather than to the other favourable changes in his life it is impossible to say. The wonderful waking dream recorded in the *Autobiography*[6] was a vision, not merely the welling up of repressed material. Muir was getting back into touch with his deeper self; his imagination was awakening, though he—and evidently the analyst—did not realise what was happening. The analyst advised him to stop the waking dreams, which he was able to do. Muir later thought this advice had been wrong, but remained grateful to Nicoll for what he had done.

The dream ended with a vision of angels flying in ordered formations, yet in their movements expressing "the very extravagance of complete liberty", and with the dreamer and his wife flying united, each with one wing. It gave symbolic expression to, among other things, his new-found sense that union and freedom are not necessarily opposed, and helped to confirm him in the conception of immortality at which he was arriving partly under the influence of John Holms. The Nietzschean eternal recurrence is a kind of immortality; all things eternally recur, and the superman is able to accept this

[4] Nicoll, *op. cit.*, p. 177.   [5] Nicoll, *op. cit.*, pp. 177-8.
[6] *A.*, pp. 159-62.

recurrence with joy. But now he saw that the eternal recurrence of his own personality, of "the second-rate, ramshackle structure which [he] had built with time's collaboration" would be but another name for hell. "In time, form and substance are synonyms of separation and bondage, and what the soul strives for and is made for is boundless union and freedom. I realised that immortality is not an idea or a belief, but a state of being in which man keeps alive in himself his perception of that boundless union and freedom, which he can faintly apprehend in time, though its consummation lies beyond time."[7] The man of personality wears a mask, asserts some parts of himself at the expense of others, maintains his separateness; and so is necessarily in bondage, because inwardly divided. His marriage was beginning to show Muir that paradoxically union and freedom go together, and the dream gave him an apprehension of this combination in a larger context. The strength of his poetry was to arise a good deal from its being the expression of "perception" rather than just of "belief". Nevertheless it is nonsense to say that immortality is "not a belief". To say that the soul is made for a state which is to be reached beyond time is to express a belief, whether he likes it or not. If one perceives something one believes that it exists.

In the meantime he was working as sub-editor on *The New Age* and writing for it. The *We Moderns* series ended in September 1917. From then until May 1920 his contributions appeared irregularly and numbered only thirteen in two and a half years. They included nine under the heading "Re-creations in Criticism"—fragmentary observations on literary subjects, hard-hitting, sometimes penetrating, but too self-consciously paradoxical; and his first two proper critical articles—on Hardy and on Shaw. It was a good sign that in the latter he was breaking away from the aphorism and beginning to develop a sustained argument at some length In the autumn of 1919 appeared three interesting articles, "New Values",[8] in which, not realising that he himself was soon to be analysed, he showed his interest in the new psychology.

[8] *A.*, p. 170.
[7] *New Age*, 18 Sep. 1919, 16 Oct. 1919, 20 Nov. 1919.

Psychology is producing a transvaluation of values. Man can save himself spiritually only by breaking away from traditional authority and traditional opinion. Psychology is providing a firmer basis for belief in the truths of intuition as against those arrived at by the conscious reason alone; psychology is able to test the truths of intuition. He compares writings which express only the conscious part of the writer with those which come out of the unconscious. "Everything in literature which incites to create, which expresses more than it says, comes out of the unconscious, and goes to it. . . . Intuition uses language in the same manner as poetry. Words become untrue in the degree in which they become exact."

In the early summer of 1920 he began his career as a regular reviewer (I believe there were occasional unsigned reviews earlier in the *Glasgow Herald*)—under his pseudonym "Edward Moore" in *The New Age*, and anonymously in *The Athenaeum*. After a late start he quickly established himself in two of the leading periodicals of the day. On literature he already spoke with authority and a distinctive voice.

In November 1920 he began a series of weekly articles for *The New Age*, headed "Our Generation". These continued after he went to the Continent until Orage gave up the editorship at the end of September 1922. Each week he commented on some current topic or topics—political, religious, or social more often than literary. It was his most sustained journalistic effort apart from reviewing. Like most others who have to produce something every week, he sometimes dealt with subjects about which he knew very little; but usually he wrote with conviction, often with anger. Orage, quick to scent new ideas, had by now abandoned Guild Socialism in favour of Social Credit (put forward by Major C. H. Douglas in *Credit-Power and Democracy* in 1920); and Muir jumped, perhaps rather naïvely, at this new prospect of remedying economic ills in a fairly painless way and without violent revolution. He did not know much about economics, and did not claim to; it was not his part to argue the case for Social Credit in detail—that was done elsewhere in the paper. What he was constantly hammering home was that something must and could be done about unemployment, poverty, the plight of war veterans and other evils. This was a time of growing unemployment—it rose from 700,000 to over 2,000,000 between 1918 and 1921—and of bitter disillusionment after the high hopes that had been aroused during the war. Muir castigated the Government and the prosperous classes for not caring enough about these things; and blamed the Labour Party, the trade unions and the workers generally for not being militant enough, for being too willing to accept temporary palliatives rather than trying to cure the ills. The British are too ready to accept ills as inevitable, as "visitations" of God, to speak in times of crisis of tightening belts, adapting to the bad situation instead of changing it. Labour leaders are too moderate ("The moderate is the man who sees every side of a problem without seeing into it"). He returns again and again to unemployment. The monied classes do not care enough about it, and are unwilling to make any real sacrifice. What is needed is first "to see into reality deeply enough", to "realise at every moment simply and almost as a truism that man is a spirit"; and that therefore "the indignity of men is a blasphemy against the spirit". Then men might attain "heroism great enough to face and to strive with our problems, and if it fails, to sacrifice everything out of pity to those who are suffering most".

The impotence, the lack of determination and will seen in the failure to deal with social ills, he found also in other contexts, especially in the Church of England. To a surprising extent in one who was not a Christian he looked to the Church for a lead, and was dismayed at not getting it. One might expect him, as a left-wing intellectual, to acclaim "modern" churchmanship, and the attempts by Church leaders such as Canon (later Bishop) Barnes to come to terms with modern thought with science, psycho-analysis, etc. But he shows no respect for compromise. The Church should deal with these things, but from its own centre of faith. It is no sign of vitality in the Church that a priest should give a series of lectures on psycho-analysis. "It is on the contrary a sign of spiritual poverty; a sign that the truth of religion, which works from within outwards setting its mark upon, and in doing that transforming, every aspect of life in a single, living, intuitional act, is so feeble that its votaries have to go outside it, have to choose undigested 'subjects' from the purely secular world, to add, finally, a little 'religion' in their mere criticism of them." Canon Barnes compromises religion in his attempts to reconcile it with science. The modern Churchman's faith is "not primarily for and in religion, but for reason and in reason," and secondly in morality. So-called "social" Christianity also is feeble. "It assumes . . . that our problems would be solved if everybody became good, and the good it takes to be something given, which everybody is supposed to know. . . . But no religion has ever existed which did not contain a tremendous truth, and which was not beautiful and did not exert the terrible attraction of beauty. . . . No human problem can be solved by goodness alone, but by the discovery of truth and the pursuit of beauty." Social Christians are not prepared to think about how society might be reformed. Their suggestions will merely make religion "something which will enable an inhuman system to work more sweetly".

Muir would not wish much attention to be paid to this early journalism of his. In these articles he was sometimes uncharacteristically ill-tempered and carping, sometimes too confident on matters of which he was ignorant. He adopted the stance, distasteful to him later, of a prophet denouncing his contemporaries for spiritual impotence while himself having nothing very precise or securely-held to offer. But the articles were a brave, though presumably vain, effort to disturb "the heavy national sleep", to waken men to compassion, to positive action in politics and to the search for a living faith. Some of the central themes of his later work are already present. A small example of this is a remark made in passing in an essay on Dean Inge, "in the Protestant churches the Word has never become flesh", which foreshadows the line in a late poem, "The Word made flesh here is made word again."

Through *The New Age* Muir came in contact with a lot of interesting, some eccentric and cranky, people. *The New Age* circle used to meet at the Kardomah café in Chancery Lane and later at another café near the British Museum. He was shy and unsure of himself, and probably took no prominent part in these meetings, but was liked by everybody.

Paying tribute to Orage after his death in 1934 Muir wrote

F

of his disinterestedness, his passionate concern for the good of mankind combined with an intense and steadfast employment of reason. "He was a charming companion, an enchanting talker, whether witty or serious or both, and a constant friend." Behind these qualities was something formidable arising from his "incorruptible adherence to reason, which was in him an objective passion".[9] From the number of causes which he espoused at various times, however, one suspects that he had no real centre in himself, no true originality. He was a midwife of ideas, not a creator; a sectarian, whereas Muir was trying to be free. As Professor Janko Lavrin, who knew them both well, put it to me, Muir was master of his -isms, while Orage was subject to his. The first part of this last statement was only just beginning to be true. Up to then Muir had subjected himself to a number of more or less alien -isms, and was only beginning to find his own centre. He needed to be free of discipleship; so his relation with Orage, for all his admiration, was not easy. Dmitri Mitrinović, a Serb with an "erratic, soaring mind"[10] and a picturesque personality, was a frequent visitor to the Muirs. Even Muir's charitable account leaves one with the suspicion that Mitrinović was a bit of a crank and a poseur, though an entertaining one. Janko Lavrin describes him as a man with a "home-made Messiah complex", concerned to be a saviour rather than to save any one. He wrote in *The New Age* as "M. M. Cosmoi". Another Serb with a more authentic inner experience of the spiritual life, who wrote as "Uran-Gavran", was Nicolas Velimirović, an Orthodox Priest who later became a Bishop. Others who wrote in the paper and whom Muir could have met at this time included Ezra Pound and G. K. Chesterton, an Irishman called Kennedy a translator of Nietzsche, and A. M. Ludovici, also a Nietzschean; Ramiro de Maeztu, a Spanish writer on politics whom he had read in Glasgow; "Michael Arlen" with his man of-the-world pose; Arnold Haskell; Paul Selver, translator from the Czech; and Herbert Read. His chief new friend from this circle was Janko Lavrin, who was then working in Nottingham, where he later became Professor of Slavonic Languages, and who often came to London. Lavrin hoped to get him taken on by the

---

[9] *New English Weekly*, 15 Nov. 1934.   [10] *A.*, p. 174.

Extra-Mural Department of Nottingham University; Muir
went down and gave a brilliant lecture, but was not appointed,
presumably because of the lack of paper qualifications. Lavrin
introduced the Muirs to some artists, and they went to studio
parties. They had some contacts with a colony of Bloomsbury
through Valerie Cooper at 8 Fitzroy Street, a centre for
Dalcroze dancing, and Mrs Muir had friends in the educational
world. It was all exciting, but life was becoming too hectic.
There was the work for *The New Age* both as contributor and
assistant editor, the drama reviews for *The Scotsman* which
meant late nights, the social life, and the exhausting psycho-
analysis. He needed a time of quiet to discover himself.
Luckily the means to get it came at just the right time. Early
in 1920 *We Moderns* had been published in America and had
been favourably reviewed in the newly-established weekly, *The
Freeman*, a left-wing periodical receptive to new ideas, of which
Van Wyck Brooks was literary editor. Muir began to contribute
to it in December 1920, and was soon asked to send articles
regularly; he was to get sixty dollars an article for one or two
articles a month. It was the assurance of an income from *The
Freeman* (*The New Age* paid very little) that enabled the Muirs
to give up their jobs in the summer of 1921 and to leave for the
Continent. The years that followed, peaceful and comparatively leisured, were just what he needed. It was not the last
time that encouragement and practical help came to him at a
crucial moment from across the Atlantic. After a few weeks
with his mother-in-law at Montrose they sailed from Leith to
Hamburg at the end of August.

II

They went from Hamburg through Berlin to Prague, where he
had been given introductions by Paul Selver. Prague had been
recommended by Janko Lavrin as a good centre to start from
and as offering the best beer and best ham in Europe. In
February of the next year he wrote to his sister and brother-in-
law, Mr and Mrs George Thorburn: "In spite of more expense
than we expected both Minnie (a family name for Willa at this
time) and myself are very glad that we left Britain, life here is
a hundred times more pleasant; there is not the constant

atmosphere of calamity and anxiety which there is in London or Glasgow; and the continental peoples seem to have such a knack for making everything pretty that one is constantly being delighted or surprised as one walks down the streets. Even in Germany, where things were supposed to be so bad, I was absolutely astonished at the difference between Berlin and London. In Berlin there was a feeling of cheerfulness, of comfort, of contentment, especially of hope for the future that came like a breath of fresh air after London." The difference was a good deal in himself. For the first time in his life he was abroad, where everything was new and different and asking to be looked at. For the first time since childhood he had leisure; and he had no anxieties about money (or only transitory ones; several times his cheques from America were stolen in the post, and they were broke at Christmas in Prague). So he "began to learn the visible world all over again" and "spent weeks in an orgy of looking".[11] He realised that his fears were gone; there was nothing to spoil his enjoyment of this new world.

The world around him in Prague really was a delightful and exciting one, in some respects superior to any urban life he had known. "The theatres", he told his sister, "are a revelation. . . . At present they are producing works of Shakespeare, Molière, Alfieri, Goethe, Calderon, Marlowe, Synge, Yeats, Wilde, Ibsen, Chekov and a host of others. In addition to this there is opera. And the town of Prague is about half the size of Glasgow! Then there are orchestral and other concerts practically every night in the week, all of them cheap."

Czechoslovakia was newly independent. The feeling of nationality overcame class-consciousness, and every one mingled naturally in theatres, cafés and cabarets. The Muirs became friends with Karel Čapek, and were welcomed by other writers; they learned to speak Czech. They noticed the respect and affection in which Čapek was held by people of all classes, a sign of the higher status of writers there than in Britain. He had plenty of free time to look, to enjoy, to think, and to plan works more important than his periodical journalism. He told his sister in February that the was "trying

[11] *A.*, p. 189.

to concoct a book of lyrical philosophy to contain partly narrative, partly aphorisms and partly poetry." This does not sound a very promising project and nothing came of it; but it shows that imagination was already stirring in him. An important step towards his becoming a poet was taken in Prague in his rediscovery of the visible world in "an orgy of looking". He needed also to turn in, to recover contact with his childhood and his deeper self; and then to bring together the inner and the outer worlds.

Early in April 1922 the Muirs moved to Dresden, and in the autumn to nearby Hellerau. In December he wrote to the Thorburns:

> We've been in Dresden now since the beginning of April. It is a very pretty, but very bourgeois town; there is a fine art Gallery, with a fine collection of Rubens and Rembrandts, an opera house which was at one time the finest in Germany, and which is still very good; a states theatre where the acting is intensely bad; any number of concerts, and cabarets which are really pleasant and unoffensive, and where the Germans, for a sum a little less than a penny, can sit of an evening drinking schnapps and listening to singers of comic songs, who are amazingly like the English ones. We live at Hellerau, a little village about two miles away from Dresden, set on the edge of a pine forest which stretches away for seven miles. The central interest of the village is an Eurhythmics School for teaching dancing, in which there are girls from all the nations in Europe —there is connected with it, a "free-school" for children, run by A. S. Neill . . . in which Minnie now teaches for a few hours a day. There are naturally, with this atmosphere, the usual complement of Communists, vegetarians, simple-lifers and so on. Among the youth of Germany there is a very strong movement called the Wandervögel (Wander Birds) of young people who live as simply as possible, go walking in bands every week-end in the woods, singing old German songs, and sleeping at nights under the trees. They are of all ages from fourteen to twenty; they are out against their parents' authority and do as they please; but, unfortunately they are a bit too serious, regard smoking, drinking, the cinema and fox-trotting as inventions of the devil. Nevertheless, they are promising as a protest against the Germans' terrific respect for the law. In Germany in summer you will see public roads

lined with cherry trees hanging with cherries (the property of the State), and though there are any number of children about, these cherries are not picked.   There is something rather fine about that, though to the Scotch it seems more than human.

Living is in most respects terrifically cheap in Germany; except for such things as clothes, boots, and now books, which are almost as dear as they are in England.   A pint of beer is less than a penny, I get good Virginia cigarettes, better than Gold Flake, for 12 a penny; you can have good Rhein wine for about 3d. a bottle—it costs about 5s. in England.   Our bill last month for our rooms and all our food was for the two of us less than £3, and we lived fairly well.   The people in general, however, are much poorer than the English papers make one think.   The working class is relatively well off, on account of the strength of their unions, but the middle class is very hard put to it to keep a roof over their heads and feed themselves. There is a general bitterness against the Versailles Treaty and the French, who are hated, but a disposition to be friendly to the English who, for some reason, are rather liked.   I've met a lot of interesting Germans, have made some progress in German, and read a good deal of German poetry.   Minnie speaks the language almost like a native.

I've been writing a lot of poetry again, two samples of which you might have seen in *The New Age*.   I have collected 12 of my poems, three in Scotch, and have sent them to Heinemann in London for publication, but have received no reply yet.   I am in negotiation for the publication of a volume of essays in America [*Latitudes*] and I am preparing a volume of aphorisms which I intend to try my luck with in London in the next few weeks.   If any of these projects come off, I may reap a little fame from them, especially the poems, which are easily the best things I have yet written.

This letter shows that even at the time he was able to look with a certain detachment at the somewhat cranky, yet agreeable, people with whom they associated at Hellerau.   There were three schools in the same building, pursuing somewhat divergent aims in reasonable but not complete harmony; an Eurhythmic School, founded by Dalcroze, for some sixty pupils, mostly adults; a German High School, dedicated to culture and aestheticism; and Neill's small school with children from many nations freely expressing themselves.   In the evenings the less puritanical members of the community would meet in a *lokal* to drink beer, wine and benedictine (which could be had for 9d. a bottle), to talk and sing. Later Muir realised clearly the rather sentimental and escapist nature of the life there. They lived in a climate of new ideas, believing themselves to be without prejudices and thinking that a new life could be brought into being by the simple exercise of freedom. But in fact they normally observed the usual conventions and "were annoyed when anyone violated them, for it caused, to our surprise, all sorts of inconveniences".[12] Looking back later at *The Freeman* articles he wrote at that time he realised that he had to some extent just been playing with ideas without really being concerned with their truth. Nevertheless the kindness, the gaiety, the aspiration after innocence and reconciliation were real.

On the surface he seemed to be immersed in the life of this gay and rather sentimental paradise; at a deeper level something much more important was happening. He had leisure, and no anxiety about making a living. During the day, while his wife was at the school, he would walk in the woods, sometimes with a charming impoverished Junker, Ivo von Lucken, often alone. Having recovered fresh contact with the external world at Prague and having felt his fears slip from him, he was now able without damage to himself to turn in again, to go over again the years he had lived wrongly in Glasgow and beyond them to renew contact with his childhood. This reaching back into the past took place at a time when he was happy—happier than he had ever been—not at a time when he might be suspected of wanting to escape from adult difficulties. In Glasgow he had wanted to escape from a present which he could not face; but he had then been cut off from his past; he escaped into various distractions and into dreams of the *future*. His return into the past now was not an escape, but a process of self-discovery, a facing of things which he had not been able to face before. It was probably at this time that the dream about his mother, already mentioned, came to him. He was now able to weep for her the tears which he had not been able to weep at her death. The latter part of the dream, the resurrection,

[12] *A.*, p. 200.

refers, I think, not, or not only, to his mother, but to a buried
part of himself. The intuitive, feminine part of himself, in
Jungian terms his anima, was coming to life; and in doing so
was giving him the power to respond more vividly to the present
as well as to the past. He was recovering inner wholeness, and
with that his imagination was wakening. In the letter to the
Thorburns he spoke of writing poetry "again"; but in fact he
was writing poetry for the first time, poetry which was the
expression of an authentic personal vision.

In looking against the direction in which time was hurrying
him, he says, he won a new experience, the ability to see life
timelessly. Memories coming to life in the present give an
effect of timelessness, and this is intensified when they are
revived by something in the present resembling the past, as
when the sight of horses ploughing in a field brought back to
him his childhood feelings about the horses on his father's farm.
Past and present seem to exist together, and therefore in some
dimension other than the normal procession of time. The
resurrection dream gave him a hint of how the past may not
only be recovered, but also transformed. This was a problem
which was to worry him for a long time.

It is curious that the conception of time which Muir arrived
at intuitively is closely paralleled in a more systematic way in
the books of his analyst, Maurice Nicoll—*Psychological Commentaries on the Teaching of Gurdjieff and Ouspensky* (1952) and
Living Time (1952).

Nicoll represents man's life in a diagram:

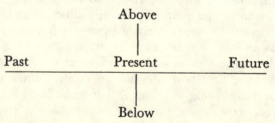

He comments:

> Every moment of a man's life can be represented in this way.
> The point of intersection of the vertical with the horizontal line
> is *now*. But this point only becomes *now* in its full meaning if

a man is conscious. When a man is identified there is no *now* for him. If he is asleep in Time, being hurried on from past to future, identified with everything, there is no *now* in his life. There is not even the present moment. On the contrary, everything is running, everything is changing, everything is turning into something else; and even the moment so looked-forward to, so eagerly anticipated, when it comes is already in the past.

It is only this feeling of the existence and meaning of the direction represented by the vertical line that gives a man a sense of *now*. This feeling is sometimes called the *feeling of Eternity*. It is the beginning of the feeling of real 'I', for real 'I' stands above us, not ahead of us in Time. . . . Eternity and Time meet in Man, at the point called *now*.[13]

Nicoll says in another place: "The vertical line represents the line of *transformation*, and this line cuts at right angles the horizontal line of Time, which is the line of *change*."[14]

What was happening in Muir can be well expressed in Nicoll's terms. Since his childhood he had merely been carried along the horizontal line of time, as most of us are for nearly all our lives. In Germany he experienced a sense of *now*, a feeling of Eternity, of real "I" and of transformation. These experiences were made possible by what had happened in London at the time of the psycho-analysis, by his repudiation of willed self-assertion. While one is trying to be a personality one is always conscious of oneself; one is confined within one-self and within the horizontal line of time. True self-knowledge makes possible self-forgetfulness, and this releases from time. Knowledge of one's real self goes along with, is inseparable from, knowledge of immortality, of oneself as a spirit not confined within time.

For parts of this time John Holms was in Dresden and Hellerau. It is worth trying to understand why Muir regarded him for many years as his chief friend, the person to whom, after his wife, he owed most among all those he knew in adult life. Though thought by his close friends, Hugh Kingsmill and Peggy Guggenheim as well as Muir, a man of genius, he produced nothing but a few slight, fragmentary pieces of writing.

[13] Nicoll, *Psychological Commentaries*, (London 1952), vol. I, p. 102.
[14] Nicoll, *op. cit.*, vol. I, p. 105.

Except for his M.C. in the War his life offers no evidence of concrete achievement. He drifted about the Continent for some years, left his wife for Peggy Guggenheim with whom he lived in stormy comfort in Paris and England until his death in 1934, a death caused partly by his constitution having been weakened by alcohol. Those who did not know him well found him vain, sensual, self-absorbed and supercilious. This is part of the truth about him, but Muir saw something else. Holms gave him, he wrote in a note soon after his death, a greater feeling of genius than any other man he had met. "What made his talk unique was its reality, the fact that it was never trite and never second-hand but always concerned with real things. . . . His benevolence came out very strongly in his talk : it was as if he was looking at things with a fraternal eye and helping them to find themselves. . . . He gave me more strongly than anyone else I have known the feeling of the reality of goodness as a simple almost concrete thing. Sometimes he seemed to breathe a goodness so natural and original that one felt that the Fall had not happened yet, and the world was still waiting for the coming of evil." At the same time he had "an equally strong sense of evil, and a profound conviction of sin."

Muir had been meeting a good many cranks and charlatans and many others who, without conscious insincerity, were adopting fashionably progressive opinions and attitudes which arose from no personal vision. Holms was a truly original person; and so was able to help Muir to see with his own eyes and to trust his own intuitions. For all his sophistication he retained something of his childhood vision, and shared with Muir the perception of immortality as a state of boundless union and freedom. He showed him "the irreducible second-rateness of a man of personality";[15] for it is not by becoming a personality that the union is to be attained. He had a vivid appreciation of poetry and a caustic intelligence, and so was able to give both encouragement and trenchant criticism when Muir was starting to write. Muir's first poems were discussed in letters between Holms and Hugh Kingsmill, and no doubt in conversation. From Dresden in July 1922 Holms wrote to

[15] *A.*, p. 181.

Kingsmill: "Muir is developing in an extraordinary way—half pathetic and half remarkable—he's writing a lot of poetry—one in particular, in spite of very bad patches, is really damned good. . . . At any rate I was immensely surprised when he showed me it—it's really remarkable. He really is a delightful fellow—if only he had a little more vitality. I am fed up with cranks—I think I told you of the school at Hellerau near here—psycho-analysis is damned interesting, but with the fools who are immersed in it one has to forget that and protect oneself by humour."

Later the same month he sent parts of the poem later called "Ballad of the Soul". "I've just seen another he's written; some really excellent things in it too—also had its root in a dream. If he hasn't a dream to inspire him, his verses are commonplace." He went on to complain of "the general pressure here of barren heartiness".

In December he wrote: "Muir's poems though patchy (they become less so) are really astoundingly good and as original as anything I have read. . . . [The ballad ones] have more of the ballad spirit than any imitations I have read—in his case the form is entirely natural—he writes in ballad form more quickly and easily than in any other. A pure question of race." He reported that Muir had sent his poems to two publishers without success, and was trying AE who had a reputation for spotting merit. In the following March he told Kingsmill that Muir had got his poems back from AE with "a remarkably stupid letter. . . . They are very patchy, but extraordinary good—and utterly original—when they *are* good."

Holms' presence at Dresden and later in Italy was in some ways trying, especially for Mrs Muir, and one of their moves was to get away from him. But the surface irritations were unimportant in comparison with what the friendship gave.

By 1923 cold winds from the outer world were destroying the happiness at Hellerau. Inflation was making life intolerable for the Germans. The Muirs with their dollar cheques were still well off, but felt guilty. They took their German friends into Dresden for good meals, but felt that they had no right to be in the country. So they fell in with Holms's suggestion that they should share a house with him for the summer at Forte

dei Marmi in Italy. By the time they got there at the end of
May Muir had written a large part of a long poem, *Chorus of
the Newly Dead*. It is curious that in the *Autobiography* he dates
the conception of this poem a year later in Austria, giving a
circumstantial account of walking in the woods on the
Sonntagberg and feeling within him the stirrings of the poem.
These stirrings took place in the woods near Hellerau, and later
were unconsciously transferred in memory to the Austrian
woods, where he was still working on the poem.

III

The Muirs spent most of the summer of 1923 with John and
Dorothy Holms at the tiny Casa Pellizzi at Forte dei Marmi
on the already fashionable coast north of Pisa. Holms's less
agreeable characteristics were more in evidence close at hand,
and relations in the house were strained at times. In Prague
and Germany they had known writers and been to a certain
extent part of the life of the place, but here they were merely
tourists. In these circumstances Muir wrote little, if any,
poetry, but spent most of his time drowsily enjoying the sun
and the sea like other tourists. Only two incidents stimulated
his imagination and gave him glimpses of the real Italy. One
was a visit to a lonely farmhouse in the Carrara mountains,
where they took refuge from the rain. The courtesy and
dignity of the peasant family there made him "dimly aware of
a good life which had existed there for many centuries", and
he was struck by "delicacy and purity of these faces bred by a
tradition so much older than ours, and embodying virtues
which we had forgotten".[16] For a long time he had been looking
into the future and dreaming of what "we moderns" were to
construct. Now he is looking more deeply into the present and
finding in it values coming down from the past. The other
occasion when he saw beneath the touristy surface of Italy was
at a religious celebration at Lucca, where he and his wife saw
old peasant women kneeling in prayer, "their faces streaming
with tears as they gazed at the statue of their Lord", while not
far off "a fair was in full swing, with booths displaying giants
and dwarfs, clowns and conjurers. This was an immemorial

---

[16] *A.*, p. 212.

part of the solemn day, and it seemed to us in no way incongruous."[17] This was an isolated experience at that time; it was not until much later when living in Italy in 1949-50 that such feelings were able to be fitted into a framework, and led him to a realisation of the Incarnation.

In August he went for a fortnight to Salzburg to join his friend Francis George Scott at the International Music Festival. In an article in *The Freeman* he told of his journey from Florence through Trieste and Innsbruck and of some of the people, characteristic of their nations, whom he met on the way— earnest Germans who had come through considerable hardship to Florence, American philanthropists who seemed disappointed to find less poverty than they had expected in Germany, etc. In another article he wrote of the Chamber Music Festival at Salzburg, praising the work of Stravinsky, Hindemith and Schoenberg, but finding most contemporary composers unadventurous. Dull works, he said, were received with approval, while a cold reception was given to the "immature but sincere and promising string quartet of the young Englishman, Mr. W. J. Walton". Walton was then only twenty-two, and this was his first appearance as a composer on an important occasion. It is pleasant to find Muir in his only attempt at musical criticism so quick to recognise new merit in music, as he was so often to be in literature.

On the way to or from Salzburg he spent some time in Florence, where he was persecuted night after night by a vivid dream, in which as a young man of twenty dressed in Renaissance costume he leapt out of a dark archway to plunge a dagger into the breast of a man passing by, the warm blood spurting out over his hand waking him. He speculates whether this dream might have been the resuscitation of an event which had happened long ago in the hotel, once a palace, where he and his wife were staying. But I think such vivid recurring dreams always spring out of some problem, usually not consciously recognised, in the life of the dreamer. A Freudian psychiatrist who has examined Muir's dreams for me interprets some of them in terms of the Oedipus complex, and regards this one as the killing of a father. A more immediate

[17] *A.*, p. 213.

cause may be suppressed irritation with John Holms—a more dominating and superficially vital person than himself, who was his literary mentor and who assumed an "indulgently authoritative" tone as a guide to Italy. If there was a mixture of affection and admiration with some, probably unexpressed, irritation in Muir's feelings for Holms at this time and if Holms was in a way in the position of a father, then it is possible that this complex of feelings may have become connected with a similar, deeply-hidden, complex with regard to his actual father (whom he had loved, but whose influence in so far as it involved a rejection of "profane" literature as sinful he had had to throw off). Hence, perhaps, the violence of the dream. This is all speculation, and may seem unprofitable, since it is impossible to know. What is of some importance in relation to Muir's poetry is that by his vivid dreaming, by recording his dreams and thinking about them he kept more than usually in touch with that part of the mind from which dreams come, and that his dreams threw up images of horror as well as of beauty. His life was mostly quiet and uneventful; he was always gentle and courteous; yet the impulse to aggression must have existed in him as in other people. It manifested itself, with other dark passions and fears, in dreams. So the poetry of this quiet man has in it fears, nightmares, violence as well as beauty and peace.

They were back at Forte dei Marmi in September, and then in October left the Holmses and went to Salzburg, which Muir, having seen with F. G., now wanted to show to his wife. His imagination and his senses were stimulated by Salzburg much more than by the Italian towns. Two years later he set his first novel, *The Marionette*, in Salzburg, and in presenting the fragmentary impressions of the town of the half-witted, extremely sensitive boy Hans he was resurrecting his own. A re-reading of *The Marionette* years later brought back more memories of things seen. It is sometimes said that he lived too much in an inner world of reverie, and was less responsive than a poet should be to the actual world around him. This is not true. His memories of Salzburg were vivid and strongly charged with emotion—memories of "streets suddenly twisting to the right or the left, the powerful circular slew of the houses giving them a pitiless look"; of the stations of the Cross on the Kapuzinerberg changing with the light and the fluctuations of the spectator's mood: "In bright autumnal days the slanting light irradiated every detail", while "in rain the wood looked soft and crumbling and the figures painted on it seemed to be weary of their stations".[18] A simple scene could move him strongly, the sight from a hill of people in the distance moving along tiny roads over the green plain calling up the archetypal image of life as a pilgrimage. He was strongly responsive— with senses, emotion, imagination—to the physical world.

In December 1923 they moved to Vienna where they lived in the Jewish quarter. Here, and earlier in Salzburg, they were painfully conscious of anti-semitism, which was fed by the hardship caused by inflation. Many Viennese families had been ruined by inflation, and it was tempting to find a scapegoat in the Jews. Just before Christmas he wrote to the Thorburns:

> The Scottish election results, combined with the recent temper of the Glasgow group in Parliament, gave us quite a thrill [In the recent elections the Conservatives had failed to win a majority, and in January Ramsay MacDonald with Liberal support formed the first Labour Government.] Things have changed enormously since I lived in Glasgow, only a little over five years ago (it seems far longer) [It was really shorter.] The Scottish members should make a move for Scottish Home Rule, and then they would have the field to themselves. Do you know if that idea has taken hold of the Socialist parties in Glasgow or not? There's a man C. M. Grieve, a Socialist, running the idea in *The Scottish Nation*. . . . When I see things stirring up so much I would like to be back to take a hand in the work. We will certainly (D.V.) be back in Scotland to stay next summer. We'll try to get a small cottage in the Pentlands. not far from Edinburgh. . . . We're beginning to have an intense desire for Scotland.

His interest in Scotland is rather played down in the *Autobiography*. He was never to find a secure and settled position there, but he would have liked to have done so.

In the spring of 1924 he was suddenly told that *The Freeman* was to cease publication—his last contribution appeared in

18 *A.*, pp. 215-16.

March. At about the same time he stopped writing for *The New Age*, of which Orage was no longer editor, and he was not regularly contributing to any other periodical. So the Muirs were left without means of support in a country where living was no longer cheap. However A. S. Neill came to the rescue, and was glad to welcome them back to his school, which had been transferred to a wing of what had once been a monastery high on the Sonntagberg above Rosenau looking out over the plain of the Danube. Neill put a roof over their heads, but could not give them jobs nor an income. So they were still pretty well broke when a few weeks after they arrived at the school they got a telegram from B. W. Huebsch, the American publisher, asking them to translate three of Gerhart Hauptmann's verse plays for a hundred dollars a play. (Huebsch was the proprietor of *The Freeman* and may have had a suspicion that the death of the paper would put them in difficulty; but he does not remember whether this was his reason for offering them translating work.)   In the circumstances they naturally jumped at the offer, though they had had no formal training in German, having picked it up by talking, reading and singing with friends in cafés. By chance they had found a means of making a steady living, one which was to take up an inordinate part of their time during the next fifteen years.

In spite of the translating he was busier on his own creative work on the Sonntagberg than he had been since the Hellerau days. In May he sent a poem, "Remembrance", to Holms, the first he had written for a long time. He was working on his *Chorus of the Newly Dead*, and was much excited by it; and was writing a novel about Glasgow life, of which he wrote to Sydney Schiff:

> The idea is not bad, but it requires more skill than I've been able to acquire yet. I am going to call it 'Saturday': and my subject is, in fact, that day, which in an industrial place like Glasgow, and to the bulk of the people in the British Isles, has an atmosphere quite different from that of every other day. I am going to try to render this atmosphere, suggesting as a background the other working days in the week. The feeling of pathetic freedom which workmen have on the day when they stop work at twelve instead of six, I know well, for I have

felt it myself. There will be a central figure: and in him will
be worked out the gradual disintegration of the day . . .: the
hope of the morning, the freshness of the afternoon after work,
and the gradual loosening and demoralisation of the evening,
the slipping of happiness through one's fingers.[19]

He had already written a first draft of about half this
novel, and he continued to refer to it during the next two
years; but, though a good idea, it was not within his power to
realise.

The few months on the Sonntagberg were happy ones, and
in his dreams later the place had "a supernatural radiance".
In one such dream he and his wife were walking, hand in hand,
down a street, irradiated with light, in a ruined town. "The
cobbles shone, and tender green grass began to sprout between
them; as we went on the grass steadily grew longer, the house
walls crumbled, sending out green branches from the stone, and
in a little square where we found ourselves next trees began to
rise and blossom, filling the air with perfume, while farther
away we heard the plashing of fountains and the singing of
birds."[20] This is a beautiful dream, but there is something a
little disturbing about it. In childhood he had had a sense of
unity between the human community and the natural life
around it. This had been broken during the Glasgow period,
and he was now recovering it—but not quite. For the town
in the dream is a ruined town, and as nature advances the
houses crumble. In order that he may feel completely at one
with nature human life, except himself and his wife, has to be
dissolved away.

In July Neill moved his school to England, first to Lyme
Regis and later to Suffolk, where it became famous as
Summerhill. I fancy there must have been some difficulties in
running a very "progressive" school in a Catholic country. The
pious coming up from the plains to the great Baroque church
next door, which was a place of pilgrimage, may have been
startled by the sight of Neill's children bathing naked. The
Muirs returned to England too, having been away three years.
Just before this Mrs Muir had written, for their American

[19] E. M. to Schiff, 7 May 1924.   [20] *A.*, p. 225.

G

publisher B. W. Huebsch, a penetrating and witty account of Muir's life and character:

> Lived on a small island containing one tree (known as The Tree) till he was fourteen, avoiding school, ostensibly herding his father's cows (i.e. dreaming in the pasture while they ravaged the corn and turnips) and being spoilt by his mother because he was the youngest.
>
> At the age of fourteen went to Glasgow: saw trains, elevators and street cars for the first time in his life. Learnt to use a knife and fork, and to wash daily. Attended church and was twice 'saved' before he struck Pascal and Nietzsche. Acquired a minute knowledge of the seamy side of Glasgow life, and a remarkable vocabulary. Developed a natural gift for contradictiousness.
>
> Wrote his first book 'We Moderns' in the office (during office hours) without being discovered by his employers. Notoriously unpunctual, but seldom brought to book, because his fellow clerks spoilt him a little, just as his mother did. Received brilliant testimonials when he left to go to London, certifying that he could above all things be trusted with cash.
>
> Went to London with 60 dollars, abetted by his wife, a reckless woman from the Shetland Islands, with whom he speaks in the barbarous dialect of these regions. In London he learned to choose wines and order drinks in Soho: escaped whenever possible to the country for week-ends.
>
> Went to Prague because it was in the middle of Europe, and he knew nothing about it. Perhaps also because he could speak neither German nor Czech. After eight months of Prague, went to Germany, and succumbed to its influence completely. Stayed there for a year, began to write poetry, take sun-baths and wear sandals. Tried Italy next, and learned to swim: but driven by a longing for the North (disguised mother complex) returned to Salzburg and to Vienna. Can't live in a city in spring-time; and so is at present marooned on a mountain in Lower Austria. Future movements completely uncertain.
>
> *Personal Characteristics.* Gives a general impression of quietness, gentle kindliness, and a little reserve. Black hair, blue eyes, very slim, small hands and feet, looks ridiculously young and won't say how old he is. Has an enormous forehead, like a sperm whale's: a fastidious, fleering and critical nose: an

impish and sensuous mouth, a detached, aloof, cold eye. Witty when at his ease: elegant when he can afford it: sensitive and considerate: horribly shy and silent before strangers, and positively scared by social functions. Among friends, however, becomes completely daft, and dances Scottish reels with fervour. Smokes cigarettes continually: likes to lie in the sun by the hour: enjoys being petted: and is beloved by cats, dogs, small children, and nearly all women. (Women always want to mother him when they see him: but he has a horror of having his independence encroached upon.)

Passionately devoted to football, although now too short-sighted to play. Watches football matches for hours.

An unusual combination of clear thinking and passionate intuition.

V

Latitudes & Early Poems

DURING these years abroad, leisurely though they were in comparison with most of his life, Muir nevertheless wrote a great deal. For *The New Age* he continued his weekly column of social and political comment, "Our Generation", up to the end of Orage's editorship in September 1922—with, one suspects, flagging enthusiasm. This kind of thing was not his *métier*, and he was discovering where his real strength lay. Between October 1922 and January 1924 thirty-one more prose contributions by him appeared, mostly under the heading "Causerie de Jeudi" and mostly on literary subjects. To *The Freeman* during his time abroad he contributed about eighty articles, reviews and collections of aphorisms. He wrote enough short poems to form a volume, and most of *Chorus of the Newly Dead.* He began a novel, and with his wife began to translate some of Hauptmann's plays into English verse.

Latitudes, published early in 1924, contains most of the essays contributed to *The Freeman* up to the previous May. The rather apologetic preface shows him already repudiating some of the opinions expressed in the semi-philosophical essays, which were the earliest written; so it is a good book in which to follow his mental growth, but not a fair one to judge him by. Not long before his death, when an expanded edition of *Essays on Literature and Society* was being planned, he read *Latitudes* to see if there was anything in it worth reviving, and wrote to Norman MacCaig: "I hadn't read the book I should say for thirty years, and it was a humbling experience. So much mere nonsense combined with overweening confidence, arrows clumsily notched and shot mainly into nothingness. And yet there were things here and there, choice forlorn fragments,

that seemed to be worth doing something with again. . . . So
that I shall have something to add to the book the Hogarth
Press want, but not very much."[1]   A late notebook contains
comments on the essays on the Scottish Ballads, Nietzsche,
Dostoevsky, and Ibsen; so I presume they were among those
he thought of preserving.

The earliest-written essays in *Latitudes* are reminiscent of
We Moderns. The main emphasis is on the rejection of static,
absolute values and on the assertion of life as eternal becoming.
Art is play; it releases us from the bonds of fixed systems. It
"does not moralize or humanize us, nor remind us of eternal
justice; it carries us into a world which is neither necessary nor
necessitated, but perfectly arbitrary and free; and gives us
freely something inconceivably rich and magical".[2] Love too,
"in which the irrationality of woman and of man meet in
infinity",[3] is play, taking us into a world of enchanted folly
from which comes renewed life. One can easily see the
relationship between what he says here and his life at the time.
He needed not only to escape physically from the restrictions
of a life of routine in Glasgow, but also internally to free himself from the Scottish bias towards the purely intellectual and
the narrowly practical. As a young man he had been more
thrilled by speculations about life than by imaginative embodi-
ments of it; and he had kept his intellectual life quite apart
from his workaday routine. Now he was freeing himself from
bondage to system, but was still inclined to keep things rigidly
apart. Imagination is opposed to intellect, freedom to order,
art to morality.

The first nine essays in the book, written later, are more
mature. The division between the two sections comes at about
the same time as he began to write poetry. Imagination,
wakening in him, made it impossible for him any longer to
separate things so neatly as before. He had made a special
realm for it, but it would not stay in it; for it "cannot stop until
it tries to unite all experience, past and present, serious and
trivial".[4] The same awakening as made him a poet enabled
him to be a critic also. An essay on "Psychology in Literary

[1] E. M. to MacCaig, 22 May 1958.   [2] *L.*, p. 141.
[3] *L.*, p. 164.   [4] B.B.C. "Chapbook", 3 Sep. 1952.

Criticism" shows the kind of critic he wanted to become. Most current criticism, he says, is either amiable gossip or professional analysis, the latter producing a dismally post-mortem effect. The badness of criticism arises from the conception that books are dead things and that in considering them the critic is getting away from life. For the true critic literature is a living thing, and he himself is an artist who "chooses for treatment that expression of life which is art". The critic must be a psychologist, though one who is concerned with the mind as revealed in the literary qualities of the work, not with the vulgar and irrelevant details of the writer's life; and he must be a philosopher, able not only to feel beauty but also to discover what significance it holds. The first seven essays in *Latitudes* show him beginning to put these principles into practice. There is no mere gossip, no killing dissection. He patiently tries to penetrate deeply into the vision of life contained in the works discussed.

He was already, for a British critic, remarkably unprovincial, dealing expertly with German books and taking an interest in Italian, Russian, and Swedish works in translation as well as in French, American and British writings. He was quick to recognise the promise of new, at that time little known, writers. He gave high praise to C. M. Grieve's first book, *Annals of the Five Senses* (1923), saying that "except Mr. Joyce nobody at present is writing more resourceful English prose";[5] and wrote warmly, though critically, of early work by Edith and Sacheverell Sitwell, J. C. Powys, and Llewellyn Powys.

In critical prose he was by the summer of 1924 approaching maturity, in poetry he was only a beginner. But the poetry is the more important; for in it the deeper part of himself was at least trying to speak. *First Poems*, having been rejected by other publishers, was brought out early in 1925 by Leonard and Virginia Woolf at the Hogarth Press. It contains twenty-four poems, of which only six were printed in the 1952 *Collected Poems* and only nine in the 1960 collection. Manuscript lists and annotations in his own copy show that he considered restoring several more, some of which he extensively revised. Against a few of the poems he wrote "bad" or some stronger

[5] *The New Age*, 15 Nov. 1923.

expression of disapproval; these include "Betrayal" and "Ballad of the Soul", which probably owe their survival among his collected works to the editor of the 1952 collection rather than to their author.

One principal theme of the volume is suggested by the titles of the first three poems, "Childhood", "The Lost Land", and "Remembrance". In the first he recreates, with some success, the timeless and secure world of his days on Wyre. In the poem he is again a child, lying on a sunny hill securely bound to his father's house below. He lies as still as the grey, tiny rocks around him; and they like him are alive—they "sleep". But more often that world is a lost land, as in the poem of that name, which I quote in full in its revised form in order to show the quality of some of the work which Muir rejected:

And like a thought ere morning I am gone;
My furrowing prow through silence whispers on,
I float far in through circles soft and dim,
Till a grey steeple lifts above the rim,

From which a chime falls far across the waves.
I see wind-lichened walls the slow tide laves,
The houses waver towards me, melt and run,
And open out in ranks, and one by one.

I see the prickly weeds, the flowers small,
The moss like magic on the creviced wall,
The doors wide open where the wind comes in,
Making a whispering presence, salt and thin.

And then I look again and do not know
This town where foreign people come and go.
O, this is not my country. To the roar
Of angered seas I wander by the shore,

Where towering cliffs hem in the thin-tongued strait,
And far below like battling dragons wait
The serpent-fanged caves that gnash the sea,
And raise a barren barking constantly;

And stop where in moon-blasted valleys stray
Dreadful and lovely mists at full noon-day.
I gather giant flowers discrowned and dead,
And make a withered chaplet for my head,

And sleep upon a green embattled mound
With childhood's labyrinths engirdled round;
And I have been here many times before
And shall return hereafter many more,

While past huge mountains and across great seas
That haven lies, and my long-sought release.

This is based on a dream, which he had while he was being psycho-analysed,[6] though it takes a different direction at the end. In the first three stanzas he is approaching the lost land; he is almost there. But suddenly he is among foreign people in a country not his own. What the significance of this country with its dreadful and lovely mists and flowers that wither in his hands is, one cannot be quite sure; the images were given to Muir in his dream, not thought out to convey something. Perhaps the dream was a warning of the impossibility of recovering the lost land by nostalgic yearning into the past, and of the danger of trying to do so. That way one may get caught in a misty region divorced from life, where the flowers are dead. The dream goes on to point by images to a more promising way. The dreamer comes upon a brown clay image of an old woman; he feels a warmth in his breast, as of a sun filling his body with light and power, and is able to bring the image to life as a young girl. The dream seems to be saying—"You cannot get back to the Bu nor be a child again, but you have a source of power within you *now* by which you can give life to what seems dead, make the old young". The poem does not make use of the latter part of the dream, but ends with the poet still yearning for the haven which lies far off.

Two things must be clearly distinguished—nostalgia for childhood, which may be a weak, escapist mood, a refusal to accept the responsibilities of adult life, and desire for that state which Muir calls Eden. Eden is known in early childhood

---

[6] *A.*, pp. 63-4.

more naturally and easily than it can be later, and so the revival of childhood memories is one means of keeping a sense of it alive in oneself, but it can be re-entered only through the present moment, only by the man one is now. This desire is natural to man, and is not an escape. Indeed it is the reverse of an escape; for the recovery of an ability to experience freshly like a child makes a man unusually vulnerable, strips away the protective mask worn by most adults. The dream pointed Muir away from nostalgia towards a recognition of the powers within himself in the present. Like the other resurrection dream it represented the revival of the intuitive, imaginative part of himself. It is noticeable that the escapist mood is associated with mist, whereas what the true imagination perceives is solid and clear. In "The Lost Land" when the speaker seems really to be entering that land he sees the prickly weeds, the small flowers, the moss on the creviced wall; later, when this land is lost, he is among mists. The poem, stopping short on the note of yearning, suggests that Muir had not with his conscious mind appreciated what, I believe, his subconscious was telling him through the dream.

The best of *First Poems* are those which do not merely reach into the past, but which bring together past and present and try to reconcile conflicting emotions. In "Horses" past and present, awe and delight are mingled, when for a moment, watching "lumbering horses in the steady plough", he recovers the feelings he had had towards the horses on his father's farm. The poem, like "The Lost Land", ends on a note of yearning as the vision fades and he is left pining for that dread country

> Where the blank field and the still-standing tree
> Were bright and fearful presences to me.

The poem which most successfully achieves a resolution of the tensions contained in it is "Ballad of Hector in Hades", in which his childhood memory, suppressed for thirty years, of his ignominious flight from Freddie Sinclair came to the surface as a poem about Hector being chased round Troy walls by Achilles. The reason for his flight, and for his suppression of the memory of it, was, I think, fear not of the boy, but of elements in his own nature which now, thanks partly to the analysis, he was able to face. So in the poem Hector flees in terror, but at the moment of being caught is suddenly "rid of fear", is released at the moment when fear might be expected to reach a climax. This surprising ending comes not from the story of Troy but from within the poet; it corresponds to a common experience, of inexplicable fear followed by release when the dreaded thing happens and is found tolerable or when one comes face to face with the dreaded thing in oneself. Like many of Muir's this poem is the end product of a long period of unconscious working on an experience from the past. It is effective, especially in the description of the dream-like precision with which Hector sees small things in his flight, but the words at the end are inadequate to convey the change of feeling. Muir's unconscious was supplying him with images and ideas out of which poems could be made, but he needed long practice with words before he was to be able to do full justice to the material offered. Sometimes the words are inadequate because weak and banal, sometimes because he strains for effect and overwrites.

In the Hector ballad the material from the unconscious was given form by being linked to a story. When the material came up as a dream, a succession of images linked only by the logic of the dream, it was less suited for transfer straight into a poem. Shapely poems are not produced by the unconscious mind alone any more than by the conscious mind alone. On "Ballad of the Soul" (originally called "Ballad of Eternal Life"), based on the waking trance he had experienced in London, Muir commented much later: "The dream was wonderful, but the poem is all wrong". The trouble was that he was trying merely to reproduce the dream, not working creatively on it. The visions he describes are of great interest from a psychological point of view, but the poem does not help the reader to see nor to feel them more vividly than the prose account does. Too many of *First Poems* merely reproduce dreams; later, as in "The Combat", he learned to use them better, to make something new out of them.

Three of the best poems in the volume—"October at Hellbrünn", "When the Trees grow bare" and "Autumn near Prague"—are based on more recent experience and show that his poetry was already beginning to profit from the "orgy of looking" he had indulged in at Prague. These poems at the same time describe actual autumn scenes and convey the poet's mood.

> The gossamers forge their cables
> Between the grasses
> Secure, . . .

The word "secure" here alone in its line has great force, conveying a sense of the strength of natural processes even when manifested in the slender gossamers. These poems evoke not the lushness of harvest but the calm which follows it.

> The wrinkled sun-memoried leaves fall down
> From black tall branches

and the poet is unburdened of thoughts which have oppressed him. The tumult of summer is over, is a mere memory; there is sense of calm, of exhaustion, and at the same time of vitality held in suspense in the earth which

> Far withdrawn,
> Lies asleep.

A young girl goat-herd seen in a field is at one with the natural scene, for she

> Sits with bent head
> Bowed to the earth
> Like a tree
> Dreaming a long-held dream . . .

and the poet too assimilates himself to the scene, as the clamour of his own strife seems to come to him in his new serenity from afar. The peace, the exhaustion, the sense of energy withdrawn but still existing in suspense, the coldness and clarity, the sense of having been unburdened and of bareness—these are all features at once of the landscape and of the poet's state. Some of the poems in this volume might make one fear that this young poet was living too much in an inner world of his own; these three showed promise for the future in the bringing together of inner and outer.

Another good poem is "Ballad of the Flood", which tells of Noah surviving the flood and in the end making his home on

Mount Ararat. Muir may have been led to the subject by his sense of having escaped great dangers and of having at last begun to find his home, his right place, his true nature; but he rightly does not bring himself in at all, but tells the story objectively in a simple ballad way. John Holms says that "this poem was written at an astonishing speed, in two or three days I think".[7] There is a tenderness and a humour in it that are not found elsewhere in *First Poems*. It is not merely an attempt to reproduce the Biblical narrative, but contains strange and original touches of imagination.

This poem and "Ballad of the Monk" are of interest for being written in Scots. The main literary influence on him at this time was that of the Scottish ballads he had known as a child; and it was natural that he should experiment with the language as well as the form of the old ballads. This was a very different thing from Hugh MacDiarmid's attempt, begun at about this time, to revive Scots as a language for all purposes. English was always Muir's language for reflective and lyrical poetry.

Muir began his *Chorus of the Newly Dead* at Hellerau, and continued to work at it, off and on, until the summer of 1925. What he meant to achieve in it he explained in letters to Sydney Schiff:

> I wished to get a certain pathos of distance in contemplating human life, and I found this the most unconditional way. In this "chorus" there will be types like the Saint, the Beggar, the Idiot, the Hero, the Mother, the Rebel, the Poet, the Coward; and they will all give some account of their lives as they see it from eternity, not in Heaven or in Hell, but in a dubious place where the bewilderment of the change has not been lost. There will also be choruses for all the newly dead in which some kind of transcendental judgment will be passed on these recitals. . . . The atmosphere I am aiming at is one of mystery and wonder at the life of the earth. There will be no dogmatic justification, and as little mere thought as possible; no mention of the name of God, but an assumption of infinite and incalculable forms behind the visible drama.[8]

[7] Holms to Kingsmill, 22 Jun. 1925.
[8] E. M. to Schiff, 7 May 1924.

The poem is not directly personal, but an unacknowledged, probably unconscious, motive for the choice of subject may have been the need to give the "pathos of distance" to his own contemplation of the life he had known in Glasgow from his new serenity in Germany. Some of the *First Poems* look back to childhood. The *Chorus*, in so far as it is connected with his own life, looks back to Glasgow, and tries to see meaning in the narrow and unsatisfactory life he had lived and seen others live there, the problem being seen within the larger one of understanding why immortal spirits should descend into the restricting conditions of time.

The list of characters was changed as the poem evolved. The first four speakers pose the problem. The harlot has been confined in a narrow, sordid life in one mean street; the coward has been oppressed by inexplicable fears, and nature appeared to him hostile:

> He saw Life only in its wounds that bleed.
> Nature he knew but in the grappling greed
> Of waxing roots, the gluttony of the weed.

The beggar has been shut out from the lust and glory of the world, sitting

> by doors forever close;
> I knew each blackened stone,
> Heard on hot walls the sunlight doze,
> And heard dry pavements groan.

They all had a sense of alienation, of having come in to a place which was not their own; and yet they seemed to have been fated to enter it. The idiot

> did not know the place, the alien throng;
> The light was strange to him, bound by the awe
> Of a once-broken long-forgotten law.

There was a strong sense of necessity:

> It was decreed. We cannot tell
> Why harlot, idiot or clown
> Lived, wept and died. We cannot spell
> The hidden word which drove them down.

The last three speakers do not give any clear or easy answer to the question why the sufferers should have lived, wept and died; but they have had glimpses of a larger context. The poet imagines that the world of time may be coming to an end:

> Perchance by now last autumn is on the earth;
> A million leaves, a million mortals fall, . . .

Contemplating the end of time we find that we have a "stubborn love of passing things"; in earthly life there have been visions of beauty which shall surely go with us into whatever lies ahead. The Chorus meditates on how they had once before stood, as now, "and longed for life". Their entry into earthly life had been fated, but had also been desired by them. Life is seen as a track through a glittering wood, with existence lying unending around it. The travellers cannot leave the track

> But sometimes there the bonds were torn
> 　Asunder, and the forests seemed
> To wake in everlasting morn,
> 　And changed the brightening branches gleamed.

The next speaker, the hero, is the traditional dragon-slayer. The scene of the combat is vividly presented, and this is one of the best sections of the poem, even though it is not easy to understand. The fight is almost entirely mental:

> Day, month and year went o'er me;
> I felt my foe before me;
> 　Close, mind to mind, I fought.
> Intense in toil and slumber
> I pierced in legioned number
> 　The lying mists of thought.

Once the mists of thought are pierced and the dragon is found the fight is virtually over. One is reminded of "Ballad of Hector in Hades". Though the hero seeks his foe and Hector runs away, in both cases the difficulty is in reaching the point of confrontation, which when it comes turns out to be less bad than has been feared.

In the speech of the mystic some effort is made to sum up all that has gone before, but the different visions are laid side by side rather than being included in a whole. He has seen, like the first speakers, "the tiny demon shapes" in natural things and

> The squat façade of tortured stone
> Close ambushed in the sultry street.

Like the poet he has seen beauty, and he knows that

> Behind all beauty Beauty lay.

And he has seen

> That stationary country where
> Achilles drives and Hector runs,
> Making a movement in the air
> Forever, under all the suns!

> And that ghostly eternity
> Cut by the bridge where journeys Christ,
> On endless arcs pacing the sea,
> Time turning with his solar tryst!

The stationary country is presumably eternity conceived as containing all the events of time existing together in an eternal present. Does the second stanza quoted mean that the conception of things in which Christ entering into time forms the bridge between time and eternity is only an idea in the minds of His followers, the word "ghostly" having almost the force of "illusory"? Whether or not the Christian answer is intended to be definitely dismissed, no other clear one is given, and we are left simply with a rather vague feeling that there is one.

Finally the Chorus chants in rather Tennysonian but moving stanzas on the passing of the earth and of time.

> And lovely now the standing plains of corn
> Which countless dying eyes in parting see,
> And million trees bowed with red fruit forlorn,
> And dusk on every no more wakening lea. . . .

> Then saviours will arise, and fainter clay,
> And evening realms casting long-shadowed towers,
> And ransomed peoples turning all one way,
> In ranks beside red westward-facing bowers;
> No fruit, but only hills of empty flowers;
> Men, blazoned beasts, and rocks, and flowers, and peace.
> Last light will fall from them and Time will cease.

The problems of evil and suffering have been left behind without really being answered, and we are left uncertain how we are supposed to see the relationship of time and eternity. In these final sections he does not quite achieve what he told Sydney Schiff he hoped to do: "The Poet begins the new movement, away from suffering to its transcendence, and the Hero emphasises that moment; but I have another figure, I don't know what to call him, perhaps the Mystic, in which all life will be affirmed. Then there will be a grand final chorus —this is what I must prepare for—which will sum up everything and convey some of the glory even of those who pass through life apparently deprived of what it can give, the beggar, the harlot, and so on."[9] The final chorus conveys a sense of the glory of life in only a vague way, and does not succeed in gathering up within it the experience of the earlier, deprived characters. But the poem remains a brave attempt to deal with a large theme; it contains some impressive visions and some lovely lines and stanzas, and deserves reprinting. It was a very original poem to have written in the early 1920s. Muir was then and ever after indifferent to fashion. At its best it is reminiscent of the work of the great romantics, Blake, Coleridge, and Shelley; but it is not imitative of them. At its worst it displays the same kind of faults as decadent sub-romantic verse of the later nineteenth century. As Kingsmill wrote to Holms: "The supreme merit is that he has a vision of a world of his own, which he repeatedly evokes in marvellous phrases. I mean by a world of his own a concrete world, bright and vast and barren generally, inhabited by Blakean beasts. His nature is in intimate touch with the primaeval world, in some way or other. . . . I think its fault is rhetoric, whenever the inspiration flags. His desire for power comes out in flamboyant adjectives."[10]

Two printed copies of the poem show that, much later, Muir made sustained efforts to revise it. He tried to cut out poetic diction, clichés, and declamatory phrases such as "vast inarticulate memory" (altered to "uncomprehended memory"). In a few places he wrote in complete new lines which show the

[9] E. M. to Schiff, 1 Feb. 1925.
[10] Kingsmill to Holms, 26 Oct. 1925.

difference between the mature poet and the apprentice. For instance near the beginning of the final Chorus, in place of

> And now the earth is but a phantom show
>> Whose lighted shapes through deepening darkness wend

he wrote

>> Earth's roads on their appointed circuits go,
>> All things to the last stations calmly tend.

And at the end of the poet's speech he altered the commonplace

>> Where, in what distant night, have these been hurled?
>> When shall dawn rise on those lost mounts again?

to the more precise and striking

>> Now to a ball that universe is curled,
>> And to a seed that paradise of grain.

But it was not possible by tinkering here and there to make the poem satisfying to his mature eye. Towards the end of his life he began to write a completely new poem on the same theme, in which he hoped more adequately to embody his original idea, but he did not get far with it.

H

VI

England and France

AFTER finding his vocation and writing quite a lot of poetry in Germany and Austria Muir wrote surprisingly little poetry in the next few years. Five poems, none long, appeared in periodicals between 1927 and 1931, and were published with one other in a fine limited edition in 1932. Letters show that he wrote, or at least began, some others during this time, but presumably he was not satisfied with them. The pace quickens after 1932; for in 1934 *Variations on a Time Theme*, consisting of ten poems, appeared, followed in 1937 by *Journeys and Places*, including nineteen new poems. The harvest of twelve years was not great in quantity, and contains little of his very best writing. Unusually for a poet he was not to come fully into his own until he was over fifty.

All this time he was working hard to make his living as critic and translator, and he was hampered at times by illness and other worries. Putting it in Maurice Nicoll's terms these distractions tended to keep him on the horizontal line of time, hurrying him along from past to future without allowing him the leisure and the peace to be conscious, except intermittently, of *now*. He had begun to discover himself, but in 1935 he still had to confess to Stephen Spender that he only rarely felt in contact with that solid foundation in himself from which all true originality must come.

His novel-writing was another cause of retarding his development as a poet. During this time he published three novels, wrote a large part of another, planned still others, and wrote some short stories. In the novels he was trying, not altogether successfully, to shape material coming to consciousness from the deeper levels of his mind. He could combine creative work with criticism, but not so easily two kinds of creative work. He wrote to Sydney Schiff: "I find that the novel demands a degree of concentration greater than I had expected; unless I feel a continuous strain I doubt whether the result is worth while. . . . My struggle to attain an imaginative prose is almost as great (though I have been writing prose all those years) as my first struggle to write poetry."[1] The novels contain material which might have found more satisfactory embodiment—as much of it later did—in poetry or in straight autobiography. Nevertheless they contain passages of great power and beauty, and deserve to be better known.

During these years there is a discontinuity between his outer and his inner life. He travelled and saw many interesting people and places, but very little of what happened to him or that he saw entered into his imaginative work, even the novels. In the novels he was trying to come to terms with his past, and in them and in the poems to deal with certain big problems which were preoccupying him. It seems that to some extent he lost the vivid sense of contact with the external world which he had won for a time in Germany and Austria and which he was to recover later. His next great period of spiritual advance was to be in the years 1937 to 1941, and this was to make possible the major poetry, the astonishing production of an aging man, that he later wrote. In the mean time he had to wait, to improve his command of words for the time when inspiration would come, and to do lesser things—to become perhaps the best reviewer, and one of the best critics and translators of his time. He was patient, not trying to force poetry out of himself by the conscious intelligence alone.

II

Back in England in July 1924 the Muirs went to stay for a few days with a new friend, Sydney Schiff ("Stephen Hudson", the novelist). In his last review in *The Freeman* Muir had praised "Hudson's" *Prince Hempseed*, knowing nothing of the author and thinking he had discovered a new writer. Schiff was a wealthy man. Something of a recluse as far as society in general was concerned and intensely disliking publicity he took great delight in the company of friends. His wife, Violet, was a sister of Ada Leverson, Oscar Wilde's "Sphinx". He

---

[1] E. M. to Schiff, 12 Jul. 1926.

had been quite elderly when he had published his first book, of short stories, in 1916. He had then started on a series of novels, later combined in *A True Story* (1930), one of which Muir had reviewed. As a result of the review he wrote to Muir, enquired about his circumstances, later found a cottage for him to rent in Penn, Buckinghamshire, near his own house at Chesham, and showed him much kindness.

They went on up to Mrs Muir's home in Montrose, and he soon afterwards wrote to Schiff: "Scotland has been a sad disappointment to us after all the longing we had for it, so shut in, unresponsive, acridly resolved not to open out and live."[2] They fell in with Schiff's suggestion that they should live near him, rather than in Scotland as they had intended, moved to Penn in the following January, and stayed there until the autumn. They were busy with bread-and-butter work, translating Hauptmann and reviewing for *The Nation and The Athenaeum*, and had little time for the writing they most wanted to get on with, his novel and her book on women. From Penn they went up to London occasionally, and saw a good deal of the Schiffs at Chesham.

Wyndham Lewis paints a satirical, fictionalised picture of Schiff and his circle in his *Apes of God*, Part IX. The satire against pseudo-artists in this book is weakened by the fact that many of the characters are thinly-disguised, and much distorted, portraits of actual people. Lewis could create a grotesque imaginative world which has its own vitality, but his persecution mania and his personal animosities made him wholly unreliable as a commentator on people he knew. Provided one bears this in mind there is no harm following Lewis's Zagreus (in some degree a spokesman for himself) to a large luncheon party at the Keins (Schiffs) and seeing how the Keiths (Muirs) are presented. Keith takes little part in the animated conversation and, when he joins in, speaks in a "faint toneless voice". The "energetic face" and voice of Mrs Keith are, however, more in evidence. When the talk turns to Pierpoint (a mysterious figure who never actually appears, but who is often quoted with reverence and who seems to stand for the author, the true artist, as against the Apes) Mrs Keith is

[2] E. M. to Schiff, 2 Aug. 1924.

heard to say, "Pierpoint is what we call in Scotland a puir wee . . .", the doubtless uncomplimentary concluding word being drowned in laughter. Meantime "Mr Keith lay back with one arm over the back of his chair, smoking, with half-closed eyes—'detached', faintly smiling, freckled, spectacled".[3] Zagreus privately tells his companion the history of "Keith of Ravelstone, who tends the shadowy Kein". A "very earnest, rather melancholy freckled little being" he was, after living in great poverty, swallowed by Mrs Keith and later taken by her on the grand tour to the remoter capitals of Europe. There he discovered in the latest book vamped up by Kein in his dotage a "new writer". Kein, delighted to find at last an admirer, discovers all about him by correspondence and on his return from foreign parts "opens his mouth and swallows him, in fact sucks him into every pore of his rickety old person and closes the lid".[4] Those who knew the Muirs later will recognise some superficial truth in parts of this. Muir was shy and quiet in noisy company, not striving to shine, speaking little and in a gentle (though not "toneless") voice, sometimes detached. Mrs Muir was more energetic, never afraid to voice forthright opinions in down-to-earth terms about the most eminent persons. But essentially the picture is all wrong—of Schiff as well as of the Muirs. Muir was never "swallowed" by anyone. His relationship with Schiff was one of mutual admiration and affection. Schiff may at the start have seen himself in the role of the kindly patron of a young, poor and unknown writer, but Muir's letters show that he never surrendered his independence. They show him writing with increasing authority on literary matters, though quite without discourtesy or chippiness. He was the better judge of literature, and was not falsely modest. At the same time he had the generosity to be able to accept kindness—though not, I think, any financial help apart from a small loan—from a rich man without any rancour. What his marriage meant to him is suggested by a passage in a letter to Schiff:

> The most profound union that can exist is that between a man and a woman in love. But the most essential thing in that

---

[3] Wyndham Lewis, *Apes of God*, (London 1930), p. 298.
[4] *Op. cit.*, p. 303.

union, it seems to me, is the unconscious out and in flowing of life between the two, which postulates both a physical and a spiritual correspondence between them, and is very like a process of nature, and is in any case as old as the hills. But this process strikes me as more like a free give and take, the freedom of two people who are united in one thing (their feeling towards each other) than like a unity. What is it that gives one thoughts, images and so on, in the centre of oneself? It is one's unconscious which is one's own from the cradle, but which a great experience can set free—a union with someone one loves.[5]

It was his marriage more than the psycho-analysis that set free his unconscious, gave him the thoughts in the centre of himself which were the source of his poetry.

In spite of the friendship with the Schiffs the Muirs had already, within a year of returning to England, decided to go abroad again. England was too expensive for them; by living more cheaply abroad they hoped to have more time for their creative writing. In October they went up to Montrose to stay with Mrs Muir's mother, and there fell ill. She had a miscarriage, and was seriously ill for a time; and he had a threatened appendicitis, which passed off. Apart from reviewing he was working hard to finish a collection of essays on contemporary writers which came out in 1926 as *Transition*. This was his most mature book yet, full of original perceptions and without the stridency and overstatement of his earlier writings. He was writing little poetry, but still regarded himself as primarily a poet. He wrote to Schiff:

I have often said to you that I value my poetry more than my criticism (though I think that the latter approximates far more closely to excellence of form); and it is for this reason, that I feel art is for me the only way of growing, of becoming myself more purely; and I value it for myself, I know it is my *good*, the only real good for me, and the personal feeling, the personal integration seems to me more and more the thing that really matters. Given that, other things will become right, for one will be alive, and have therefore some sort of criticism of life. And it does seem to me, however uncertain the future may be,

---

[5] E. M. to Schiff, 8 May 1925.

that this being alive, this capability of renewing oneself . . . is
the thing which chiefly matters. I think you are profoundly
true when you say that this state is not final, that it 'seems to
have an unlimited extension at both ends'; and your saying
so makes me convinced that you are in the preliminary state
for creation again, that this feeling will not rest until it has
been resolved. Can equilibrium be reached? Or if it is
reached is it anything more than a point which becomes once
more a point of departure? I cannot think so, and I cannot
wish it so. There is something constant in us, I feel; but we
can only feel it when we are growing through creation, and
when the habitual has no longer any hold over us.[6]

The life of Montrose probably still seemed narrow to the
Muirs, but they had the interest of meeting there C. M. Grieve,
who was working on the local paper. Things were stirring in
Scottish literature, though few knew what was happening.
Grieve had already published *Sangschaw*, containing his earliest,
and some of his best, lyrics in Scots, as well as *Annals of the Five
Senses* which Muir had praised highly in a review. He had
printed some of Muir's work in *The Scottish Nation* and in
Scottish Chapbook, had praised him in *The New Age* both as
critic and poet, and was soon to hail him as "incomparably the
finest critic Scotland has ever produced".[7] The two men met,
went for walks together, and relations were amicable; but the
temperamental differences were already evident. Grieve
remembers that whereas he wanted to talk about literature,
Socialism, etc., Muir was most keen to tell him of his dreams
and visions. Muir wrote a year later to his brother-in-law:

> When we were in Scotland last time we heard a lot about
> Scottish Nationalism from C. M. Grieve who wrote *A Drunk
> Man Looks at the Thistle*. It seems a pity that Scotland should
> always be kept back by England, and I hope the Scottish
> Republic comes about: it would make Scotland worth living
> in. Grieve is a strong nationalist, republican, socialist, and
> every thing that is out and out. He thinks that if Scotland
> were a nation we would have Scottish literature, art, music,
> culture and everything that other nations seem to have and we

---

[6] E. M. to Schiff, 17 Dec. 1925.
[7] *Contemporary Scottish Studies*, p. 111.

haven't. I think that would probably be likely; but I feel
rather detached, as I've often told Grieve, because after all I'm
not Scotch, I'm an Orkneyman, a good Scandinavian, and my
country is Norway, or Denmark, or Iceland or some place like
that. But this is nonsense, I'm afraid, though there's some
sense in it.

In March 1926 they were able to leave for St Tropez in the
south of France. They had been asked by B. W. Huebsch to
translate Lion Feuchtwanger's *Jew Süss* for a fee of £300, which
seemed—and probably was—a generous offer, though in view
of the tremendous success of the book they would have done
better if they had had a small royalty. But in the mean time
this was riches.

III

They rented a furnished house a quarter of a mile from the
town of St Tropez—a pleasant house with a large sitting room,
small kitchen and two bedrooms, with large grounds containing a quarry and almond and pine trees, all for thirteen
shillings a week. The town he described as "a little fishing
village . . . a rather primitive, but pretty place, where most of
the inhabitants, I believe, are Communists".[8] Though they
loved the house they never got used to the life around them.
St Tropez was not the crowded tourist resort it is now, but was
already the centre of an international colony of artists and their
hangers-on, many of them people whose lives were left without
purpose, direction or joy by the cult of untrammelled freedom.
In notes for the *Autobiography* he mentions a "German lady who
stopped us one day and told us we must not stand aside from
the general crowd—we had no idea we were doing so". They
were not deliberately standing aside in a priggish way. They
were busy, and living their own lives.

During that hot summer, while the free lovers pursued
their immature *affaires* around them, they recovered their
health, spent much time bathing, and worked hard. Their
translation of the 150,000 word novel *Jew Süss*, begun at
Montrose, was quickly finished, and appeared later that same
year. He continued with his reviewing, and by November

[8] E. M. to Thorburn, 21 Nov. 1926.

had finished the first draft of his novel, *The Marionette*. Mrs Muir too was working on a novel, *Imagined Corners*. In October they moved to lodgings in Menton near the Italian border, "a much more civilised place"[9] with more congenial company.

This was the year of the General Strike, and Muir at times felt half guilty about his isolation from practical affairs and the struggles of his former comrades in Glasgow. He wrote to his sister in November: "If it were not that I feel I am doing work now that justifies itself, I should like still to be taking an active part in the Socialist movement, for it is unbearable sometimes to look on and do nothing. But one can't do two things, and it is better to try to become a good writer than to be a bad writer and a bad Socialist. I am of course a Socialist and shall always be one; but I can't do anything, not because my hands are tied, but because all my energy is going into something else."

The Marionette was his most important production during his stay in France. Some preliminary notes for it were written in Austria in 1924, but it was not begun until two years later. By the end of November 1926 the first draft was sent to Holms, who in January wrote to Hugh Kingsmill:

> In sending it to me Muir said he was very satisfied with it, particularly the second half, which I hadn't seen; this was very curious, since the first half had a good deal of merit, with some really fine things, whereas the second half was so bad, almost from any point of view, that I am surprised the publisher took it. . . . So I told Muir that if I were him, although the book was with the publisher and coming out in the spring, I'd delay it till he had rewritten the second half. His incapacity for self-criticism is extraordinary, coupled with his immediate recognition of faults when they are pointed out. He agreed at once and is now rewriting the second half on a plan that should be really good if he brings it off.

Holms's strictures were quite justified, and the revised version, which he saw at the end of March, was a distinct improvement. He then wrote: "Muir's novel is fairly near it [the borderline of sanity] too; I've seen the proofs and like it better than I did. . . . Even now I don't think it's successful really as a

9 *Ibid.*

whole; but it's very remarkable and clearly written by someone with genius".   It was published in England and America in the summer, was quite favourably reviewed, but did not sell well.   Muir himself was quite pleased with it at the time; but later spoke slightingly of it, as of all his novels.

The Marionette is the best of his novels.   He did not have the kind of imagination which a novelist needs, and found it difficult to create living individual characters and a solid fictional world.   He tells us that the characters possess such and such qualities, but when he comes to show them in action he gives them, the central ones, his own sensibility, and they live with their creator's life rather than with a fictional life of their own.   In *The Marionette* he came nearer than in the others to overcoming this defect, and it is well worth reading for its own sake.   But I am concerned with the novels here more as revelations of the author's inner life than from a literary critical point of view, and I shall examine them with this end in mind.   In Prague he had awoken again to the outer world of actual things, and had indulged in an orgy of looking; and in Salzburg had responded vividly and freshly to things seen. At the same time his imagination had awoken and presented him with perceptions which seemed much more real than the ideas he had been trifling with; and his dreams too seemed to have a reality and meaning of their own.   His childhood had come alive for him again, and he had a longing to re-enter that lost land.   Were his imaginative perceptions true perceptions, not mere fantasies? How was he to combine the inner and the outer worlds, to live as an adult in the everyday world and to keep alive his perception of a deeper reality associated with childhood? He dramatised these and other problems by showing in Hans, an extremely sensitive half-witted Austrian boy, a much more extreme case than his own of these difficulties.   Hans responds vividly to things, but is afraid of them. As a boy "he saw nature as a terrifying heraldry.   The cat, the lizard, and the wasp were embattled forces armed for war, carrying terror and death on their blazoned stripes, their stings, claws and tongues".[10]   Later when taken for walks by his father he still sees everything freshly like a child.   He is

10 *M.*, pp. 7-8.

frightened by the noise and bustle in the Salzburg streets, by the falling of a fir-cone, by the smallness of things seen from the top of a mountain, by a dog and by salamanders. He retreats into a succession of fantasy worlds. First he has dolls and a dolls house, and builds for them an imaginary life. Then he is taken by his father to a special performance of *Faust* at a marionette theatre, and his fantasy world is enriched. He imagines himself as Faust and in love with Gretchen. The actual world around seems inane and clumsy in comparison with the world of his dreams. Then during a final visit to the marionette theatre there is an accident; the Gretchen puppet's ankle is broken, and it falls to the floor. Hans is greatly disturbed. His father has the puppet repaired and gives it to Hans, saying that Gretchen is all right again. But Hans has come to doubt the reality of the marionette world; Gretchen seems, at times, like one of his own dolls, and he is confused. In order to restore the illusion his father has a Faust suit made for him and he strikes attitudes in it before a mirror. (This is the part suggested by Holms). Sometimes he recognises that he is just playing, but sometimes the pretence seems to pass into an action outside himself, not created by himself. He sees in the mirror another Hans, who seems to be trying to show him something. This other Hans must, he thinks, live in another house, in a distant place; and one day he sees this house quite distinctly, its garden, flowers, three trees, etc. He sees himself there on a bench, but younger and quite peaceful, with his father, also younger. Knowing of the life of the other Hans and the other father in that other house he is able to feel greater affection for his father in ordinary life. (Here, for the first time, the imaginative life is shown as feeding the daily life.) Later Gretchen begins to enter his vision of the other house.

One afternoon he wears his Faust suit for the first time out of doors; he goes into the garden in it with the Gretchen puppet and dreams of the other house; his dream is shattered by rude boys on the wall shouting "loony" and throwing stones. He stops wearing the suit and playing with the Gretchen puppet. One day he undresses the puppet and sees that it is constructed in the same way as his dolls. This makes him doubt whether the world of the other Hans and Gretchen and house exists. He wishes to reach it again, but is unable to. He takes the clothes off the puppet and chops it up, and comes to believe that in doing so he has destroyed the other Hans and Gretchen. He sees in a vision the other house and garden, and in the garden many pairs of inanimate figures lying in leaves. He suffers a mental collapse. On recovering he has a dream in which his father comes to tell him Gretchen is dead; they go to a room in the other house, where Gretchen lies dead; Hans weeps by a marble mantelpiece, then goes to the dead girl, feels a glow of life from within himself being communicated to her; she comes to life and they go together through a radiant town into green fields. This dream seems to release him. His father puts together the pieces of the puppet, but Hans is not much interested in it any more.

This is something more than a story about a half-witted boy in a state of pathological withdrawal from life. Hans sees more, not less, than ordinary people. His senses are more acute, his imagination more vivid. He responds to things with unbearable intensity, sometimes with terror, sometimes with delight and love. The successive worlds of his imaginative creation have real value, embody real perceptions. When he sees the other house and in it the transfigured images of himself and his father and Gretchen living together in peace and love, and when this vision enables him in ordinary life to see his father as loveable, something more is happening than a wish-fulfilment dream. This is, as Muir might later have put it, a vision of Eden; and the boy is *right* to see the everyday fallen world as, in comparison with it, inane and clumsy. Where he is wrong is in clinging to the dolls, dressing up and infantile attitudes in general. The imagination sometimes leads us to a perception of another world, a reality underlying and giving significance to the more limited world perceived every day by the senses. Toys, puppets, works of art, images in general may help to lead to this perception, but may become dangerous if taken as more than means. Hans is on the way to a cure at the end when the vision of the other house is restored to him in a dream and when at the same time he is no longer much interested in the Gretchen puppet for itself.

In *Hans* Muir dramatises some of the dangers to which a person of exceptional sensitivity is subject. The artist must keep awake, awake with his senses to the external world and with his imagination. To be fully awake is dangerous. The perceptions that come are terrifying and painful as well as beautiful, and are difficult to reconcile with one another. The artist, "a shrinkingly sensitive mirror", may, hurt by contacts with the external world, withdraw into himself and then be overwhelmed by an uprush of images from the unconscious. It is safer to be half asleep, as most of us mostly are; but then one is no longer an artist.

The answer for the artist is in creation. What arises from the unconscious must be given form. Muir had dealt with this problem earlier in an essay "Against Profundity", in which he inveighed, with some immaturity and overstatement but also with real insight, against the modern tendency to introspection: "Life is comprehended only in the throwing of it outward, cleanly and completely; what introspection shows us is only what introspection itself has tortured and thwarted, the suffering, passive body of our vivisected selves. . . . The soul is unfathomable; it can only be expressed. . . . This is how the soul has been enriched, and diversified; not by a withdrawal into itself, but by an expression outward which breaks one bond after another, and in which the hidden riches of one's soul rise up and are revealed."[11]

Though he knew the danger of introspection he knew that as a poet he must keep open the channel into his deeper self. He knew that he had experienced something of great value in his childhood and more recently in dreams, and that he must keep alive these perceptions in himself; and he was aware of the danger of regressing, of looking for the "lost land", "Eden", "the other house" solely in the past and by introspection. His Hans, the boy who was unable to grow up, was among other things a warning to himself of one of the dangers to which a person of his temperament is subject. His main help in avoiding this danger was, of course, his wife. As she says, if Edwin had one foot in Eden, she had firm hold on the other.

[11] *L.*, pp. 184, 185.

IV

About the end of May 1927 the Muirs returned to England. They were expecting a child, and needed to establish a settled home. The commercial success of *Jew Süss* had led to their being asked to do more translating; with that and the reviewing they could reasonably expect to be able to make a living. They wanted to be near London so as to be in touch with editors and publishers. After a short time they found a furnished house (Hazel Cottage, Dormansland) near Lingfield in Surrey, where, and later at the White House, Dormansland, they stayed until the end of the next year. There in October 1927 their son Gavin was born. During the dry hot summer they enjoyed walking through the woods to see the horses charge down from the start on Lingfield race-course. But life was mainly hard work. He was writing a book on the novel, *The Structure of the Novel*, finished early in the next year, and had undertaken to provide Jonathan Cape with a life of John Knox by the end of 1928. So two books were on hand at the same time, as well as a great deal of translating, most of which was done by Mrs Muir. After May 1928 he gave up regular reviewing for a few years.

The Structure of the Novel is his one work of literary criticism in which he was able to develop a sustained argument at length. It is lucidly and wittily written, and is full of original insights both into general principles and into particular novels. It is close-packed, and does not admit of fair summary; so I shall not try to discuss the ideas contained in it here. More than most theorists Muir shows a catholic appreciation of novels of different kinds, and does not seek to impose any particular pattern. The one thing he demands is that a novel must be a work of art, present an image of life. "For the object of this argument is to show that the plot of the novel is as necessarily poetic or aesthetic as that of any other kind of imaginative creation. It will be an image of life, not a mere record of experience." The writer must "transform his vague and contingent sense of life into a positive image, an imaginative judgment. . . . If in most novels this transformation does not take place, then we know what to think; they are not literature, but merely confession. If again in the period novel

the writer contents himself with drawing a picture of the contemporary changes in society, we know once more that this is
not literature, but journalism."[12]

The Structure of the Novel is much the more valuable work,
but it was the *Life of Knox* which seems to have excited him the
more at the time. He agreed to do it, not only because the
terms were good, but also because he thought that, having been
brought up in the shadow of Knox, he might be able to get
something vital to himself into it. This personal interest is the
source both of the book's strength and of its weakness. In
Knox Muir was hitting at things in Scottish life which had
hurt him and damaged Scottish culture. This makes the book
lively and in parts amusing and exciting. On the other hand
he lacked, as he later realised, the detachment and the
historical knowledge to paint a fair and comprehensive picture.
He hauls Knox into the twentieth century, and arraigns him
from the point of view of the modern liberal, making little
apparent effort to get back into the sixteenth century or into
the mind of his subject. He had neither the knowledge nor
the historical imagination for the task he had been set. Eight
years later he gave generous praise to a life of Knox by Lord
(then Lord Eustace) Percy, by implication admitting the
limitations of his own by calling it "probably the best book that
has ever been written on Knox", and by commending the way
in which Percy "continuously shows Knox in relation to the
whole European situation, as well as to the Scottish and
English".[13]

The biography came out in June 1929. One curious result
is mentioned by Muir in a letter to his sister: "Who do you
think I've just been interviewing on account of having written
the Knox? Lord Beaverbrook! He's enchanted by it, and
disagrees completely with it. He's offering me work, but how
that comic incident is going to turn out I can't say. . . . It's
the most comic thing that ever happened to me, but I rather
liked the old rascal." Beaverbrook thought that Muir's power
in denunciation might be useful, but soon found that he would
not write to order.

[12] *S. N.*, pp. 149-50.
[13] *The London Mercury*, vol. xxxvii, no. 218 (December 1937), pp. 213-14.

The Structure of the Novel was the first of his books to sell reasonably well, and is the only one of his early prose works that has been kept in print. His reputation as a critic was now firmly established. The Knox also had a modest commercial success, being received with undue enthusiasm in some quarters in Scotland. He was contemplating at this time a series of short stories, and told Huebsch that he had ideas for about ten, some of which had already been written. He was slow in realising his limitations as a writer of prose fiction.

He was trying to express his deeper self mainly in prose. But during the time at Lingfield he did publish two poems in periodicals which show that, though inspiration came seldom, he had grown in ability to give it adequate expression when it did come. These were "The Enchanted Knight" (originally "The Trance") and "Tristram's Journey" (originally "Tristram Crazed"). The former shows a great advance on "The Enchanted Prince" from *First Poems*, in which the mood is similar but in which both the scene and the emotion are left rather vague. The Prince lies on an ancient mount, and looks sleepily with half-raised eyes at wild weeds springing in the ditch nearby, at the houses on the hills "so inaccessible and so clear"; and at the dimly-seen heights further away where peaks seem to battle in the haze and dragons to rear in the sky. He is cut off from the world immediately around him—the houses are inaccessible though clear—and has but a vague possession of the imagined world further away. The knight's situation is like the prince's, but is much more effectively conveyed. We see a clear picture of him as he lies "in the bare wood below the blackening hill"; of his rusted armour and of the spider's web stretched "from his sharp breast-plate to his iron hand". The ordinary activities of life go on around him; the plough drives near. In dream he sees his "ancient friends" pass, but he cannot rise and join them. He cannot even brush away the "insulting weight" of a withered leaf which drifts on to his face. Many people experience something like this in dreams—a despairing sense of helplessness and immobility when something urgently needs to be done; and in waking life a similar feeling is not uncommon. Muir had known a sense of alienation from things and from people in childhood and in Glasgow. More recently he had felt unhappy at being merely an onlooker at the time of the General Strike; his ancient friends in the Labour Movement had gone out to battle, while he lay by the sea at St Tropez and wrote books, one of them the story of a boy whose dream life cuts him off from the world of every day. The poem was written at about the same time as *The Marionette*, and a similar complex of feelings lay behind it. Alternatively, or perhaps in addition, one may think of the enchanted knight, and prince, as Muir's own buried self, or a part of himself, which he was trying, not yet successfully, to revive. In *Poor Tom* Mansie Manson thinks "of that rich and bright cloud in which, as in a trance, some part of him for ever beyond his reach still lay imprisoned; so that the memory awoke in him a vague need to struggle and free himself from something or other, he did not know what".[14] It is quite unnecessary, however, to know anything about the biographical background in order to appreciate the poem. Whatever personal experience went into it has been objectified and universalised, and it stands up on its own.

"Tristram's Journey", based on chapters 17 to 21 of Book IX of *Morte D'Arthur*, also deals with a state of alienation, this time followed by discovery. What the story meant to Muir is made clear by the way he modifies the original. In Malory Tristram, believing Iseult unfaithful, leaves Tintagel and wanders deranged until captured and brought back to King Mark's castle, where he lives as an unknown wild man until made known to Iseult by being recognised by her brachet. In the poem the brachet is the means not just of making him known to Iseult, but of restoring him to a knowledge of himself and to contact with the outside world:

> There as he leaned the misted grass
> Cleared blade by blade below his face,
> The round walls hardened as he looked,
> And he was in his place.

This was the first of Muir's "journey" poems. "The Enchanted Knight" expresses a "place", a certain spiritual state;

---

[14] *P. T.*, p. 112.

"Tristram's Journey" deals with the passing from one state to another.

v

After a bit more than a year in Lingfield the Muirs moved to another rented house (The Nook, Blackness Road) at Crowborough in Sussex, where they stayed for over three years. Crowborough stands high on the Weald not far from the Ashdown Forest. They had a garden, and there were "hills, heather, gorse, and fat woody country all within easy reach".[15] At the same time they were in easy reach of London, the British Museum and necessary contacts there. They were rather isolated, not having much in common with their bridge-playing neighbours; but their nieces came down from Glasgow sometimes in the summer, and friends came to stay from time to time. The work they most wanted to get on with was their novels. His researches on Knox had given him an idea for a historical novel set in Scotland in the sixteenth century; and she had yet to finish *Imagined Corners*, begun long ago in France. But they were particularly busy with translations, four volumes of which appeared in 1929 and four in 1930; and they were hampered by illness. He wrote to his sister in July 1930: "Almost for a twelvemonth we've been having one misfortune after another; we've never had a year like it. . . . First Willa was ill with one bad throat after another; then when she was still very unwell Gavin took inflammation in the middle ear, and the doctor had to be in almost constant attendance on him; then Willa's mother and brother Willie died within seven hours of each other; and finally I had a collapse too. Finally we took a complete month's rest—we had to, for we couldn't read a book, far less try to write one. It's the first holiday we've had for three years, and we are both feeling very much better after it. . . ." In a letter to Schiff he wrote of having had a "break-down" and of his mind still being bleak and musty after his return from France. In spite of these difficulties he had managed to finish *The Three Brothers* by this time, and it came out in 1931, as did *Imagined Corners*. He had

---

[15] E. M. to Thorburn, 19 Jun. 1929.

long ago abandoned his original novel of Glasgow life, but now used his Glasgow experience for *Poor Tom* (1932).

One should not give the impression that life at Crowborough was all work and illness and trouble. Muir's nieces, Ethel and Irene Thorburn (now Mrs Ross and Mrs Abenheimer) spent summer holidays there, and remember the household as a particularly happy one. Mrs Muir created an atmosphere of fun and gaiety and humour—sometimes caustic, but not malicious; he, more withdrawn and quiet, was also gay and humorous in his own way. His nieces, like himself writing of his own parents, do not remember them ever exchanging a discourteous word with each other. Gavin was a very bright and intelligent child. After her mother's death Mrs Muir inherited some money. Some was given to the Thorburns— George Thorburn was a house painter and often out of work; the nieces were given bicycles; and for themselves they got a car for £30. He was a vague and absent-minded driver, but never came to any harm. ("There is no trust but in the miracle.")

During their month's holiday in France in 1930 they made contact again with his old friend, John Holms, who was living with Peggy Guggenheim in Paris. She wrote: "I liked Edwin Muir from the very beginning. He was frail and timid, and so sensitive and pure that you could not do otherwise than like him. You felt his talents, even though he was shy and never acclaimed himself. Muir reminded me of a man who has been asleep in front of a fire too long and could not recover from his drowsiness."[16]

Another visit abroad was in 1932 to a PEN conference at Budapest at which they represented the Scottish PEN and which he described to his sister:

> As for Budapest, we were very unhappy there most of the time: the atmosphere of misery, oppression, hatred being so overpowering. We couldn't account for it ourselves, but shortly before we left an English Quaker who had been living in Hungary for ten years told us lots of things. The people are treated like cattle, it seems; the whole country belongs to six old noble families, who, it seems, are extraordinarily charming,

---

[16] Peggy Guggenheim, *Out of This Century* (New York, 1946), pp. 120-1.

generous and humane in most ways, but who simply do not consider their servants and country labourers as human at all, and would not even think of lifting a finger if they were all starving. Then, in the train leaving Budapest Ernst Toller told us a pretty gruesome story. On the day when all the delegates to the PEN were being received in the old royal palace by Horthy, the Regent, Toller had been taken by a doctor he knew to a hospital in Pest. He spoke there to a tailor, both of whose legs were broken. This tailor had been suspected of distributing socialist (not communist, but only socialist) pamphlets. So a group of gendarmes entered his house and searched it, and when they found no pamphlets strung the tailor up by the wrists and ankles between two chairs in his own room, and beat him on the soles of his feet until they were a bloody pulp. When the tailor awakened from his faint they prepared to beat him again, and in his terror, bound as he was, he leaped out through the window, which was three storeys high, and broke both his legs. His wife, who was pregnant and had to look on at all this, died of the shock. This is the story the tailor told Toller, and it is not by any means exceptional; but quite a typical slice of Hungarian life. The ordinary people in Budapest are extraordinarily nice, I fancy, but quite cowed: the people at the top, and especially their hangers-on and lackeys, are a set of stuffed swine and butchers. And of course, on top of this, Budapest is filled with hatred of the Roumanians, the Serbs, the Czechs, the Slovaks, and as there were representatives of all those countries at the Conference, the atmosphere wasn't exactly harmonious. Still we met lots of nice people, had the amusing experience of seeing Marinetti in action, and the real pleasure of listening to Toller —he's a magnificent orator when he gets well started.

And on our way back through Vienna we had Broch's company for three days [they were translating his *The Sleepwalkers*], which was worth the infernal torments of Budapest. He's the greatest man there is, I think, and so intensely sensitive, so shy, so easy to hurt, that life must be a torture to him—though he loves gaiety and simple kindness, almost intensely.

The Muirs had their special difficulties at the Conference. They were delegates of Scottish PEN, an independent centre, but were at first treated as part of the large English contingent.

He was therefore put in the, to him of all people unwelcome, position of having to push himself forward and insist on being treated as the head of a delegation.

It might seem that at Crowborough the Muirs had been living in an ivory tower apart from the main stream of events. But Muir was in some ways more emotionally involved in the troubles of the 'thirties than the mainly middle-class writers who dealt more directly with politics. Few of them saw the effects of unemployment in their own families; and they had to reach out from their inherited environment to try to make contact with the working and lower middle class. Muir had been a poor clerk for eighteen years, and knew the life of an industrial city from the inside. Now his sister was married to a man who was often unemployed; and she herself, though an intelligent woman, had to go out to work as a domestic servant. Troubles abroad too were to hit him personally, engulfing or driving into exile people he knew well. But, even if they did not live mentally in an ivory tower at Crowborough, they did feel rather out of the stream of things there; and in October 1932 they moved to a large, dilapidated house (7 Downshire Hill) in Hampstead.

The chief works produced at Crowborough were the two novels and a few, a very few, poems. A note written at Menton in February 1927 tells us something of the genesis of *The Three Brothers*:

> I had thought of this first as a story with two brothers, one good, one bad, a perfectly simple allegory of the dualism of the soul. Now it has become more intricate: I do not see the simple story any longer and the final business [?] may be more like a novel than a story. (I think just now I am becoming more interested in people and less in nature than I used to be. In my Chorus I was concerned with human life in its general outlines, with birth, death, fate, etc: in "The Marionette" this is also the case. Now, after this concern with life in general I find myself filled with curiosity over individual cases: How do they live? How do they go through with it, easily, hardly, in all their different ways? [If this concern of mine is real, as I feel it is, then it probably means that in regard to my own life I am becoming more positive. I hope that this is so: it is what

I need most: and it would fructify me, or rather give me a
whole new province to roam in.])

There is no indication that at this stage the novel was intended
to be a historical one. Probably it was only when collecting
material for his life of Knox more than a year later that the
idea of making his brothers grow up in sixteenth century
Scotland occurred to him. He may have hoped by this means
to "distance" the material taken from his own experience. If
so he was not entirely successful. Reading *The Three Brothers*
we hear some interesting discussion *about* the sixteenth century,
but we do not feel ourselves to be in it. The parts of the novel
that live are those which are based on experience, not research.
The real subject is not sixteenth century Scotland, but the
passage from boyhood to early manhood of the three brothers,
and behind that Muir's own search for maturity. The central
character, David Blackadder, having been brought up in the
country by a kindly father, goes in early manhood to Edinburgh,
where he experiences a series of shocks which make him keenly
aware of suffering and evil and shake his faith in the meaning
of life. His vision of horror is conveyed by description of scenes
of violence in the streets and of his dreams—such as the dream
of the black worm in his hand already quoted. Sensitive, shy and
intelligent he is not able to adapt himself to what surrounds him,
as his twin-brother Archie is in a thoughtless, animal-like way.
Archie has seduced and so been the cause of the death of a
girl whom David had loved. Waking from his dream of the
worm David hears his brother's steady breathing in his sleep;
and this "steady breathing took on an unbearable self-
complacency. . . . He lay wondering why Ellen was violated
and dead, and Archie sleeping peacefully not more than six
feet away, his dreams undisturbed. That callous and im-
penetrable rhythm was stronger than anything else in the
world; death would break it some time in his brother's body;
but when it was broken there, then in myriads of bodies like
Archie's it would still beat on; nothing could touch it, or impede
it, or distract it; and this was what God had created."[17] There
are signs here of the original scheme in which the twins were

<hr>

[17] *T. B.*, pp. 266, 270.

to have been "one good, one bad, a perfectly simple allegory of the dualism of the soul." Characteristically evil is identified with indifference, insensitivity, and good with a capacity to suffer and sympathise. It would be quite wrong to think that Muir was here identifying himself with the sensitive David and some one else with Archie. It was the indifference he found in *himself* that shocked him, the dualism that is found in *every* soul. David sees the black worm in *his own* hand.

Listening to his brother's even breathing, David's thoughts turn to God, who also seems indifferent to the suffering for which as creator He must surely be ultimately responsible. He had believed in God in the Heavens, and Him he had faced with bewildered faith; now he was confronted by the God of Nature, and from this new God he revolted. "For if God were the moving principle of the universe, how could he turn from the cruelty of the Universe to Him, who was its burning centre and axle?"[18] In the end he becomes calmer, and reaches a tentative faith that there is a road and a meaning in life though we cannot see them clearly here. It is not the passages in which such thoughts are merely discussed that give the book distinction, but those in which they are conveyed poetically, in images. David *sees* things with clarity and intensity—both actual scenes and the images and visions in which his thoughts present themselves to him. Near the end he has two impressive waking visions. In one he sees a stationary eternity in which all the events of time are frozen:

> I saw ships heeled over for ever at the same slant by an invisible and eternal storm, and the wind like a solid rock leaning against the sails, and the ocean a stationary fury of mountain crests which would never subside. I saw Caesar with the knife in his breast, and I thought: There is the moment when the point does but touch the heart, and that moment in the retina of His eye is eternal, and in that moment is Caesar eternally stationed between life and death, and is neither alive nor dead, or is both alive and dead. . . . I saw Judas innocent and Judas guilty; and he was innocent for ever and guilty for ever. And I saw one embrace an eternity, and one murder an eternity, and one act of mercy an eternity. . . . And all these

---

[18] *T. B.*, p. 273.

beyond computation, without beginning or end, for all was as it was, and so remained.[19]

In the second vision he sees the Last Judgment, not at all like that in the Bible, but described with powerful and original imagination. These passages came out of Muir's recent experience, not from his Glasgow years; he was becoming increasingly preoccupied with the problem of time.

The Three Brothers was no great commercial success, but was highly praised by Rebecca West in *The Modern Scot*.[20] She recognised that the characters have a symbolic significance, and thought that in this book literature had regained a state in which comedy and tragedy might again be achieved. She complained, however, with some justification, that "Mr. Muir's people know too well what is the matter with them. At any moment they can analyse their psychological condition with perfect detachment and practised eloquence." Like many other modern writers Muir was hampered as well as helped by knowledge of psychology.

The same stricture can be applied to *Poor Tom*, in which even more than in the other novels the weight of the actual past bore too heavily on the fictional structure which the novelist tried to create. I have used it extensively in relation to the Glasgow years, and so shall say no more of it now.

The preoccupation with time, found in parts of these two novels, is seen also in the few poems written, or at any rate published, during the Crowborough period. Two poems, "The Stationary Journey" and "The Threefold Place" (originally called "Transmutation"), published in periodicals in 1929, gain by being read together, since the second seems to suggest an answer to the question implied in the first. The wakening of his imagination had come when he had looked back over his own life and been able to see it timelessly, had experienced, in words he quoted from Proust, "a moment liberated from the order of time". But does this looking at life timelessly liberate one from time? This seems to be the question implied in "The Stationary Journey", in which he looks back not just over his own past but over the whole history of the earth. Past time

[19] *T. B.*, pp. 331, 332.   [20] *The Modern Scot*, vol. II, no. 1 (April 1931).

flits before him like a cinema reel played backwards, and then in an architectural figure he sees all the events of time frozen in a stationary present.

> For there Immortal Being in
> Solidity more pure than stone
> Sleeps through the circle, pillar, arch,
> Spiral, cone, and pentagon.

This vision, similar to that quoted above from *The Three Brothers*, liberates from time in the sense that one is no longer being hurried forwards or backwards by it; but it leaves the events of time untransmuted. It leaves Judas eternally guilty as well as eternally innocent. He then sees another vision, "the mind's eternity" which liberates from the distresses of time and restores the unfallen world; but asks whether this is more than a dream.

The poem originally called "Transmutation" ends on a more hopeful note. He sees an autumn field, in which are standing corn and cut sheaves; heroes come walking from the woods, are scattered on the ground like leaves by a silent wind, and birds build nests in their helmets and shields. There are "Sweet cries and horror on the field./One field." Horror because so far this is another stationary journey, all things existing together in one field. But he looks again and sees that there are not one, but three fields:

> One where the heroes fell to rest,
> One where birds make of iron limbs a tree,
> Helms for a nest,
> And one where grain stands up like armies drest.

The three fields are presumably the past, the present and eternity; these are in a sense separate, not one. Eternity is not just the events of time frozen, but a different dimension. There is the possibility of transmutation, of Judas being forgiven, not eternally guilty. Originally there was an additional stanza, which is poetically inadequate but makes the meaning clear:

> So my deep dread is lightly taken away,
> Now that to three the old blind mass gives way.
> In this won space Beauty and Hope and Faith
> May walk and draw terrestrial breath.

The poem is the better without this rather banal and too abstract stanza; its exclusion in 1932 shows that Muir knew that he must work towards a more complete fusion of thought and image. The poem is spoilt by the explanatory lines, but is a little puzzling without them.

VI

At the beginning in Hampstead, in the winter of 1932-33, the Muirs had their troubles, but their time there was to be a happy one. The lavatory was condemned and dismantled, bricks fell down the kitchen chimney, plaster fell from the dining-room ceiling, and the roof leaked; but these difficulties could be dealt with, and they found the house charming. By Christmas they were in money trouble, as he told his brother-in-law the following March: "Immediately after we took the house I lost my job with Secker, on which we were depending for a livelihood. (They couldn't afford to keep me on any longer). At Christmas we were down to £1.10.0, with no job in prospect, the rent due, myself down with the 'flu. In the first week of the year I got a job from Gollancz, also a huge book to translate; and the same week *The Listener*, quite out of the blue, offered me the job of reviewing novels for them. So that out of hopelessness we were raised in a few days to comparative comfort." He had done little reviewing since he stopped contributing regularly to *The Nation and The Athenaeum* in May 1928. His work for *The Listener* was to provide a small, but assured, income for many years. He contributed an article of about 1500 words about once a fortnight, dealing usually with three novels. The jobs he mentions with Secker and Gollancz were as publisher's reader.

Such things as a leaking roof and temporary lack of money did not worry him deeply. It was larger anxieties that gave the sombre tone to the poetry written at this time. In the letter, already quoted, to George Thorburn he wrote:

> It's a dreadful world that we're living in just now: like the Dark Ages, when one civilisation was breaking up and another forming with painful fragmentary slowness. But that seems to be how great changes take place; we're in the trough now, but something eventually is bound to come, some new form of

society; the present misery convinces me far more of that than I was ever convinced during my early idealistic Socialism. . . . I'm translating; Willa is finishing her second novel [*Mrs. Ritchie*]; I'm thinking of another; also writing some poetry, inspired by this present world we find ourselves in. We like being in London after the deadness of the country: I find the people we meet are more human than I had expected. I've seen Orage a few times, rather a pathetic figure now, I think, without knowing it; still leading an advanced army that has long since fallen into the rear. . . .

I don't know how Scottish Nationalism is to survive in the general revolution that seems to be sweeping over all civilisation. It seems to be a counter-movement, but it may be simply another form of the general process. I'm all for it, in any case.

This letter shows that he was thinking of yet another novel —probably a sequel to *Poor Tom*, which he at one time thought of as the first of a trilogy. But fortunately poetry began to come faster, and the novel was abandoned. He was glad to see Orage again, back in London from America, and contributed to his *New English Weekly* until his death in 1934, but was less in sympathy with his ideas than before.

Despite public and private anxieties they were on the whole happily settled in Hampstead by early 1933, in love with the "sweet, battered, Mozartian grace" of their house, and with Hampstead itself with its "little shops like shops in a village, the sense of seclusion and leisure on the verge of a great city".[21] They enjoyed the greater opportunities they now had for social life and friendship. Though busy they were always hospitable, and though never financially secure enjoyed and generously shared whatever prosperity they had. One of those who became a friend at about this time was George Barker, then a very young man making his start in literature. He recorded his impressions more than twenty years later in *The London Magazine*. He wrote a novel.

It made no money, but it did gain me the friendship of Edwin Muir, who, having written about the book, asked me to call and see him in his house in Hampstead. I went one wet evening

---

[21] *A.*, pp. 237, 239.

in the autumn and met for the first time a phenomenon I hope
never to forget: the extraordinary gentleness that prevails in
the presence of many men who are truly poets.

I think with gratitude of evenings spent in his quiet company, because here I learned that words were not only
delightful things in themselves but also—this mysterious fact
still fascinates me—that they stand for far more than most
people either think or are. Muir was like a silent clock that
showed not the time but the condition, not the hour but the
alternative.

And I gratefully remember that occasion when the over-
powering caryatid of Willa Muir took up Homer and began to
recite that opening passage in the Greek, so that the whole of
the tasteful room in Hampstead gradually filled with the loud-
mouthed rolling parallels of the poem and the sea—until I was
witnessing the living demonstration of Eliot's assertion that a
poem can communicate before it is understood.[22]

But Muir was not, except socially, drawn into any group or
movement, literary or political. Just round the corner, in
Keats Grove, Geoffrey Grigson began to issue *New Verse*. Muir
knew him and, then or later, most of the fashionable writers of
the 'thirties, but he was not much, if at all, influenced by them.
Similarly, in opposition to the trend towards Marxism in the
circles he frequented, he kept to his own undogmatic and liberal
brand of Socialism. In 1935 he wrote to Stephen Spender,
sending him four new poems: "I am getting away from my
obsession with Time (a static obsession) and these poems are
stages, some losing, some winning, in the battle. I have been
coming more and more towards a socialist or communist view
of things for some time (I was in the Socialist movement in
Glasgow before the War, but the War put an end to that for a
long time). I think the *hin und her* of that development might
be as good a theme for a sequence of poems as the expression
of a communist attitude without the doubts and fears. (You
express the doubts and fears yourself, but there are not many
others who do.) At any rate I feel that I may put all this into
poetry, if I have the luck." He was drawn towards a "socialist
or communist" view, but not towards the Communist Party,
which always seemed to him a perversion of the Socialism he

[22] *The London Magazine*, vol. III, no. 1 (June 1956), pp. 51-2.

believed in. Two years later he wrote to Spender from St Andrews: "I meet many communists here, chiefly Dundee ones, and I like and respect them; but I feel I shall never join the Party, indeed I could not. I agree with the ends of Communism completely, but the philosophy, the historical machinery, deeply repel me: I cannot think of it except as a coffin of human freedom. . . . I have come to the conclusion that the whole Marxian apparatus is a terrible dead weight on the hope of Socialism, a terrible perversion of it into something else altogether, whose roots are partly in Capitalism and partly in the Old Testament." Though not yet certain of his own way, he was mature enough now not to allow himself to be led down fashionable wrong paths.

In the early summer of 1933 he went to the PEN Congress at Dubrovnik, Yugoslavia, as a delegate of the Scottish PEN. In a letter to his niece he tells of having had a gay time flirting with the editress of a fashion paper and breakfasting with H. G. Wells, whose stories he enjoyed. But the conference had its sombre side, being the first since Hitler's assumption of power. There was a passionate discussion of the persecution of Jewish and other writers in Germany. The official German delegation, writers acceptable to the Government, walked out when Wells, the Chairman, recognised the right to address the Congress of Ernst Toller, who had been expelled from the German PEN under Nazi pressure and was in exile. Toller spoke with great force, as also did Sholem Asch, the Yiddish novelist, some of whose works the Muirs translated. Perhaps influenced by this renewed contact with European writers and by his consciousness of the new barriers which were being erected among them, Muir the next year made his one excursion into periodical journalism as editor as well as contributor. With his old friend Janko Lavrin he started the *European Quarterly* to keep open communications and "to foster the growth of the European spirit in every sphere of human activity". It ran for four numbers, and contained writing of high quality. It aroused some interest abroad, but very little in Britain, where almost the only subscribers were Jews and Germans. There was not enough support to enable them to keep going beyond the one year.

He came back from Dubrovnik to find piles of work and
the bad news that his sister Clara, who had been close to him
as a child, was dead.   Soon afterwards his son Gavin, then
five, was run over by a petrol lorry, and his leg was broken.
The leg healed well and they had no reason to think that the
accident would have any long-term ill effects.   In August they
set off, with Gavin, for a holiday in Orkney—the first time he
had been there for many years.   They lodged in a farmhouse
(Grimbister, Firth) with a young couple, the Davies, whose
family had tilled the land for centuries.   The serenity of the life
there reminded him of the Italian peasant family they had
visited in the Carrara mountains years before.   Mrs Davie
remembers his gentleness, and the delight he took in the sunsets,
in helping to stook the sheaves in the harvest fields and in
hearing again old Orkney words and sayings.   They came back
by Glasgow, where he became more vividly aware than before
of the effects of the economic depression.   Driving one evening
through the mining districts of Lanarkshire he was struck by
the ugliness and desolation of everything and by the plight of
the unemployed.   "Everything which could give meaning to
their existence in these grotesque industrial towns of Lanarkshire is slipping from them; the surroundings of industrialism
remain, but industry itself is vanishing like a dream.   Airdrie
and Motherwell are the most improbable places imaginable in
which to be left with nothing to do; for only rough work could
reconcile anyone to living in them.   Yet a large population
lives there in idleness; for there is nowhere else to go. . . ."[23]
The idea of writing a book about modern Scotland came to
him; and the next year he went on the tour round Scotland
recorded in *Scottish Journey*.

In the winter John Holms and Peggy Guggenheim came to
London—to 12 Woburn Square—but for a tragically short
time.   Holms had injured his wrist in a fall from a horse in the
summer, and was to have a minor operation.   His heart gave
out under the anaesthetic, and he died on 19 January 1934.   He
was cremated.   Muir, one of the few people present, remembered the ceremony as "a dreadful violation of death, too
horrible for tears.   But afterwards, walking about outside

[23] *S. J.*, p. 2.

along a brick wall crowded with niches and urns, I cried at the thought that he had died so easily, for that was the saddest thing of all: as if Death had told him to come, and like a good child he had obeyed, unresistingly letting Death take him by the hand."[24]

In June 1934 he went to Scotland for a PEN Conference, and then set off from Edinburgh, in an old car given him by Stanley Cursiter, on his "Scottish Journey". The Cursiters went to see him off as he passed their house just outside the city; he came bowling along, stopped at traffic lights, looked up and enquired whether it was the red or the green that meant "go". The car—a 1921 Standard—evidently had quite a personality of its own; and his rather inefficient handling of it is one of the humours of the book.

Back in Hampstead the Muir's gay social life and multifarious writing went on, but their happiness was clouded by the after-effects of Gavin's accident. Physically he seemed to be all right, and he was becoming a precocious pianist; but the accident had left him nervous of traffic, and they thought it would be better for him if they moved to a quieter place. Also, life in London was too expensive, and was becoming too hectic. They were generous hosts, glad to welcome writers and other friends who knew that good food, drink, and conversation were to be had at 7 Downshire Hill. In January 1935 he wrote to Sydney Schiff: "We have been struggling along, with the usual expanse of translation, and getting, I am afraid, very little original work done. London is an expensive place, and we have definitely decided, whenever we are able to do it, to go up to Orkney to live for a year or two, where we could live on a third of the money we spend here, and so would have at least half our time for original work. Orkney is my native place, and Willa too has taken an affection for it, and so the change would not be a hardship; on the contrary, we are looking forward to it keenly." It was perhaps a pity that this plan was abandoned. They were offered a suitable house (Castlelea, The Scores) to rent in St Andrews, and moved there in August.

[24] *S. F.*, p. 256.

VII

Poetry 1932-1937

I

VARIATIONS ON A TIME THEME is perhaps Muir's least attractive volume of poetry. One reason for this is suggested in a letter of his to Mrs E. B. C. Lucas, who had expressed admiration for his earlier poems: "I wonder if you like my new ones as well; I myself did not get nearly so much pleasure in the writing of them—indeed, a good deal of bitterness in some cases—whereas my earlier ones were the fruit of very fortunate moments for me. And we must write, and feel, as we can."[1] The *Variations* contain bitterness and inner tensions incompletely resolved. Nevertheless they are an advance on *First Poems* both in content and style. He tried in them to express a wider range of experience, to find images and myths to bring together his personal story and his sense of what was happening in Europe in the 1930s and of the human situation in general. The greater complexity is bought at the price of some obscurity.

The poems were not written in the order in which they are collected, nor originally, I think, with any idea of forming a sequence. He was preoccupied by time, and so the poems which came were related in theme; but they are ten poems, not an attempt at a single one. The best comment on them is Muir's own on No. II in the series, originally called "The Riders", which Miss Gwendolen Murphy included in her anthology *The Modern Poet* in 1938. He wrote to Miss Murphy:

> The point round which the poem crystallised was the beginning:
>
> At the dead centre of the boundless plain
> Does our way end? Our horses pace and pace
> Like steeds for ever labouring on a shield.

---

[1] E. M. to Lucas, 30 Mar. 1934.

These lines came to me spontaneously, without my being conscious of the possible development they implied. The development grew from a variety of associations that would have remained isolated and disconnected but for this image, which acted as a sort of magnet, and drew them into a rough pattern round it. The Horses, as I see them, are an image of human time, the invisible body of humanity on which we ride for a little while, which has come from places we did not know:

> They have borne upon their saddles
> Forms fiercer than the tiger, borne them calmly
> As they bear us now,

and which is going towards places we shall not know:

> Suppliantly
> The rocks will melt, the sealed horizons fall
> Before their onset.

Yet the steed—mankind in its course through time—is mortal, and the rider is immortal. I stated this belief tentatively in the poem, because it was written in a mood of unusual dejection. The painful emotion in the poem comes from a simultaneous feeling of immortality and mortality, and particularly from the feeling that we, as immortal spirits, are imprisoned in a very small, and from all appearances fortuitously selected length of time: held captive on the "worn saddle", which in spite of our belief in our immortality has the power "to charm us to obliviousness" by "the scent of the ancient leather".

I was not aware, or at least fully aware, of all these implications when I wrote the poem; and I have only realised during the last year that all my poems from the start have been about journeys and places: that is about the two sides of the paradox one of which implies the other.

Miss Murphy asked him about the lines about the autumn light:

> And so we do not hope
> That their great coal-black glossy hides
> Should keep a glimmer of the autumn light
> We still remember, when our limbs were weightless
> As red leaves on a tree, and our silvery breaths
> Went on before us like new-risen souls
> Leading our empty bodies through the air.

K

He answered:

> I actually saw once, many years ago, the picture as I set it down: it is one of the few things in the poem taken from observation.   It was a clear bright day in late autumn down in Sussex: the weight seemed to have left every physical object with the drying up of the leaves still sticking to the trees without burdening them.   A boy was ploughing in a field, and a moving column of breath went on before him; his own breath; but the air was so light and clear, the picture so distinct that what my eye saw was the column going on in front and the boy following it.   Why this struck me so much I can't say yet; but when I came to this part of the poem it seemed to be the correspondence I needed.
>
> '. . . The autumn light/We still remember' of which the 'coal-black glossy hides' do not keep a glimmer.   I think this is an attempt to suggest those isolated moments of pure vision which have a feeling of timelessness (and are often called timeless).   My feeling about these moments (which are a common experience, though most people are unconscious of them) has always been that they do not *go into* Time; that they do not change the actual physical body of Time, symbolised by the horses.   They may cast a momentary reflection on the glossy hides, but it fades almost at once.   This instant fading makes them 'autumnal'.   At the moment when we are aware of them we are released from the presence of Time; our limbs are 'weightless'.   Our silvery breath going on before 'Leading our empty bodies through the air' is an extravagant way of describing the state of freedom.[2]

This poem, like many of his, started from lines which came to him spontaneously, originated not from a train of thought but from an image whose implications he came to appreciate only gradually.   The title "metaphysical" which has sometimes been given him can be accepted only with reservations. He was concerned to be true to his experience, to his "simultaneous feeling of immortality and mortality", rather than to reach by conscious thought any facile solution to the problem posed by this combination.   Yet he felt that his own experience was significant, and was related to that of others and of the

---

[2] *The Modern Poet*, pp. 168-70.

race. In the third of the *Variations* (originally called "Autobiography") he—for the first time, I think—explicitly brings
together the story of his own life and the fable (the pattern
underlying the single life which relates it to the history of
mankind). Like Adam, he had known as a child a timeless
Eden and the Fall; then, both Abel and Cain, he had been
both victim and aggressor (incidents with Freddie Sinclair);
then had been overwhelmed by a flood (early years in Glasgow);
but his essential self had survived and

> Rode on the flood to Ararat's safe hill.

Then, like young Abraham among his flocks, he had been
content to enjoy "a small Eden" (period in late adolescence
when he had put away serious thoughts and enjoyed the
ordinary pleasure of a young man); then had suffered from
inner divisions, conspiring against himself like Jacob against
Esau, his brothers against Joseph. Then, like Joseph in Egypt,
he had obtained some worldly success, but this had not brought
him any nearer to his true goal. Now, like the children of
Israel, he was wandering in the wilderness searching "this
rubble for the promised land". This theme is continued in
the sixth poem, in which the children of Israel are still in the
wilderness after forty years of circuitous wandering. But sometimes a higher, though fearful, reality has made itself known to
them—in the stream smitten from the rock, on Mount Sinai,
and in whirlwinds. They believe that there is a promised land,
their own land; they do not know the way to it, but believe
that they will be led there.

Faith is never wholly lost; but in the series as a whole the
main emphasis is on the waste land, the wilderness, the sense of
imprisonment. He finds it difficult to establish any relationship between the two realms of which he is conscious, to see
any positive value in time. As he wrote to Miss Murphy his
feeling was that the moments of illumination do not "go into"
Time. (Compare the passage in the *Autobiography* where,
writing of similar experiences, he says: "I feel that they should
'go into' life; yet there seems to be no technique by which one
can accomplish the work of their inclusion".[3]) He seeks a

[3] *A.*, p. 114.

chink in time, a means of escape. Time is spoken of as a flame
which consumes itself, while a few as their flesh crumbles in the
pyre have sight of another realm beyond. He was in some
danger of depriving ordinary human life of all meaning by
making time merely a wilderness to be escaped from. Why
must one go through the wilderness in order to reach the
promised land? Is there any value in the journey itself as well
as in the goal? He approaches these questions obliquely in
the ninth poem. He finds in himself two beings, the fiend
Indifference, who can stare coldly at beauty and at suffering,
and the Soul, which pities all. (Compare the twins in *The Two
Brothers*.) If Pity could, as it wishes, put an end to all it feeds
upon, to all passion, flaw, offence, then it would die and
Indifference would have him wholly in its power. The two
beings are paradoxically dependent upon one another. So the
rather strange conclusion is reached that the Soul, which is
identified with Pity, would in the absence of real suffering have
to create for itself imaginary scenes of suffering, as in a work of
art; if "passion, flaw, offence" did not exist they would have
to be imagined. Some attempt is here made to bring together
the two halves of the paradox, but his danger at this time
remained a dualism, in which time was rejected in favour of
eternity, in which his perceptions of mortality and immortality,
of time and eternity, were laid side by side rather than being
included in any whole.

The *Variations* represent an advance over *First Poems* in
that the note of nostalgia is not so prominent. The journey
now is forward to a promised land rather than back to a lost
land. The quality of the writing also is more consistent.
There is less stiff language and inappropriate poetic diction.
The metre is handled with more consistent skill. But he has
not yet attained the luminous, close-packed simplicity of his
later work. The images are individually striking, but one does
not always know what to make of them.

II

When *Journeys and Places* came out in 1937 Stephen Spender
was among those who reviewed it. Muir wrote to him in
October: "Your review I liked very much, and I feel your

point about the argument existing outside the poem is a very true and a very fine one, crystallising something which I have dimly felt myself, and of which I have been growing more and more conscious. The remedy, if any, I think, is for me to get more outside myself, and I think I have been able to do this a little more recently". He was preoccupied with certain problems which he was trying to work out intellectually. His imagination was presenting him with images, perceptions. Sometimes he was able to achieve in a poem a fusion of thought and image, of what he thought and felt and saw. When such fusion does take place, the richness of meaning conveyed by the words is much greater than any attempt to summarise can suggest. But it does not always do so; and when it does not, one feels either that the poem is trying not wholly successfully to state an argument already existing outside it, or that we are being presented with a series of images whose significance and relations we cannot grasp. His best poems, I think, generally started from images, whose meanings he then proceeded to uncover, rather than from ideas which he then sought images to express. "The Solitary Place", originally called "I and not I", is an example of a poem of the second kind. He wrote about it to Spender:

> The theme of the poem was, as I consciously saw it, the modern historical view of the world, in which there is no reality except the development of humanity—humanity being in that case merely an I and not I, a sort of long and interminable monologue of many. This view of the world has always repelled me very deeply and even horrified me—though I have only recently been able to explain partially to myself why. The question I ask myself in the poem is whether there is not some reality outside this I and not I (that is humanity in its historical development). My own deepest feeling is that there is, and I think it is a feeling that you get in all the greatest poetry and music, in Beethoven for instance, but just as clearly in another way in Mozart. That is not the strongest argument for it, nor the real argument, but it is a sort of corroboration. . . . My own feeling is that in allowing ourselves to adopt a purely historical view of human life we are losing half of it, for history too is a sort of substitution of the technique of existence for the

content; there are ever so many things about which it can tell us nothing, otherwise why should there be poetry and music?[4]

Parts of "The Solitary Place" do more than put these thoughts into verse; the images carry suggestions more subtle and complex then the prose explanation. But I doubt whether it succeeds as a whole. Not enough is done in the poem to convey to a reader what the phrase "I and not I" is intended to mean. The argument exists outside the poem, and is not quite satisfactorily embodied in it. In contrast a better one, "Merlin", just came to him. In introducing it in a broadcast selection in 1952 he said: " 'Merlin', I can scarcely say how I came to write; it more or less wrote itself." His speculations about time here find embodiment in poetic images which he has no need to explain and to which any explanation would be inadequate.

The remedy which he proposed for the weakness diagnosed by Spender was to get more outside himself. Most of the best poems in the volume are those in which the problems are dealt with obliquely through the experience of some historical or mythical character. An example is "Troy" in which we get a vivid picture of a "brave, mad old man" left behind in the sewers after the fall of Troy, fighting the rats and believing himself still to be fighting the Greeks. One sees that the old man and the fall of Troy have symbolic meanings, but the old man and the scene exist first and foremost in their own right. Other such poems are "The Enchanted Knight" and "Tristram's Journey" which I have already discussed, and "The Dreamt-of Place". In these we are first made to *see* a journey or a place, and can then gradually feel our way into an understanding of the psychological process or state suggested. Some others, especially of the "place" poems, are more abstract and difficult to get into, though in all of them we find images individually striking and lines with a haunting rhythm.

Though he wanted to get outside himself he could not force himself to write a different kind of poetry from that which came naturally to him. As a poet he was rather an isolated figure in the 'thirties, especially in view of his links, of friendship

[4] E. M. to Spender, 4 Sep. 1935.

and of conviction, with the left-wing political poets. He wrote to Spender, sending him "Hölderlin's Journey":

> I don't know if it has rough relevance to the present world. I hope it has, but if it hasn't I can't help it; for I find that while consciously I am a Socialist, and would like to write poetry that would in some way express that fact, when I actually start to write, something else comes up which seems to have nothing to do with Socialism, or is connected with it in some way too obscure for me to detect. I expect that any feeling of pure humanity must in the end make for Socialism, for Capitalism prevents us all from being human. The end of poetry, in a Socialist society, would be this pure humanity, without inflection: I feel that is the only thing it could be. I don't pretend to have achieved it in my poetry, even in a single line; but it is something resembling it that excites me and makes me happy whenever I succeed in writing poetry at all.[5]

He did try to write a poem about the Spanish Civil War, but wrote to Spender: "I feel for the present I had better keep it to myself, it's so hopeless".[6] Ultimately he was to write at greater depth about the contemporary world than most of the political poets, but he could do this only by being true to his personal vision. Propaganda is an expression of the will, poetry of the imagination; so he did not think propagandist poetry possible. He was up to a point right in saying that the way forward for him was to get outside himself. But this was not to mean that he was to write about miscellaneous day-to-day events nor about the surface of political life, nor that he was to commit himself to any contemporary ideology. He wrote to Spender: "I think we are all far too much moved by a spirit of emulation, and when something 'new' appears feel almost in conscience bound to produce something new, whereas if we wrote from the solidest basis within ourselves we should produce something which is new. I know that in my own experience I have generally to burst through to that solid foundation (at least it always feels like that) and only rarely touch it: for to me it is the most difficult thing in the world to reach. I am very rarely on it, most of my life is somewhere else."[7] This is

---

[5] E. M. to Spender, [undated—probably 1936].
[6] E. M. to Spender, 19 Nov. 1936.   [7] E. M. to Spender, 4 May 1935.

not really incompatible with the aspiration to get more outside himself; for only standing firm on that solid foundation within could he look out at the world with his own eyes. He was soon to get a more secure foothold on that foundation. But even this early poetry is genuinely original, not spuriously "new".

Journeys and Places attracted little attention, and must have had a very slow sale since it was still possible to get a new copy twenty years later.

VIII

St Andrews 1935-1939

I

THOUGH he wrote half seriously to his brother-in-law that as an Orkneyman he was "not Scotch", Muir was never long out of Scotland without wishing, with part of himself at least, to get back there. He left to escape dreary work, but meant to return after his first long visit to the Continent. Though he did not do so, except for not very happy visits, he continued to follow Scottish affairs, literary and political, with interest, and later began to delve into Scottish history.

In the twenties there was a feeling of hope and new life among the few who took an active interest in Scottish literature. For the first time since Burns a great poet was writing in Scots, and the first works of Eric Linklater, Neil Gunn, Lewis Grassic Gibbon, James Bridie, and others were becoming known. To provide means for Scottish writers to meet, the Scottish centre of the PEN Club was founded in 1927. When Grieve left for London two years later the secretaryship passed to Miss Helen Cruickshank, and her house in Edinburgh became a meeting-place where writers could find hospitality and good company. Since part of the object was to bring back into the fold writers living outside Scotland the Muirs were invited to stay in the spring of 1932, and a party was arranged as a kind of home-coming. They came, and he wrote afterwards to Miss Cruickshank: "We haven't had an experience for a long time half so fine as this rediscovery of Scotland. The only choice left for us is to come and stay among you—you can't be resisted."

The visit to Orkney the following summer was another rediscovery, and that to Glasgow and the depressed areas round it a third. These were very different Scotlands. His

Scottish journey in 1934 gave him a chance to see them all, and other parts of the country, again, and to try to put his impressions together. Starting from Edinburgh after the International PEN Conference (called there with the idea of showing to other countries the separate existence of Scottish literature and culture generally) he went down into the borders, and up through Ayrshire, revisiting Kirkmichael where he had worked as an apprentice chauffeur, to Glasgow, where he stayed with F. G. Scott and went to see some of his old colleagues at Lobnitz; then up through the Highlands to Orkney. He did not find much in his journey to inspire him with hope. In the towns he found less extreme poverty than in the old days, but everywhere idle men and machines gave a sense of an industrial system running down and leaving people stranded in drab surroundings without meaning or purpose in their lives. In the Highlands he found still a courteous and dignified people, but they too had been deprived of their ancient way of life. Nowhere except Orkney did he find a contented and prosperous community. Everywhere else there was a sense of division—between classes, between races, between different parts of the country and between past and present. The feeling of division between past and present was particularly strong in Edinburgh, which "has a style, and that style was at one time, indeed as recently as a century ago, the reflection of a whole style of life. While the city itself remains, this style of life has now been broken down, or rather submerged, by successive waves of change, which were first let loose during the Industrial Revolution."[1] So "one cannot look at Edinburgh without being conscious of a visible crack in historical continuity. The actual town, the houses, streets, churches, rocks, gardens are there still; but these exist wholly in the past. That past is a national past; the present, which is made up of the thoughts and feelings and prejudices of the inhabitants, their way of life in general, is as cosmopolitan as the cinema."[2] He knew well that this wearing away of the distinctive characteristics of cities was going on everywhere, but felt that the process was especially damaging to a people without its own institutions. "Though Scotland has not been a nation for some time, it has

---

[1] *S. J.*, p. 20.　　　　　[2] *S. J.*, p. 23.

possessed a distinctly marked style of life; and that is now falling to pieces, for there is no visible and effective power to hold it together. There is such a visible and effective power to conserve the life of England; and though in English life, too, a similar change of national characteristics is going on, though the old England is disappearing, there is no danger that England should cease to be itself. But all that Scotland possesses is its style of life; once it loses that it loses everything, and is nothing more than a name on a map."[3] At the end of his journey his main impression was that "Scotland is gradually being emptied of its population, its spirit, its wealth, industry, art, intellect, and innate character,"[4]

Scottish Journey as a whole is not so gloomy as this summary might suggest. It contains much quiet humour, sensitive descriptions of landscape, and passages in which the poet takes over from the social critic. I am concerned with it here from a special point of view, trying to understand his attitude to Scotland at the time he returned to live there and the attitude of Scotsmen to him. Complacent Scots naturally disliked the unfavourable diagnosis of the condition of their country, and some of those who in general agreed with the diagnosis may have been repelled by the cold eye which he cast on one of the proposed remedies, Nationalism. He was in principle in favour of an independent Scotland, but did not think that a mere transfer of power from Westminster to Edinburgh would cure the ills of the country, which were basically economic. Only a more radical change, a transformation of society along Socialist or Douglasite lines, would do that. "The impulse of Scottish Nationalism at its best comes from a quite sincere conviction that the course of Scottish history needs to be changed; but it is probable that the change can come only from outside, from a change in the structure of civilised society in general, by means of which all nations will be given a new start and all peoples taken into a new federation."[5] One must admire the objectivity with which he tried to view the problems, but one can understand that an enthusiast might find his attitude too negative and passive. He seems to offer Scotsmen the prospect not of being able to do something effective in the

[3] *S. J.*, pp. 25-6.   [4] *S. J.*, p. 3.   [5] *S. J.*, p. 233.

present to improve their situation, but of having to wait for the slow unfolding of a process of historical change to produce a new society in Britain as a whole, perhaps in Europe as a whole. Muir combined to an unusual extent objectivity and strong feeling. The presence of the first in him blinded some people to the second. He did, I think, feel himself to be a Scotsman as well as an Orkneyman, did care deeply about the country, and would have liked to have found a home and a secure position in it.

II

The Muirs arrived in St Andrews late in August 1935 and established themselves in Castlelea, The Scores. This was a fine house looking out over the sea and over the Castle he had written about in *The Three Brothers*, the Castle in which Cardinal Beaton had been murdered. St Andrews was a smallish and quiet town, suitable for Gavin and for Muir himself to get on with his work without the distractions and expense of London. It also seemed to offer some of the advantages of a large one—a university, the possibility of intelligent company. Mrs Muir had happy memories of the place where she had been a brilliant student. So the chance of renting a house there seemed just what they wanted, and they were at first glad that they had come.

During that autumn they were very busy clearing up work left over from London. In that year they produced no less than five volumes of translations as well as his *Scottish Journey* and his pamphlet on Social Credit. Until the War they continued to produce translations at the rate of two or three volumes a year; he did his fortnightly review for *The Listener*, frequent reviews for *The Scotsman* and occasional reviews and articles for other periodicals. After a time they began to miss the busy social life of Hampstead, and to look around for congenial company; and then they found the limitations of the town. St Andrews was split by fairly rigid class divisions, and in none of the groups could they feel entirely at home. They had no links with the "county" and the sporting gentry who came to the Royal and Ancient Golf Club. The prosperous middle class seemed conventional and money-grubbing.

Occasionally he allowed his irritation to break out in his
private diary in a way in which he would not have expressed
himself in public: "On Saturday night went to a dance. Oh,
God. I can't get on with the upper middle classes in small
Scottish towns. All being ladies and gentlemen according to
a standard which I can't fathom. Dull and stale. I came away
deeply disgusted. Must analyse this sometime. Haven't the
mind or the spirit for it at present. But they seemed to me like
members of some savage tribe."[6] What most of all disgusted
him was the contemptuous attitude of rich people to the poor:
"The rich live on the poor; why should they sneer at them as
well? . . . In a small town where people know one another, the
blatancy of the rich becomes more obvious; they sit more
visibly on their money-bags."[7] Though living in what might
seem a peaceful and sleepy town he became vividly aware of
war—not only of the civil war in Spain and of the threat of
international war, but of war existing in the present within
society:

> Walking back from the post-office this evening in the un-
> accustomed light (for it is the end of March) I realised more
> strongly than ever before in my life that war is going on the
> whole time. I had just heard on the radio of a new advance
> of Franco's armies: bills were out saying that Barcelona was
> bound to fall. Yet not a single look of concern on any face I
> met, though this brings war and the end of liberty much nearer.
> These faces are the surface jetsam, but below there is a continual
> deadly, locked fight: shopkeeper against shopkeeper, business
> against business, master against workmen, rich against poor:
> no relaxation, no pause for rest even. All this is war: why
> haven't I felt it more clearly before?[8]

Among university people the Muirs found a few individual
friends, but the university showed no recognition of the fact
that they had a man of genius on their doorstep, someone who
understood literature from the inside. Later he applied for
posts in Edinburgh and, I think, other Scottish universities,
but without success. In some university people he found an

[6] Diary, February 1939.   [7] Diary, May 1938.   [8] Diary, March 1938.

arid intellectualism, a lack of vision and imagination:

> The other night I was at a little party for a while. Scientists mainly: good people: without refreshment: clever: honest: disinterested. But without a soul among them. I am interested by such people. Take F for instance. He is a pleasant fellow; he has an acute mind; he is an amusing talker: he's surprisingly 'human'; a good husband; an indulgent father; with a fine appreciation of painting: good to look at: engaging: but he has no soul. There's no refreshment in him. Old M [Mitrinović], the Serbian quack [?], used to say about Bertrand Russell, 'When he die, the angels, they find nothing to eat in him.' F gives me nothing to eat, and I'm no angel. Yet I'm fond of him, sorry for him as if he were a foundling. And I admire his intellect; it is a very efficient one, even subtle in some ways, though all it can grind out is bran.[9]

The sharp observation is characteristically mixed with affection and sympathy here; but occasionally, in the unpublished parts of the diary, he describes people he could not be fond of—for instance a philosophy lecturer: "He really believes in nothing: he thinks, resentfully, that philosophy is a fraud, and is envious of those who know it isn't, and are really *inside* it. Every remark, when any name was mentioned, was belittling, as if [he] had the low-down on *him*."[10] After hearing him talk at a party he found himself when walking home alone reciting desperately "A dreadful, awful bore! A terrible, terrible bore!" Confronted with people he could not like he retreated into himself. Another uncongenial person met at St Andrews was a Cambridge student: "Thick-set, quick, a born Rugger scrum-half, but intelligent . . . Tough . . . Attractive. Amusing . . . No fears . . . Yet a kind of stencil. Clipped speech. Scottish evidently, with no trace of it. Probably Loretto, or something. These people, so perfectly pressed out in spite of their lively temperments, unnerving to me."[11] He was shocked by his own ability to sum up people in this way: "The cool considering eye that a human being, however kind, sometimes turns upon another without knowing it. . . . The same glance as an animal gives another at their first encounter. I know

<hr />

[9] Diary, winter 1938-9.   [10] Diary, March 1939.
[11] Diary, February 1939.

I'm guilty of these considering glances, like everybody else, though quite unaware of it at the time. And how hateful this glance is; nothing gives me a deeper sense of the sordidness of human nature."[12]

In St Andrews he became more aware than before of the lack of an organic, united community to live in; but he still had his home, and his wife, who created around him an atmosphere of gaiety and affection in which he could do his work. In May 1938 they moved from Castlelea into another rented house, in Queen's Gardens, where they could have their own furniture. He wrote in his diary:

> I cannot help thinking that a new life awaits us in that new house. . . . A house of your own is bound up with the very thought of a right life: and a family, too. There is a solemnity about a house: it is the affirmation of two thousand years at least of human life, and, somewhere in my mind it is associated with Mary, Joseph and their Son. But if a genuine house is necessary for the good life, this must be pressed further and we must say that a genuine society is necessary too . . . I have often been conscious of an ache, walking down these streets here, looking at these people here, and the cause of that ache is the knowledge that I do not fit these people, and they do not fit me, and that this is a general disharmony, not one personal to myself. . . . This ache comes from the recognition that there is no society, no general house for us all. (Perhaps the church was once such a house.)
>
> I have often had a vague fancy or intuition of a certain state of human existence, which satisfies me more completely than any other possible image. It is a state in which the earth, the human buildings on the earth, and the earthly life of everyone will in some way be in harmony with the sky which overarches them. In childhood I had that feeling of harmony, and I can still remember it; the sky fitted the earth then: but since that time I have often been troubled by a sense of dislocation between the earth and the sky: an actual physical, or visual, feeling of something wrong.

What made him a poet was that this feeling, which exists, I suppose, in a vague way in most people, was "an actual physical, or visual" one. He *saw* an image of the state he

[12] Diary, spring 1938.

thought natural to man; he *saw* the dislocation and felt it as an ache in his bones.

Both at Castlelea and in Queen's Gardens old friends came to visit, and a new circle of friends formed. F. G. Scott and his wife came from Glasgow for their summer holidays, and differences of opinion made no breach in their friendship. Muir greatly enjoyed F. G.'s exuberant vitality. When they were together F. G. and Mrs Muir tended to dominate the conversation, but to a sensitive observer Muir was as impressive a person and one with whom a close and warm relationship could be established at once. George Bruce, the writer, F. G.'s nephew, then a schoolmaster at Dundee remembers his first meeting with Muir in the summer of 1936. "F. G. bursts into the Muir's house—Willa and he embrace, rather hug like bears. I see Edwin's face behind smiling and then laughing out loud." Later F. G. sang some of his songs, and there was much gay conversation. "By all the rules of the game F. G. and Willa ought to have established themselves most strongly in my mind, for they did most of the talking. They cut and thrust with great warmth and freedom of expression." Yet it was Muir, sitting quietly on the periphery of the group that he remembered most vividly. "No introduction was necessary. Communication had been established unconsciously."

Later that summer on another visit to St Andrews, Bruce found his uncle in a great rage reading Muir's latest book, *Scott and Scotland*, in which the conclusion is reached that "Scotland can only create a national literature by writing in English".[13] "What will Chris say to this?" F. G. roared. Bruce went on to see Muir, who, always aware of what might be said on both sides of a controversy, explained mildly that Grieve and F. G. as Borderers would naturally feel more hostility to England than himself, since the Borders had been subject to more pressure from England than the peripheries of Scotland; but he was quite unaware of the storm which his earnest attempt to state the truth accurately as he saw it was to arouse.

Scott and Scotland is not a wholly convincing book. Most people would agree in general with Muir's survey of Scottish

[13] *S. S.*, p. 178.

literature in the past. In the fifteenth and sixteenth centuries Scotland was an independent kingdom, and possessed a distinctive culture and a language (two languages, but he does not deal with Gaelic) in which writers could express their whole mind, the whole mind of the nation. Henryson and Dunbar wrote naturally in Scots, which was the language of thought and feeling together. The language of the Court and the learned had a living relation to the language of common speech. After the Reformation and the Union of the Crowns the educated turned more and more to standard English, and the Scottish language was not developed to deal with a changing world. English became the language in which educated people expressed their thoughts; but some variety of Scots remained for most people the mother tongue, the language of feeling. In neither language could the whole mind of the nation be expressed. On the one side was a rather arid intellectualism and a stiffness of language; on the other nostalgia and sentimentality, the outpouring of feeling without discipline. Writers of genius appeared; but even Burns and Scott could not achieve all they might have done in more favourable conditions.

Muir as a critic convincingly demonstrates the decline of Scottish poetry after the sixteenth century, its poverty in comparison with English poetry, and the handicap to Burns and Scott of not having a homogeneous language in which to express themselves. When he comes to the present and to suggest what should be done he is naturally more controversial. He does not, it seems to me, demonstrate convincingly that his conclusion—the necessity to turn to English—arises out of what has gone before. His survey of the ill effects of the decline of the Scottish language might be expected to lead to a plea for reviving it rather than abandoning it. It may be that it was impossible to revive it, but he does not show this to be so; and he does not take enough account of what recent writers in Scots, especially Hugh MacDiarmid, had actually done. He, as always, gives high praise to MacDiarmid's own poetry in Scots, especially to the philosophical *Drunk Man Looks at the Thistle*, which he considered underrated in comparison with the earlier lyrics; but he says that MacDiarmid "has left

L

Scottish verse very much where it was before."[14] If, as he allows, MacDiarmid had written poetry expressing both thought and feeling, it is difficult to see that the situation was unchanged. If one man could do it, it was presumably possible that another man of genius should arise and do it also, and so establish, or re-establish, a tradition. Muir perhaps underrated the extent to which a language can be created, or recreated. So it is possible to argue that he was a too quick despairer with regard to the possibilities of the Scottish language.

On the other hand he fails to use what seems to me to be the most convincing argument of all in favour of the use of English. For his statement that "Scotsmen feel in one language and think in another"[15] is no longer true of a large proportion of educated Scotsmen, and was not true even then. (I doubt whether it was true of Muir himself.) For a large, and increasing, proportion of Scotsmen, English, perhaps with some tincture of a Scottish accent and the addition of a few Scottish words, is the mother tongue, and broad Scots is virtually a foreign language. For them English is the only natural language to write in, and there is no reason why they should not, as readily as Englishmen, achieve a fusion of thought and feeling in it. This situation can be altered, if at all, only by political action. In the meantime the only sensible thing is to recognise that there is no one homogeneous language in which the whole mind of the Scottish people can be expressed, but that there are Scottish writers who have written with distinction in English, in different varieties of Scots and in Gaelic. I am not sure that this is quite such a deplorable situation as Muir thought. He thought it necessary for Scotland to have one homogeneous language in order to be able to maintain and assert its identity and to feel itself a unity. But there can be a kind of unity in diversity, and a fruitful interchange between different traditions even within one nation. To try to make the best of the diversity is an immediately practicable policy, whereas to seek for homogeneity is not. I think Muir in later life would have agreed with this. In 1951 he wrote: "Because of his [Hugh MacDiarmid's] example there has been a revival of the Scottish language, a language which has proved

[14] *S. S.*, p. 22.   [15] *S. S.*, p. 21.

that it is full of vigour, colour and potentiality. A new poetry
without the mark of parochialism which used to cling to
Scottish verse, has been written in it, along with a poetry by
Scotsmen in English, and the remarkable work of Somerled
Maclean in Gaelic."[16]

These things can be rationally debated, and were by some
of those, such as Neil Gunn, who reviewed *Scott and Scotland*
critically. But to Grieve the book was a betrayal of the Scottish
Renaissance movement, a sell-out to the Anglo-Scottish
"Establishment"; and for many years afterwards he pursued
Muir in books and articles with bitter personal attacks which
did nothing to advance his cause. A strange feature of the
situation was that it was just before *Scott and Scotland* appeared
that Grieve had himself turned to English as his principal
medium in poetry. He may have been quite justified, for his
special purposes at that time, in doing so; but this abandon-
ment of Scots by its greatest practitioner was a greater blow to
the prospects of the language becoming established than anything Muir could say.

Muir was surprisingly little bothered by the controversy.
He was uncombative, but tough. He must have been a bit
hurt by some of the personal attacks, but never answered in
kind, and continued to speak and write with admiration of
MacDiarmid's poetry. I do not know whether his poem, "The
Letter", is connected with this controversy, but from its date
—it was first published in November 1937—it seems quite
possible. In any case it is a characteristic demonstration of his
inability to pursue a quarrel. When friendship is threatened
by "the outward eating rage/And murderous heart of middle
age", he thinks first of mortality:

> Look long enough and you will see
> The dead fighting with the dead.
> Now's the last hour for chivalry, . . .

and then of immortality:

> Look again until you see,
> Fixed in the body's final station,
> The features of immortality.

---

[16] *Catalogue of an Exhibition of 20th Century Scottish Books* (1951).

Try to pursue this quarrel then.
You cannot. . . .

Meanwhile the Muirs were gathering a new circle of friends round them at St Andrews. Among these were Oscar Oeser, then lecturer in Psychology at the university, and his wife, Drury. Mrs Oeser writes to me: "I found him a shy, gentle, humorous and affectionate man of such wonderful quality that it was impossible not to grow fond of him at the same time as one revered him for his integrity, his sensitivity and his gentle toughness. He was in some ways a rather puckish character, e.g. his dry, sly humour about people and happenings." He was working very hard, she says; on Mondays he was never available, for he was finishing his reviews. On Saturday afternoons he used to go to the local soccer match, walking through the streets with an abstracted air. On Saturday evenings, she, her husband and the Muirs often used to dine together. "In their house we listened to records of Mozart, and especially *Don Giovanni*, Edwin's favourite opera, and talked books; in our house we talked books and politics and perhaps listened to some Bach. From a woman's point of view Edwin was a specially delightful person when he got just a little drunk with wine. Then some of his shyness and inhibitions disappeared, and if one were sitting by him, he would become what I can only describe as chastely affectionate and very beguiling. He would bend towards one from time to time and kiss one, gently, lightly and with leisurely enjoyment, looking slightly mischievous . . ." This letter touches on two qualities in him which may seem contradictory but are not really so— his abstractedness, which led some people to think of him as remote, and his capacity for affection. He lived much in an inner world of his own thoughts and imaginings, was shy, and would not waste his energies in unnecessary battles with those he could not get on with; but he remained very open to experience and to people. All his friends testify to the speed with which he established more than polite relationships. In congenial company he dispersed with preliminaries, and people felt they could open up to him on important and intimate subjects. This openness to experience left him vulnerable right into old age; and enabled him to remain a poet to the end.

He was remote neither from people nor from concern over the large events of the time. The Muirs and the Oesers formed an informal club to discuss the questions of the day. It met on Sunday evenings at members' houses in turn, and included a Congregational minister, two teachers from a girls' school, two trade unionists, a dustman and others. One of the trade unionists was the father of Tom Scott the poet, then, by his own account, rather a brash and fiery young apprentice in his late teens. Tom Scott had formed another group to discuss literature, and this met in the Muirs' house, which he remembers as having been the centre of intellectual life in St Andrews at that time. After first meeting him Muir predicted that he would be the only member of the group to achieve anything in literature. To the passionate and impatient young man Muir, with his capacity for detached, cool judgment, seemed rather frightening and remote; he would state his opinions gently, but with great authority; at times he would look at a person with a quizzical, summing-up look (the look which he himself expressed so much dislike of in his diary). Scott was aware in him of an "inner radiance"; he "glowed with faint distant radiance", as he put it to me.

Another young man who came to sit at Muir's feet was Douglas Young, whose father came in to St Andrews every Friday morning to have his beard trimmed. Douglas Young would go to breakfast with the Muirs and show him his poems, translations, etc. He was impressed by his extraordinary objectivity and consistency as a critic, his independence of the mood of the moment. He would always give an immediate and sure judgment, and was always a helpful and honest critic.

So, even in St Andrews, he was not without friends and followers. If he was, as he says, more unhappy there than he had been since the time of his obscure fears and the course of psycho-analysis that helped to dispel them, it was not primarily because of external circumstances, but because of dissatisfaction with himself. As he acknowledges, his critical attitude towards others was a good deal due to this self-dissatisfaction.

Approaching fifty he had not arrived at any secure faith, and the powers which he knew within himself had not come to full flower. He was astonished, he wrote in his diary, by the contrast between the strange powers within him and the triteness of his life. "Sometimes I encourage myself with the thought I am still developing, still reaching out to something, until I remind myself for the thousandth time that this is only another way of saying that I have perpetually remained short of fulfilment. Perhaps that is why I am haunted by a dream of standing on a ship and watching the green hills drawing nearer and nearer across the sea: and how green they are! Have I dreamt this often, or only once? I cannot tell any longer; the picture is so vivid when it rises, and it may rise at any time, which shows that it is never away."[17]

Other dreams were more unpleasant: "A horrible dream, with blind debased faceless human shapes moving slowly. An image of lust without sensuality: horrible. The heads something like the heads in some of Wyndham Lewis's drawings."[18] But seldom was the vision of horror unrelieved: "My dream that I was to be publicly executed, which makes me understand the 'last words' of the great Elizabethans. You are raised up in a sort of ecstasy."[19] A curious waking dream-like experience combined a vision of the skull beneath the skin with one reminiscent of the dream of approaching a green land in a ship: "Sat in my bed looking at myself in a mirror hanging on the wall opposite. My face, especially the bony expanse of forehead, *came out*, and I saw the skin and flesh shrivelling from it, and the bone beneath: a terrifying, absolute vision, like the stripping off of time. And simultaneously a feeling of journeying on, with that forehead as a prow, beyond time, and the assurance that the naked bone, there, would flower into angel's flesh, and sprout angel's hair, fragrant and beautiful beyond conception. An assurance, or was it quite an assurance, or more than assurance? I don't know what it was."[20] Here he has become the ship, and receives a possible assurance of attaining a state of blessedness, which in the other dream was symbolised by the green land. If this state is conceived

[17] Diary, May 1938.   [18] Diary, August 1938.
[19] Diary, May 1938.   [20] Diary, August 1938.

as the green land of childhood, then it recedes and can never be entered; if it is placed beyond time then it can be entered, and one pre-condition is humility. Perhaps this is part of what the dream suggests, but Muir characteristically does not claim to know.

The green land, if understood as childhood, could not be re-entered; but strength for the present could be got by reviving memories of it. Early in 1938 he was more unhappy than he had been since 1919; and as in the earlier period he worked towards a cure by self-discovery and by returning to the sources of strength in the past. He began to collect material for an autobiography; or rather, perhaps, he began a process of self-discovery which then led to the idea of writing the autobiography. In his diary he justified this concern with himself:

> The problem: to discover what I am; to find out my relation to other people. The first an inward problem, the second an outward one. For when I understand myself I will have changed myself; and when I understand my relation to other people, I will have to set about changing society. At present the emphasis is on changing society, as is natural: I sympathise with and take a small part in it, by membership of discussion societies and so on. But I still feel I must take stock of my own life, and though that is in appearance an investigation of the past, I know it is important for the future: because of this change that it must bring about. I come much in contact with socialists and communists. Some of them are far better, wiser, more solid and real than I am; but others seem to have no inward life at all, which means that they are not quite real: and how can unreal people produce a real change? . . . The more you observe yourself the more you observe other people and the world in general. So introspection needs no apology. The great sin is to let everything go past in a sort of dream or stupor; aware neither of yourself nor of the world: the ordinary state of human life.[21]

He wrote to Sydney Schiff: "I am taking notes for something like a description of myself, done in general outline, not in detail, not as a story, but as an attempt to find out what a

[21] Diary, April 1938.

human being is in this extraordinary age which depersonalises everything. . . . It may be that I have found at last a form which suits me." [22]

In the 1937-1939 diary there are frequent notes of scenes and incidents, mainly from childhood, set down when his memory recovered them. The memories may in themselves seem trivial; their importance was that they reminded him of, and in some degree recreated in him a capacity for, a way of seeing which most adult people completely lose. For instance one day in a café in Edinburgh he recovered the memory of a sailor suit, a yellow cord and a whistle he had had as a boy. He tells of this in the *Autobiography* (pp. 19-20). In the diary he says more of the meaning of the incident to him:

> I can still feel the deep delight which that yellow cord and that yellow wooden whistle gave me. And ever since simply because I have at last remembered them they have been more real, and in some way close to me, than a thousand things in my life which are of infinitely greater intrinsic importance. The cord and the whistle had a delightful odour as well as texture and colour. How bright things were in childhood! and how bright they remain. And not only bright but close, closer than we can endure to have anything at all after we have lived for some time. It is as if the child confidingly laid his cheek against all the lumber of the world, against the oddest things, bits of glass, pebbles, tram tickets. He still trusts things with a trust incredible to us later; and takes them completely into his arms. There is no truer story than the story of Eden. The idea that an equally true, or rather a truer and better story, can be constructed out of scientific hypotheses elaborated during the last century with an anthropoid ape as their foundation, is to me a strange and absurd and above all blind piece of folly. [23]

After the recovery of the childhood memory in the café he went to the B.B.C. to rehearse a broadcast and then to a restaurant for dinner. Again he had a visionary experience, but this time a more than usually intense seeing of the actual scene before him. He sat at a window, and saw what would usually appear quite ordinary things happening in the street below, combined in such a way as to give him a special feeling,

[22] E. M. to Schiff, 17 May 1938.   [23] Diary, June 1938.

"half nightmare and half aesthetic pleasure. I think I must have had an intuition of the impossible thought that countless absolutely different things are always happening at the same moment in a fixed scene, a static world". A girl got off a tram; three young men came out of a pub opposite; at the end of the street a long, thin, furry dog shot past. A big woman with blind, hanging face and blind, hanging breasts, with the legs of a tall man and enormous feet, went past at immense speed, yet with a sort of blundering gait; "she was terrifying and pitiable. . . . And all were going about their own business; and all were related in some way to each other, like the different themes in a very obscure and difficult piece of music. I sat in astonishment, delight, and horror, feeling, as one feels only a few times in one's existence, the inexhaustibility, absurdity and enormity of human life. I felt that there was literally nothing that could not be said about human beings, for this simple scene seemed incredible to me." The recovery of the childhood memory had led him to a new sense of the inexhaustibility of human life in the present; and that in turn led to a renewed sense of immortality. He goes on in the diary: "This mood lasted for some time, and it led me by stages to a more frequent one in which I nurse the fancy that if we could see every human being as an immortal spirit, and not merely as a prospective one (as the ministers do), it would change the very basis of imagination, and through that of life itself. I have occasionally tried to do this, for moments at a stretch, but I know that it is impossible as a consistent way of seeing. It is a truth, but it is a truth which we cannot look at, though if we could it would glorify us." He tried to think of various people as immortal spirits. Children and old people he found easy. Then, seeking a really difficult subject, he thought of a prominent St Andrews citizen who had acquired a fortune and even some public respect by all sorts of flint-hearted rascality. "I found I could see him as an immortal spirit; but as an evil one; and when I reached this point my dream of the glorification of life through this way of seeing received an unexpected check, for I had thought that this vision would of itself bring reconciliation to us poor human creatures; and instead I saw that it would only deepen in our consciousness the pattern of good and evil.

And that would be unbearable; to see life like that is bearable only for a few moments at a time."

Such experiences are necessarily fleeting. A few days later he was in Edinburgh again, "went to the same restaurant, sat again at a window; but nothing happened". The people merely looked "ordinary and lost"; and looking at them he felt "neither grief nor satisfaction, merely that indifference disguised as meaningless acceptance, in which we live for the ninety-nine hundredth part of our lives. . . . I sat and looked at them almost contentedly through the scales which covered my eyes, like a mildly damned spirit, a spirit pickled delicately in a very weak, almost unnoticeable but quite effectual, solution of damnation, while something far within me, as faint and forlorn as a hunter's horn in an immense forest, cried that I wanted to see".

Moments of special seeing are recorded quite often in the diary from the summer of 1938 onwards—both in waking life and in dreams. After an evening walk that August he wrote:

> Wonderful light on the sunken burn from the sunset. I wandered on, sometimes by myself, sometimes with G[avin] and once had the sudden realisation that my dreaming pleasure in nature, in grass, weeds, flowers, trees, *paths* . . . comes from familiarity, a trustful feeling to all these things, as if they were old friends! all memory, like *friendship*." A few days later, at Gavin's eager request, he got up at half past four to see the sun rising. "We went along the East Sands, the light growing stronger and stronger: the land no longer rich and dark, but picked out in primitive colours: I was struck by the red roofs of the farms, as if red were newly created. Then I became conscious of light in itself, not as a mere medium for revealing objects: the whole world seemed to be over-flooded with light, flowing in a level river from the eastern fount. . . . And then, in a few minutes, deliberately, in great circumstance, in great majesty, the sun rose: deep golden yellow, molten, a living fire. . . . The deliberation of the whole magnificent process overwhelming. I was struck particularly by the feeling, as the sun rose, that it was creating all the objects it fell upon: the towering range of cloud round it, the cliffs along whose foot we were walking: they all *appeared* as if at a word of command, a spell broken: as if for the first time."

Characteristic notes jotted down the following March were:
"My love of ploughed fields, especially of harvest fields, and
stacks where all is gathered—the most satisfying sight there is".
"My shocked hatred of nature deflowered—as for nature round
Glasgow: slum grass, scabbed and aching trees, and desecrated
ground—a feeling of blasphemy."

He was acutely sensitive to the physical world—much more
so than some critics, or even some of his friends, realised. But
he seldom confined himself to pure description or to a merely
aesthetic response. He was a farmer's son who saw natural
scenes practically, in relation to the life of man, as well as a
poet and thinker who sought to grasp the significance of what
he experienced.

His dreams were still troubled. On 6 August 1938 he
recounted:

> Had a dream last night about roads, forbidden roads: I think
> connected with forbidden occupations, smuggling perhaps. I
> loved these roads, which wound through pleasant fields and
> woods; but I always had to take them during the night time,
> for they were watched. Smuggler's roads, but I was not a
> smuggler: I merely loved the fields, and roads and the freedom,
> and the soft night. In the dream I met a man in stiff town
> clothes, with a soft hat. He asked me the road to Guardbridge
> [a town near St Andrews]. The actual road to Guardbridge
> came into my mind, an uninviting, macadamised road,
> almost straight, featureless. The thought of it was unbearable
> to me. I told the man how he could get to Guardbridge by
> foot-paths, through woods and fields. . . . At the same time
> I had a vague feeling that the paths I recommended did not
> actually exist: neither do they. A saddening thought this
> morning.

The straight road perhaps suggests the methods of enquiry
most favoured in the modern world—materialistic science and
reason—the footpaths intuition and imaginative exploring of
realms of mystery and beauty. The climate in the modern
world is such that the dreamer cannot help feeling some sense
of guilt in using the footpaths, and having recommended them
to another he is stricken with doubt as to whether they actually
exist. A dream of a few days earlier had suggested a greater

confidence in art as the revelation of a really existing order.
He could not remember much of it except the general feeling—
"the feeling that I was suddenly realising the liberating greatness of art, which I saw as a creation of order out of chaos,
occurring before my eyes. I saw things visibly moving into
their places, though what the things were I cannot remember:
and when the movement was ended (it did not take long) there
was arrangement and order where confusion had been before.
It was as if I saw the Word that was in the beginning moving
and creating order."

During that summer of 1938, after a period of depression,
he seems to have experienced an intensification of his inner
life. Fortunately at just that time he found a new friend with
whom he could share these experiences, Dr Alec Aitken, then
a lecturer, later Professor of Mathematics, at Edinburgh
University. A mathematical genius and also interested in
poetry and music Aitken had by a different route reached
similar intuitions about time and other things to Muir's. Muir
wrote in his diary on 16 July: "Dr. Aitken: a wonderful
fellow. He supports me without knowing it in this effort [to
change and improve himself]. A letter from him this morning:
the time he saw wasps' wings and sycamore leaves opening in
slow motion: it gave me a lovely feeling. I wish I had more
time: and was not so driven." Soon afterwards he wrote to
Aitken:

> We were so glad to get your letter, for we both felt at once an
> affinity with you, which probably goes deeper than any of us
> knows yet, and I assure you that such spontaneous friendship
> is rare to us, as to you. I want it to continue, and I'll do any-
> thing I can to make it continue. I feel that in some ways our
> experience coincides, though I feel that yours, in the things
> you mention, has gone further than mine and is more exact.
> The sycamore leaves and wasp-wings opening and shutting in
> slow motion gave me an extraordinary feeling of beauty: I
> can faintly visualise it, and when I do, for some reason I have
> a picture of brilliant light, more intense than actual light. I
> can't conceive with my mind at all the sonata of Beethoven
> heard in an instant; it is too much for me; you must try to
> describe it some time.

He goes on to describe as the most beautiful experience he had ever had the waking trance in London years before, and then to speak of Gavin whose sensitivity was causing his parents worry as well as pleasure:

I don't know whether he is feeling the reflection of a breakdown of my own. I did have a severe breakdown in my youth, caused by the death of four of my family, my father and mother and two brothers, in the space of two years. I have not got over that yet, in spite of the time between. And I had a breakdown of some obscure kind when I was six, which I feel has altered all my life: not absolutely, of course, and even "altered" is a questionable word: one's life is what it is. I merely mean that there was a profound change at that time, a sort of convulsion which I can't entirely put down to growth; perhaps the first intimation of guilt; but that is conjecture. I'm very attached to Gavin and very moved by him in all sorts of ways, powerfully and happily. The enormous feat of intellectual digestion made by a child in the first few years of his life, thrown into a world he knows nothing about, is extraordinarily moving. To see him seizing upon these foreign things, grappling with experience before he knows it is experience, distinguishing and reasoning about the objects which make up the world, gives me a better opinion of mankind, and of myself.

He thanks Aitken for what he had said about the *Variations:* "Willa is perfectly true when she says that we expect nobody who comes to the house to have any knowledge of my poetry, and so we assume the opposite. What you say about the poem warms my heart. But when you came I was too moved by some of the things you said to consider that I was a poet, or to care about it, except essentially, in recognizing that the world you spoke about was the world from which what I like best in my poetry was drawn, largely unconsciously."

He had probably never met an advanced mathematician before, and was intrigued to find that there is a pathway through mathematics to the realm of experience he had reached through poetry. In his next letter he wrote: "Thanks more than I can say, for your letters, and what is in them, and for the Eddington. . . . I was conscious, very soon after I met you, that mathematics, as you know it, is the pathway into a strange world which can be reached by other means, by music and poetry: and though the mathematical way is closed to me, or at any rate obstructed by endless things which I do not know, I think we meet in the place, or at least have sometimes, by different routes, found the same place." He sends a volume, presumably *Journeys and Places*. "When I look through it, I really seem to see a faint glimmering of mathematics somewhere in it." He thanks him for his encouragement, and for his understanding of his poetry. "I've acquired a certain reputation, not a big one, by going on writing poetry; but that is almost worthless, for it is not a matter of understanding, and understanding is the only thing that is of any use to a man who is saying what he thinks, in poetry, mathematics, or any other form of utterance."

Another person from whom he got encouragement and understanding was Walter de la Mare, with whom he had been corresponding for some time. He met him only once, on a visit to London in 1938. Long afterwards, near his death, de la Mare wrote: "Why do I always remember so vividly giving you a little bunch of violets in Piccadilly, near the gates into the Park?" and: "It seems preposterous that we have met only that once. But how vividly memorable *onces* can be."

The experiences of that summer gave him a renewed sense of the glory of the physical world, of the mystery and inexhaustibility of human life, of immortality and of the liberating greatness of art. He was right in thinking that new life might come to him in the new house. But the following winter was a difficult one. Like others he was oppressed by the threat of war. Because of his contacts with European writers he was more intimately in touch with events on the Continent than mere newspaper readers. He had been much worried about Hermann Broch, who had been imprisoned after the German invasion of Austria. "He is such an extraordinarily sensitive creature, that it makes my heart sore to think of his position. It is terrible to think that men like Hitler have power over such men as Broch. We both met Broch in Vienna several years ago, and in a few days came to love him."[24] Now Broch had

[24] E. M. to Schiff, 17 May 1938.

got out of Austria, and came to stay. "Strange and fine creature. Talked about many things, the three of us. The pettiness of the Nazis. Benches in the streets of Vienna: 'Here no Jew may sit'. Parks. 'Jews enter here at their peril', with a death's head as a device. Mean and ignominious exercise of power." Anxiety over the Munich crisis caused a return of the stomach trouble which was apt to affect him in times of stress. Then Mrs Muir had a bad illness, had to have an operation and was in a nursing home for quite a time. This meant not only anxiety about her, but also the need to do all the routine money-making work of reviewing and translating without her help at a time when his own health was not strong. But Mrs Muir recovered quite quickly—"Willa is getting better and better; she is my heart" he wrote in his diary at the end of February. And the spring brought a sense of renewal, crystallised in the sight of schoolboys playing marbles: "Coming back from Willa in the nursing home saw two schoolboys playing at marbles. The afternoon soft and spring-like, then gentle rain falling. I suddenly realised that marbles come in spring, and the whole feeling of the wet soft earth, and these days when marbles 'come round' returned to me."

He described himself to Sydney Schiff at this time as "an anti-Marx socialist, a man who believes that people are immortal souls and that they should bring about on this earth a society fit for immortal souls", but said he was not sure that he agreed "that the only hope of the world lies in the gospel of Christ".[25] Very soon after this came one of the turning points of his life, recorded in the diary entry for 1 March, part of which is given in the *Autobiography* (p. 246) in a modified form, but which is worth giving in full as originally written:

Last night going to bed alone (Willa being in Cottage Hospital) I suddenly found myself (as I was taking off my waistcoat) reciting the Lord's Prayer in a loud emphatic voice—a thing I have not done since my teens—with urgency too, and deeply disturbed emotion. As I recited it I grew more composed; my soul, as if it had been empty and needed replenishment, seemed to fill: and every word had a strange fullness of meaning,

---

[25] E. M. to Schiff, 16 Jan. 1939.

which astonished and delighted me, and gave me not so much hope as strength. It was late; I had sat up reading; I was sleepy; but as I stood in the middle of the floor half undressed reciting the prayer over and over, the meanings it contained, none of them extraordinary, indeed ordinary as they could be, overcame me with joyful surprise, and made me seem to realise that this petition was always universal, always adequate, and to life as it is, not to a life such as we long for or dream of: and for that reason it seems to sanctify common existence. Everything in it, apart from the Being to which it is addressed, refers to human life, seen realistically, not mystically. It is about the world and society, not about the everlasting destiny of the soul. "Our Father which art in Heaven" means merely "Our Heavenly Father", not our earthly father. "Hallowed be thy name," defines our human relation to him. "Thy kingdom come", means "Thy kingdom come here on earth", so that God's will may be done on earth as in heaven. It means that we should desire that human society might be directed in accordance with the perfect laws of heaven. "And forgive us our debts as we forgive our debtors". Excuse our failings, and our offences against You, as we excuse those who offend against us. "And lead us not into temptation but deliver us from evil: For thine is the kingdom, and the power, and the glory, for ever. Amen."

I never realised before so clearly the primary importance of "we" and "us" in the prayer: it is collective, for all societies, for all mankind as a great society. "After this manner therefore pray ye." Not "My Father which art in heaven", not "Give me this day my daily bread", not "Forgive my debts"; not "Lead me not into temptation"—as Protestantism almost succeeded in persuading us. And this collective form of prayer was the form enjoined by Jesus. It would be called now, in the jargon of the fashionable revolutionaries, political.

The difference here between "I" and "we" tremendous: there is no end to the conclusions that follow from it. In "we" it is man, or mankind, or the community, or all the communities, that is speaking: it is human life, and therefore society is the formal embodiment of human life. And to pray as "we" is not only to embrace in the prayer all human life, all the aspirations of mankind for the perfect kingdom when God's will shall be done on earth; it is for the individual soul a pledge for all other souls, an act of responsibility, and an act of union which strengthens him from within and at the same time lends him infinite strength from without. Yet how many centuries this prayer has been recited as if it were the multiplication table. If the revolutionaries had any sense they would bring out the implications of this prayer, which contains the whole philosophy of a desirable life in this world. But "Hallowed be thy name" is enough to restrain them, and bring a sneer to their faces.

From this time on he recognised himself to be a Christian. "I had a vague sense during these days that Christ was the turning-point of time and the meaning of life to everyone, no matter what his conscious beliefs; to my agnostic friends as well as Christians."[26] He turned to the Bible, especially the Gospels, but not to any Church. One reason for his shrinking from belonging to any Church is given in a diary entry in the following August: "Walking along towards the pier last night suddenly saw for some reason that a church which is not an universal all-inclusive church is by virtue of that evil, because it rejects man: all such churches are fond of the doctrine of Hell and send a great number of people to Hell."

This time he had come to Christianity by his own route— not in response to a revivalist's appeal to emotion, nor by any chain of reasoning, but as the culmination of a process of self-discovery which was at the same time a discovery of the nature of man. At the time he had only a vague sense that Christ was the meaning of life, and he did not say anything about it in the first version of his autobiography, *The Story and the Fable*, finished later that year, nor include the diary entry for 1 March 1939 in the extracts put at the end of the book. He did not want to commit himself to any system of dogma nor to any group. He needed time to work out slowly and in his own way the implications of his new experience.

The Story and the Fable was finished in December, and came out the following summer. It is the greatest of his prose works, written in a beautifully lucid, quietly rhythmical style, not mannered but always expressive of his individuality. By its nature it is necessarily centred on his own life, but conveys an unusual sense of impersonality. He is able to look at himself

[26] *A.*, p. 247.

M

with detachment; he does not dramatise himself, nor try to excuse himself. He was interested in his own life in the same way as he might have been in the life of another if he could have known it as well, not because it was his own but as a means of penetrating to some understanding of the meaning of human life in general. As he wrote in his diary: "The Eternal Man has possessed me during most of the time that I have been writing my Autobiography, and has possessed me too in most of my poetry." *The Story and the Fable* puts one in touch with a man of great charm and goodness, but in reading it one feels that one is getting to know not just the author, but oneself also; for we all live the Fable.

A much lesser work written at about this time was *The Present Age*, a survey of English literature since 1914 contributed to a series edited by Bonamy Dobrée. It came out in the summer of 1939. It was written rather hastily at a time when he was busy and strained. He later had a low opinion of it, writing to Dobrée in 1951: "There is one thing I am particularly troubled about, and that is my unfortunate book in your series on English literature. I don't want to have it reprinted if it can be avoided at all, for I am heartily ashamed of it." He need not have been ashamed. The book is not satisfactory as a historical survey of the literature of the period, and the bibliography is inadequate; but it contains vigorously independent and often wittily phrased assessments of particular works and writers. In saying "this book is concerned with history rather than with criticism",[27] he was submitting it to the wrong kind of judgment. In so far as the two can be distinguished he was a critic (a rarer thing) rather than a historian.

[27] *P. A.*, p. 143.

IX

The Translator

MUCH of the Muirs' time between 1924 and 1940 was taken up by translating. They produced over forty volumes of translations, almost all from the German. Some of these, especially the novels of Lion Feuchtwanger, are very long, and some, especially the works of Kafka and Broch, present very difficult problems to the translator. Most of the work was done by Mrs Muir; she was the more brilliant linguist, and wanted to free her husband for other things. Books by Hans Carossa and by Baroness Hatvany were done entirely by her, and were published under the name of Agnes Neill Scott. (The enthusiastic praise which the translation of Carossa's *A Childhood* won in the *Times Literary Supplement* is the more impressive for being uninfluenced by a well-known name.)

The translating was undertaken initially to make a living rather than because of any special interest in the books concerned. Muir did not think much of the plays of Gerhart Hauptmann with which they started, writing to Schiff: "I really think it has not been the labour that has exhausted us so much as the stupidity of the originals";[1] nor were the voluminous works of Lion Feuchtwanger of a kind to make a special appeal to him. But as time went on they began to make their own suggestions as to what should be translated. I shall consider here only the three authors whom, I think, he most admired, and who might therefore be thought to have had some influence upon him. Some of the other books were well worth translating—for instance the war novels of "Ludwig Renn" and Ernst Glaeser, and works by Scholem Asch, Heinrich Mann and Robert Neumann; but I can see no evidence of their having had any effect upon him.

It was in 1929 that their really important work as translators began when they persuaded Secker to commission a

E. M. to Schiff, June 1924

translation of Kafka's *The Castle* (1930). This was followed
by Kafka's other two novels, *The Trial* (1937) and *America*
(1938), and a considerable proportion of his short stories. In
Kafka they were tackling a major writer, whom they greatly
admired. They divided the work equally between them,
literally tearing the books in half, then going over each other's
part to iron out differences of style. I do not know that any
one has detected where the breaks come, nor which of them
did which half.

In an essay in a symposium on translation[2] Muir explained
the special difficulty of translating from German, especially
from Kafka:

> Translation is obviously a difficult art: I use that word, for if
> translation is not an art it can hardly be called translation.
> Yet it is a secondary art, and at best can strive for but never
> reach perfection. My own experience is mainly of translation
> from the German, and there, as a beginning, one must change
> the order of the words, and to do that with a great prose work
> is to commit an irremediable but unavoidable injury against it.
> I am thinking of Franz Kafka, whom my wife and I spent
> years in translating. The word order of Kafka is naked and
> infallible; it not only expresses his meaning but is involved as
> part of it; only in that order could he have said what he wanted
> to say. Yet the fine order has to be disarranged, the original
> edifice of the sentence dismantled and put up again. And the
> result can never be quite satisfactory, simply because the words
> run differently.
>
> No other modern writer has made them run more easily
> and naturally than Kafka, so easily and naturally, indeed, that
> his style never strikes one as being acquired by study and
> practice, but simply to be there, like the intonation of a voice.
> So our main problem was to write an English prose as natural
> in the English way as his was in his own way.

The translations do read as good, natural English, and
convey, I am told, something of the flavour of the original.
Another special difficulty about Kafka, apart from the word
order, is the presence in his writing of several levels of meaning.
When the meaning is dense, as in Kafka, the words conveying

[2] *On Translation*, ed. R. A. Brower (Cambridge, Mass. 1959), p. 93.

ambiguities and complexities of meaning, literal and symbolic, it is often impossible to find English words which will express the same combinations of significance. The translator has either greatly to expand the original, losing the concentrated effect, or to simplify, possibly even to falsify, by choosing to express only what he regards as the most important of the meanings. Whether the struggle with words involved in this kind of translating had any effect on Muir's own writing one cannot say with any confidence; but it is possible that it did. Part of what he says about Kafka, about the words running easily and naturally, the style seeming "simply to be there, like the intonation of a voice", might be applied to himself.

In 1936, when translating *The Trial* he thought of writing a story in the manner of Kafka. He wrote to Spender: "I have an idea for a story about the present state of things in Germany dealt with in the style of Kafka, with elaborate investigations and arguments. I think it is not a bad way of approaching the subject. . . . I admire him more and more: his fascination is simply endless: and a feeling of greatness comes to me in every sentence."[3]

Kafka entered far more deeply into his translators' minds than the other writers they had tackled. "At one stage Kafka's stories continued themselves in our dreams, unfolding into slow serpentine nightmares, immovably reasonable."[4] The likenesses between the imaginative worlds created by Muir in some of his poems and by Kafka in his stories are due mainly to the sharing of a common vision, but it is possible that there was some influence too. Muir had been preoccupied with the image of a journey before 1929, but it is noticeable that this becomes more prominent in his poetry after that date. The idea of life as a journey is in itself, of course, a commonplace one; but it is used to a considerable extent in the same way in both writers. Both can express a sense of frustration, of terror, of nightmare, of roads going wrong, of the goal being almost completely inaccessible, of loneliness and alienation, without ever entirely losing the sense that there is a goal. Kafka expresses the frustration and terror with greater power and through a greater variety of concrete images; whereas Muir in his later

[3] E. M. to Spender, 19 Nov. 1936.   [4] *A.*, p. 240.

works gives a fuller and more serene vision of the goal. There is not in Muir to the same extent as in Kafka a sense of the irreconciliability of the divine and the human law. Muir's view of life was his own, but Kafka may have helped to give him confidence to express it, to show him that it was expressible. At the end of an essay on Kafka he wrote: "The influence of Kafka on modern writing, particularly on the work of such English writers as Rex Warner and William Sansom, comes from his art, not from his view of life; from what he does, not what he says. He has provided imaginative writers not merely with a way of looking at life, but with a way of dealing with life. In an age obsessed by the time sense, or, as it is called, the historical sense, he has resurrected and made available for contemporary use the timeless story, the archetypal story, in which is the source of all stories."[5] Some critics have complained that Muir was always writing the same poem; and it might with equal half truth be said that Kafka was always writing the same story. As Muir says: "Kafka starts with a general or universal situation, not a particular one. This being so, it does not matter where he begins his story, for the situation is always there, and always the same." This is not such a restriction as it sounds, for "the meaning of a universal situation is inexhaustible".[6] Kafka's stories can be interpreted on several levels—psychological, political, and archetypal. One can say that the son Kafka was seeking reconciliation with his own stern father as well as that he was seeking for grace or God; that the sensitive Jewish outsider was constructing images of the impersonal commercial machine in which he worked for a time, and of the oppressive German bureaucracy of his day and even, prophetically, of Nazi tyranny, as well as that he was telling the archetypal story of man's fallen condition. Similarly Muir's "broken kingdom" is within himself and other individuals; it is Scotland, or Europe at war, or the good town after its freedom has been lost; and it is the fallen condition of humanity. The universal situation can be entered at any point.

More perhaps than any major writer before him Kafka used images from dreams and images that have a dream-like

[5] *E. L. S.*, p. 124. (1st ed.)   [6] *E. L. S.*, p. 120.

quality to give concrete expression to psychological states. In doing so he may have helped to give Muir confidence that his imaginative experiences were significant and could be used.

The other important writer from whom the Muirs translated and whom they much admired was Hermann Broch. The long trilology, *The Sleepwalkers*, appeared in 1932, the slighter *The Unknown Quantity* in 1934. *The Sleepwalkers* was very difficult to translate. Muir wrote:

> Those who have read it will remember that the first book is written in one style, the second in another, and the third in a whole medley of styles, the object being to reproduce by these verbal fluctuations a sense of the disintegration of values in Germany in the years leading up to and following the first World War. This must have been a difficult feat for Broch himself, and so difficulty itself became an essential quality of his prose; his attempt to express the almost inexpressible. He had to show the writer battling with his own style, and indicate his intention as part of his performance. With Kafka one is conscious only of the performance.[7]

Muir thought *The Sleepwalkers* a great novel, and was much disappointed by its reception in England.

Muir was not much, if at all, influenced as a writer by the example of Broch. He did not write any more novels after 1932, and in style he followed the seeming naturalness and simplicity of Kafka rather than the self-conscious difficulty of Broch. But there is something in common between his and Broch's central interests and between their ways of looking at life. Broch's central theme is the disintegration of values. In the middle ages there was a system, a centre of values in God. When the medieval system broke up, there was no centre left. Commercial, political, military, aesthetic, and other values were pursued increasingly for their own sakes in isolation from one another. This led progressively to men being unable to understand each other because they were enclosed in separate value systems. This line of thought is familiar, though it has seldom been so effectively embodied in a novel as by Broch. What was unusual about his vision of disintegration was that it led him neither to despair nor to nostalgia for the lost unity. He

[7] *On Translation*, ed. Brower, p. 94.

regarded the process as having been made necessary, as Muir put it, "by the bankruptcy of medieval logic itself, by the fact that medieval theological thought, a closed deductive system, could not resolve its own antinomies, and so had to allow reason to start anew from the fact of the empirically given world, or rather from the multitude of facts presented by that world." The process of disintegration is fated and necessary, and "when it is consummated the Platonic idea is fated to return, the community of men bound together by one aim, united by one faith, must necessarily return, because the very laws of human reason, the needs of the human soul, make it inevitable. Throughout the book these two perceptions run parallel: the perception of a historical process through which civilisation is passing, and the perception of the everlasting human need of salvation".[8] The perception of disintegration is the more immediately apparent in the novel, but the other perception is present in the persistent, even if outwardly ineffective, search of such characters as Joachim von Passenow and Esch for order, relationship, and salvation, and, less effectively, in the final paean to the unforfeitable "brotherhood of humble human creatures", to "the oneness in which all light has its source and from which springs the healing of all living things".[9] Broch is particularly good at conveying a sense of the separate inner worlds which his characters inhabit. Each, as Muir might put it, lives in the labyrinth of his own loneliness, though he wishes to break out and establish relationships.

Though the translations from Hans Carossa were done by his wife Muir too loved his work, and found in him, especially in his *A Childhood* (1930), a kindred spirit. Carossa re-creates the child's feeling for animals and things and natural forces, his sense of an immutable order. "This," Muir wrote, "is Carossa's rare distinction as a writer that he not merely describes things, but quietly, as if by an act of mystical legerdemain, restores them to their places—where alone they are truly what they ought to be." Carossa was a doctor, and

---

[8] E. M., "Hermann Broch" in *Modern Scot*, vol. III, no. 2 (August 1932), pp. 103-10.
[9] *The Sleepwalkers*, p. 648.

he describes pain realistically without softening it. "He sees it as a mysterious and terrible force; but in the powers which rise to combat it he discerns the order of the world, and remembers that we all rest upon it. He has a constant sense that at every moment, no matter how terrible, the reconciling powers which hold the universe together are near us."[10]

The Muirs' work as translators ended in 1940. War reduced the demand for translations from German; and they took other jobs which meant they had no time for translating. During the war two novels by the Hungarian Zsolt de Harsányi appeared in translation with their names on the title page; but their contribution was only to give some polish to the English. Hermann Broch, by then in America, wanted them to translate his *The Death of Virgil;* but at the time this was proposed, in the autumn of 1940, other commitments made it impossible for them to undertake it. In any case they felt that by this time the philosopher in Broch had to a large extent driven out the artist.

[10] *The Bookman* (New York), vol. LXXII, no. 4 (December 1930), pp. 404-8.

X

The War Years

I

THE first two and a half years of the War were critical ones in Muir's life. Externally his fortunes reached a low ebb, and he endured much anxiety and suffering; at the very same time his spiritual life deepened, and he came into his own as a poet. There was no dramatic change, but the considerable advance poetically between *Journeys and Places* (1937) and *The Narrow Place* (1943) was related to, and in part caused by, this deepening of his spiritual life. He attained a more secure foothold on the solid foundation within himself, of which he had written to Spender.

The Story and the Fable was finished in December 1939, and translating work kept the Muirs busy until the following spring. After that the income from translating stopped, and reviewing did not bring in enough to keep the home going. So they began to look for jobs. She could have got a good teaching post if she had been willing to leave St Andrews, but they did not want to split the family; so she took a badly-paid post at the school where Gavin was a pupil. He also applied for teaching posts, but without success because of his lack of a degree—a startling demonstration of the modern preference for paper over real qualifications. Eventually in the autumn of 1940 he got a clerical job in the Food Office in Dundee, stamping ration books and doing other such routine chores in the back office for £3 a week. After twenty one years he was back again as a clerk, earning less than he had in 1919 and doing less responsible work. Many, he fully realised, were suffering far worse hardships at the time; and he passes over this period quickly and without complaint in his *Autobiography*. But it was an absurd waste of talent. He allowed himself one wryly humorous comment in a letter to Aitken: "I found that my lack of an academic degree is a most astonishing obstacle:

in Scotland nothing but a certificate of some kind seems to be recognised as really meritorious—a curious example of the preference of faith to works, for surely by this time I've done some work that should count."[1] He got up at seven in the morning, and travelled by train to Dundee, changing at Leuchars Junction. One day a friend saw him standing in the corridor of the crowded train jotting down notes for a poem; this was probably "The Wayside Station", the station in that poem being Leuchars. In the evenings he took classes in English literature as well as going to Home Guard parades and taking his turn on guard duty at the telephone exchange, armed with a shot gun and no ammunition. The Home Guard he enjoyed; for it brought people of all classes together. There was a new sense of unity and common purpose in the town, and he felt himself more a part of it. All this time he was also writing his reviews and occasional broadcast talks. It was too much. He overstrained his heart carrying sand-bags in the Home Guard, had pains in the chest and was told that he must rest completely for six weeks or he might not live for a year. This was in the spring of 1941. He lay in bed alone all day, while his wife and son were away at school, his meals being brought in from a neighbouring boarding-house, and was astonished at the tranquillity which, in spite of his anxieties, he was able to attain. When he got up in the summer Mrs Muir, who had not been well for some time, had to take to bed; later in the summer she seemed to be on the upgrade, but in the winter was worse again. Early in January 1942 she was taken to a nursing home for an operation, and for a few days her life was in danger. Sending in a script to the B.B.C. he wrote: "I have done my best, but my best is very poor at present, for Willa, after seeming to be in the way to recovery, is up and down again, and although I hardly like even to say it, I have been horribly afraid for her; she is so weak; but I hope and hope and hope she will mend." By the end of January she was out of danger, but it was a long time before she recovered, and "when she came home at last she had shrunk as if by some chemical process, and life, of which she had been so full, had sunk to its inmost source. Years passed

[1] E. M. to Aitken, 12 Jun. 1941.

before she returned to the semblance of what she had once been."[2] He saw again, almost as when in the Glasgow days he had watched the slow deaths of his brothers, the ravages of disease and of time acting on a loved person. But now the result was not fatal, and he had much greater inner resources with which to confront anxiety.

It was at about this time that his first love poems to his wife were written. Danger made him more than ever conscious of what he owed to her. At the time of their marriage friends on both sides prophesied, with some excuse for their mistake, that it would not last. He had been reluctant to commit himself, lacking the confidence to take on responsibility and not wanting his personality intruded upon. She was ambitious, a feminist, resentful of the position of women in a man's world, fully capable of making an independent career for herself; an agnostic, with a powerful and sceptical intelligence, a sharp tongue and no respect for genteel conventions. To a superficial observer it might have seemed that they were an ill-assorted pair; that she should have gravitated towards some fashionably progressive, rationalist circle; that he should have married some one gentler, quieter, more obviously in tune with the mystical side of his nature. But in fact both gained more than if they had married people more like themselves. She could appreciate in him a fineness of intelligence and of perception beyond her own, and found in him, as she could have in very few men, some one she could devote herself to, in some degree give up her own ambitions for, without a sense of waste. Her devotion was bracing, never cloying, and she remained very much herself, and different from him.

He found in her not only love and loyalty, but also intellectual companionship, and a toughness, an earthiness, which might seem discordant with his fineness but which was probably good for him. She maintained around him a protective atmosphere of love and gaiety, and at the same time kept him in touch with the earth and with common humanity. The word "protective" may give the wrong impression. Her protection was not to shield him from experience, but to enable him to remain unusually open to it

[2] *A.*, p. 249.

right into old age without damage. Alone in Glasgow he had to armour himself; with her, in the warmth she created round him, he was able to become a man without a mask, to let the fears and evil of his time pour in as well as his perceptions of glory. Unusually, he became more human, more open as he grew older. It was a union between two very remarkable and very different people, in which both became more fully themselves.

Some extracts from letters will help to show how they weathered the storms. In December 1939 she wrote to a friend (referring to her earlier and less serious illness):

> Yes, I have been ill and had an operation—a damned nuisance, for it meant that I was on the shelf for months. Last Christmas I fainted away on the floor after making a batch of amateur sweets for the family, and was kept in bed by a horrified doctor for two weeks until my silly heart was fit to stand an operation. . . . I had to be cut open and stitched up well and truly, and I lay on my back for seven weeks in all, so that I had to learn to walk all over again. The worst thing was: I couldn't bring my mind to bear on any job of work for more than fifteen minutes at a time. Consequently I was just a dead weight on Edwin, and I still feel ashamed of it. But by the end of the summer I was able to translate, and I have been working like a mad-woman; and a fortnight ago posted the last of Feuchtwanger's new novel. . . . I am now going to finish my own novel, by hook or crook, despite the war.
>
> All this with the war on top of it, has knocked our finances endways. But we are lucky; we have been commissioned to translate another rotten novel, by February, and our literal instructions are: to cut out the 'hot' bits and make it sloppy and sentimental enough for the British Public! So we shall survive as a family until about April or May. After that, if nothing happens, Edwin and I will have to look for jobs. . . .
>
> So the household lurches on, grazing rocks and nearly foundering on sandbanks, but still staggering across the seas. In our own peculiar fashion, I believe that as a family we are happy, war or no war.[3]

Her courage and gaiety and determination to help her husband pulled her through. He had similar resources, and

[3] W. M. to Miss Lehfeldt, 20 Dec. 1939.

others of a different kind. His experience of the Lord's Prayer early in 1939 was not an isolated one; it was followed by a return to the Bible, especially the Gospels, and eventually by other religious experiences of which he gives only faint hints, but which must have been of great importance to him. It did not lead, however, to the adoption of any dogmatic system of belief. He wrote to Aitken in January 1940:

I find with some dismay, after going over my life, that I have no philosophy—here am I, a middle-aged man and a professional writer, and I have no philosophy. I had a philosophy when I was twenty-seven, but it was not my philosophy. I have no philosophy now—that is no rational scheme for accounting for all the time I have lived in the world, or comprehensively for life itself. And this lack—which I must share with several million people—really does dismay me in some part of me, and gives me a troubling sense of insecurity. I believe that I am immortal, certainly, but that in a way makes it more difficult to interpret *this* life (in another way it makes it easier: I would be the last to deny that: if life were *only* this life, I would find it virtually impossible to find a meaning in it—moral or aesthetic). If we're moving towards a society which compared to this will be a sort of heaven on earth (and I doubt it), how can that society, a mere point in history, justify all the grinding cycles of suffering and cruelty and mere grey living that were necessary to lead up to it? I think Ivan Karamazov was quite right in saying that if that was how things were he would hand back his ticket. I suppose what I mean when I say I have no philosophy is that I have no explanation, none whatever, of Time except as an unofficial part [?] of Eternity—no historical explanation of human life, for the problem of evil seems insoluble to me: I can only accept it as a mystery, and what a mystery is I do not know. All these thoughts have been roused (and clarified a little in my mind) by writing my life: there is very little in the book itself about them. All I can say I have, confronted by these things, is faith, and I think that perhaps my faith is a little too easy, considering the enormity [?] of these things. But faith can produce a sentence like: 'I am the resurrection and the life' (It seems to me the most sublime sentence ever uttered, especially the order of the terms, the resurrection preceding the life, as if a real life only began with a resurrection, even in

this world—and I believe this.) So that there may be something more in faith than we can account for, a source of energy
and reconciliation which philosophy cannot reach. I do not
know: I wish my mind were more single and clear.

About a month later he wrote to the poet William Soutar
(Soutar had been confined to his bed by paralysis since about
the age of thirty, and the Muirs had visited him at his home
in Perth the previous summer):

Forgive me for not replying sooner to your note and particularly
to your poems, which ask for a much more eloquent answer
than I can give. (Poetry is the only answer to poetry.) I
should have replied sooner, but I have been writing my life,
and have managed to finish it at last (at least up to 1922)—a
curious labour, almost as difficult as living itself, but interesting
at least. The difficulty that strikes me about life is not that it
is uninteresting (as so many uninteresting people call it) but that
it is interesting in too many different ways, that is, confusing;
so that it takes a genius, and a very great genius at that, to
pierce through its countless meanings to the one that illumines
them all. I suppose the importance and necessity of religion
lies in that; for the great religious figures have this particular
gift *in exelcis*, and they can give it out to others so long as there
is a faith and a religious community. I have been struggling
with such questions in my book; the difficulty with me is that
I have the faith, but that I cannot belong to any one Christian
community. I believe in God, in the immortality of the soul,
and that Christ is the greatest figure who ever appeared in the
history of mankind. I believe in the Fall too, and the need
for salvation. But the theological dogmas do not help me; I
can't digest them for my good; they're an obstacle to me
(perhaps they shouldn't be, but they are); and so I'm a sort
of illicit Christian, a gate-crasher, hoping in my own way to
slip in 'At David's hip yet'.
I was greatly moved by the integrity and the high temper of
your poems, and of the introduction as well: they hang
together absolutely, as things from one integral centre do. You
have given these questions of Pacifism and Marxism and
Christianity and their relation to one another more thought
than I have. I have been troubled more, and perhaps too
exclusively, by personal things—the hope of finding a meaning

in life and in my own life. I feel the need to see life timelessly:
the only way in which it can be seen as a whole. . . .

I hope you did not have a Temple Dante already. The
one I sent you belonged to me, but a dear friend of mine
[John Holms?] left me another at his death a few years ago,
with his name and markings in it, and I have used it ever
since. I have got so much enjoyment out of Dante, with only
a slight smattering of Italian to help me, that I thought you
might get the same pleasure, or perhaps a greater one. I
suppose there's no one to equal him, except Shakespeare, and
they are very different.

Dante remained one of Muir's favourite writers, and one of
those from whom he learned most. In the first version of a
later poem, "For Ann Scott-Moncrieff", he wrote:

> I hurried past my prime
> To Plato and Dante to school
> And conned immortality,
> And tried to put off the fool,
> And, a being, strove to be.

Some time before this he had resumed contact with his old
friend, David Peat. Peat had had a sad life since the days in
the early twenties when he had been a successful journalist and
organiser of the Arbitrate First Bureau. He had spent much
time in mental homes, but had retained his charm and gentleness and the capacity, when not too ill, to rise above self-pity
to a concern for all mental sufferers. In order to help people
like himself and to gain understanding for them he also was
writing his autobiography, and he and Muir corresponded
about their respective books. (It is characteristic of him that
he induced Muir to omit all criticism of his father, whose
severity Muir had been inclined to think partly responsible for
David's neurosis.) In February 1940 Muir wrote to him:

I have been thinking a good deal about my own life recently,
and feeling more and more that it is not what it should be, and
I feel guilty that I have let our old friendship drop so much,
without giving it anything on which it could nourish itself. . . .
I am not writing to you because I am lonely; actually I am
happier than I have been, in spite of the state of the world,
for I have had something like a sense of the presence of God,

a sense which I have never consciously been aware of before, though I am now fifty-two; it is too new and strange for me to write about it, and so inexperienced that I am afraid of writing about it. I have believed for a long time in the immortality of the soul, but this is something different: I tremble to lose it again by my own fault. Perhaps I should not have written about it at all, for I cannot tell anything about it, but only so far feel it at times.

These last few sentences are very important. He was very reticent about his religious life, and I have come across no other direct reference to the sense of the presence of God which he writes of here. But I think this sense must have stayed with him—not all the time, of course, but the memory of it would always be there—for the rest of his life. As he says in the letter this experience was quite recent—perhaps more recent than the letter of a few weeks before in which he had written to Aitken of having nothing but a perhaps too easy faith. His early religious conversions had been in comparison quite superficial. He had, like so many modern people, been stripped of various inadequate conceptions of God and had had to go through a period of atheism in order that he might make his own discovery of Him—or allow himself to be discovered. It is largely because his faith was so humble, tentative, undogmatic and at the same time so securely based on experience that his religious poetry has such a strong appeal. The new experience was something coming to him, a grace, not an escape nor something consciously willed; yet the honesty of his self-examination must have contributed to make it possible. Some of his early associates were surprised at the young Nietzschean and socialist turning into the elderly Christian, as if in some way he was false to his early ideals. But his socialism looked beyond material ends, and his later religion included them, was in a sense a *this*-worldly one. The Lord's Prayer for him "seemed to sanctify common existence. . . . It is about the world and society, not about the everlasting destiny of the soul." Christ is the meaning of life, including of *this* life. He always reacted against any kind of religion which seemed to him life-denying.

A letter of a few months later to a new friend, George

N

Scott-Moncrieff, mentions a writer whom he discovered at about this time and who greatly impressed him, St Augustine: "I've been reading St. Augustine's *Confessions* with intense attraction and repulsion: it seems to me one of the greatest of all books; the description of the ecstasy unsurpassed by anything else I know. An enormously great and passionate mind: the only thing that nears it in elevation and power being some of Beethoven's music. And what an artist!"[4] Muir would be repelled by St Augustine's fierceness against the flesh and against those whose opinions he thought mistaken, and attracted by his honesty and tenderness as well as by his powerful imagination and intelligence. The *Confessions*, like Muir's own recently written book, is a strangely impersonal autobiography, which at the same time gives a strong impression of an individual personality. Muir was especially impressed by St Augustine's discussion at the end of Book XI of God's eternal present, which is eternity, and of time. His reading of St Augustine may have combined with his own experiences mentioned to Peat to give him a new understanding of mysticism.

This is suggested by a very interesting article "Yesterday's Mirror:Afterthoughts to an autobiography" contributed in the autumn of 1940 to *The Scots Magazine*.[5] He says that one learns about oneself by writing an autobiography. Normally the momentary self continuously ousts the permanent self, and we live "in a perpetual bright oblivion of ourselves, insulated in the moving moment." We learn about life from yesterday —"a yesterday which can never change again and is therefore beyond confusion. . . . Art is the sum of the moments in which men have glanced into that yesterday which can never change; and when we read, or look at a picture, or listen to music, we are released from the moment to contemplate that mirror in which all the forms of life lie outspread."

There are three ways of looking into that mirror:
(1) The realist's who sees a world where wrong triumphs and right suffers. He has forgotten his childhood.
(2) That of the man who in maturity has kept a memory of

4 E. M. to Scott-Moncrieff, 13 Nov. 1940.
5 *Scots Magazine*, September 1940, pp. 404-10.

his childhood. "He sees in the mirror an indefeasible rightness beneath the wrongness of things; a struggle between good and evil, and not merely the victory of evil; and to him the rightness of human life has a deeper reality, a more fundamental appositeness, than the evil, as being more truly native to man. This, to our credit, is our normal view of life."

(3) That which is given "only to the greatest poets and mystics at their greatest moments, and is beyond rational description. The world which the mystical poet sees is a world in which both good and evil have their place legitimately; in which the king on his throne and the rebel raising his standard in the market place, the tyrant and the slave, the assassin and the victim, each plays a part in a supertemporal drama which at every moment, in its totality, issues in glory and meaning and fulfilment.[6] This vision is too dangerous for us as human beings struggling in the arena; it would be safe only if we felt no touch of evil, and it is given to men only when they are at the very heart of good, and in a sense very different from Nietzsche's, beyond good and evil. St. Augustine saw it and so did Blake; it is the supreme vision of human life, because it reconciles all opposites; but it transcends our moral struggle, for in life we are ourselves the opposites and must act as best we can." Something of this vision, he says, is possessed by the child—a sense of rightness in all things. The vision of the child and of St Augustine are comparable. We return through experience to innocence; the road curves round towards its beginning.

He writes here with greater confidence than in his letter to Aitken at the beginning of the year. Any one who has got so far need no longer complain of the lack of a philosophy. The three ways of seeing discussed in the article are expressed more vividly and concretely in the poem "The Three Mirrors". The first two sections begin "I looked . . .". He had been among those who saw in the first mirror a world where wrong triumphs and everything is askew; and so one accepts that it is not by self-blinding but by deeper vision that he is now able to see in the second mirror the rightness behind the wrongness, the rightness which has a deeper reality as being more truly native to man. When he comes to the third section he begins "*If*

[6] *Cf.* "The Trophy", in *C. P.*, p. 116.

I looked in the third glass . . .". He did not claim to be among the great poets and mystics; he could not yet see directly into the third glass himself, but he knew something of what he would see there if he could, and that it was the ultimate truth.

The reinforcement of his inner resources in 1940 helped him to surmount the illness and anxieties of the following year. How he got through his own illness he described in a letter to Aitken: "The doctor told me that if I went on as I was doing, I should kill myself off in a year or two. He told me I was not to over-exert myself or to worry, and the last part of this advice seemed quite fantastic at the time; yet I found to my surprise that, if I set myself to it, it could be followed. So I've been living in a state of enforced tranquillity, and because of that my illness hasn't been altogether to the bad: it made me realise that I had been rushing on like a madman, past my true self, living my own actual unique life as if it belonged to any one at all, or to some one whom I had no concern with, someone who did not matter in the least to me. That at least is over now, and whatever job I find to do, I shall try to make sure it never returns. The result of my tranquillity—or rather one of the results—has been a little freshet of poetry: I'm enclosing some of it, not knowing how you will like it, for it seems to me different from most of my poetry: there is no effort in it, for at present I'm unable to make such things as efforts; and I'm afraid it lacks intensity, but it may have some other quality that makes up for that: I don't know."[7]

The poems sent with this letter are "The Question" (then called "The Finder Found"), "The Guess", "The Prize" and "The Old Gods". In these poems, written in a time of strange tranquillity in the midst of anxiety, Muir achieved the luminous simplicity which is a special feature of his mature work. The first of them shows that he had attained to a profounder conception than before of the meaning of self-discovery:

Will you, sometime, who have sought so long and seek
Still in the slowly darkening hunting ground,
Catch sight some ordinary month or week
Of that strange quarry you scarcely thought you sought—

---

[7] E. M. to Aitken, 12 Jun. 1941.

Yourself, the gatherer gathered, the finder found,
The buyer, who would buy all, in bounty bought—
And perch in pride on the princely hand, at home,
And there, the long hunt over, rest and roam?

The words "the finder found" have a double meaning. The
seeker finds himself, his innermost self; but also he is found.
The finding of the self turns out to be the finding of God, and
that to be a being found by God; for once God is known at
all He is known as *alive*, active. The central theme of these
poems is the discovery of man's natural shape, of blessedness
as natural. Serenity is combined with humility, and nothing
is dogmatically stated. Blessedness *seemed* natural, the *guess*
was felt as true; the finding of the true self is glimpsed as a
possibility in the future, and put in the form of a question. Yet
these humble, questioning, tentative poems are much more
impressive affirmations of life than anything in Nietzsche or in
Muir's Nietzschean writings.

II

Once he had recovered from his illness he had to get another
job. In the summer of 1941 he was negotiating for a post as
a publisher's adviser; this would have meant flitting to near
London, which he did not much want to do. He went to
England in July in connexion with an application for a job as
a schoolmaster, but was quite glad when he was unsuccessful;
for, fortunately a more attractive opportunity occurred nearer
home. Mr H. Harvey Wood, the British Council Representative in Edinburgh, was looking for some one to give a talk on
English literature to a group of Polish officers, and Stanley
Cursiter suggested he should ask Muir. An hour and a half
after the lecture should have finished Harvey Wood found him
still in animated conversation with the Poles; the lecture had
been a great success. That winter Harvey Wood was organising
International Houses in Edinburgh—a Polish House, a
Czechoslovak House, a French House, later an American
House—where servicemen and refugees from those countries
could meet each other and the people of Edinburgh. He asked
Muir to join the Council staff and to organise evening programmes for these Houses. So, in March 1942, after the

worst of his wife's illness was past, he began his eight years
association with the Council. At first he lived in lodgings
(47 Manor Place), going home to St Andrews at the week ends.
Then he got a flat in Edinburgh (8 Blantyre Terrace) and the
family was reunited. He enjoyed the work for the Council,
and did it well. He lectured a good deal himself, mainly on
poetry; he wrote scripts for dramatic entertainments; got
many distinguished poets, other writers and scholars to lecture
at the Houses; arranged concerts; and by his presence
contributed to the gaiety and friendliness of these Houses, adding
for those able to hear it the note of intellectual distinction.
The impetus given to the cultural life of Edinburgh in those
days by the Council and the presence of so many Europeans
led on after the War to the starting of the Edinburgh Festival,
of which Harvey Wood was one of the principal inspirers.
Harvey Wood tells me that Muir was good not only at the
educational and personal-relations side of his work, but also
at more mundane things: "He was a quiet but astonishingly
efficient and methodical worker. He had one surprising
ability which probably revived from his clerking days. When
we had difficulty with our accounts and couldn't get them to
balance, Edwin would take one quick look at the figures and
point out where they had gone wrong."

These were his happiest years in Scotland. Edinburgh was
more than usually full of life, and he was at the centre of it.
He was working with congenial people, had many friends and
friendly acquaintances, and was modestly glad to be doing a
useful job in wartime like everybody else. But one cannot
help feeling sorry that at this time when he was coming to his
late maturity as a poet he did not have more leisure. As
Harvey Wood says: "Most people thought (and I did too)
that he was far too good for us and for the work he was doing."
How much more, or better, poetry he would have written if
he had had more time it is impossible to say. For he always
waited for a poem to knock on the door, for inspiration. He
could not—or at least did not—stimulate inspiration in himself
by deliberately setting himself tasks. He waited—sometimes
for a long time. Then perhaps sitting on the top floor of an
Edinburgh tram, "looking at the windows flying past, feeling

as if I were in no fixed place, as if I were nowhere," he would find odd lines coming into his mind which he recognised as the beginning of a poem. Or this might happen in company, and he would withdraw right out of the conversation, and Mrs Muir would nudge her neighbour and say "birth is coming". Then he would need perhaps quite a long period of gestation, walking by himself preferably in the country, before he would write down the poem and work at it with the top of his mind. From Edinburgh he would often go out in the afternoons to the nearby village of Swanston under the Pentland Hills, where a seat has now been placed in his memory. There he would be quiet and alone in beautiful surroundings. The poem "In Love for Long" originated there, and others were slowly brought to birth.

It may be that other work sometimes interfered, and that some poems were lost through the initial knock on the door not being attended to in time:

> Do not believe I do not want your love,
> Brother and sister, wife and son.
> But I would be alone
> Now, now and let him in . . .
> And oh I dread
> He may even now be gone
> Or, when I open, will not enter in.[8]

But he had great tenacity of purpose and did, I think, usually manage to attend to the visitors when they knocked. He wrote the greater, and the best, part of his poetry during the period between 1942 and 1956 when he had regular jobs other than writing. He was best able to do his special work by accepting uncomplainingly the conditions in which he found himself and the tasks laid upon him.

One of his subsidiary activities in Edinburgh was broadcasting. The B.B.C. had shown an earlier appreciation of his potentialities than some other bodies that might have used his talents. In 1936 he had been asked to produce a script for a St Andrew's Day programme. This surveyed four centuries of Scottish history by means of quotations from documents and

---

[8] "The Visitor", in *C. P.*, p. 198.

literature linked by a verse narrative by Muir. The central theme was Scotland's need for liberty and unity, her struggle for these things and her failure. As a result of the success of this programme he was asked to devise the St Andrew's Day programmes for 1938 and 1939 also. The last of these, written after the beginning of the War, expressed by means again of quotation and linking narrative the values, especially freedom, for which Scotland had stood in the past and still stood in war. A producer commented in an internal B.B.C. memorandum: "As in everything Mr Muir has written for us, there is a feeling of greatness about it." Another undertaking of a similar kind was a series of seven half-hour programmes in 1941-42, entitled "The Book of Scotland". He himself suggested the scheme, and the title, explaining: "Perhaps the phrase was unconsciously drawn from 'The Book of Life' mentioned in the Bible; I thought of the leaves as living leaves, turned by Time, in the living volume of Scottish life." The seven programmes dealt with the high points of Scottish history and literature from St Columba to Scott. Even the scripts convey a sense of a great and tragic story. Some of those who heard them brought to life still remember them as inspiring—and true; for they encouraged no false hopes.

In the mean time he had established himself as performer as well as provider of scripts. Sympathetic producers helped him to overcome his initial nervousness, and to become an effective, though not spectacular, broadcaster. He never developed a radio personality separate from his every-day one. He was always himself, the same man talking as his friends knew in private life. From 1937 onwards he gave a large number of talks on literature, mainly reviews of Scottish books, and a few on other topics. For about a year, in 1943 and 1944, he edited as well as took part in "Chapbook", a magazine programme on Scottish affairs.

One or two of his early scripts were criticised by producers as being too involved and too abstract. He had to learn to appeal at once to a wide audience, to compress and simplify, and to express his meaning as far as possible dramatically and in narrative rather than by abstract statement. It may be that the effort to do these things helped him to achieve concreteness and simplicity in his poetry. In any case he made a distinctive contribution to Scottish broadcasting, especially in the war years.

After the comparative isolation of St Andrews the Muirs had many friends and a busy social life in Edinburgh. All those I have talked to stress his gaiety and charm as a companion. Any impression of solemnity which the poems may have given to some readers is quite false to the man (and I believe to the poems too). His friends recall pictures of him sitting on the floor talking and laughing among a group of Poles, of him singing in a pleasant tenor voice ("almost in tune", one friend tells me, but that may be unfair) at evening entertainments in the International Houses, of him and Neil Gunn coming singing into the house rather late for dinner and of Mrs Muir throwing rice at them. Morley Jamison, the writer, and his wife lived with them in Blantyre Terrace for quite a long time. He saw Muir angry only once, when a conductor did nothing to help an old woman off a tram and pressed the start-bell before she was properly off. Hew Lorimer, the sculptor, shared a room with him at the British Council, and also stresses his quiet gaiety and the fun of his company. With Lorimer he was less reticent than with most others about his religious experiences; he would not talk about them except with people he was sure would be sympathetic. To him he talked of his rediscovery of the Bible, which until 1939 he had not read much since boyhood. Now he was bubbling over with enthusiasm. The splendour of the Gospels seemed to him much greater than that of other parts of the Bible, even than other parts of the New Testament. One day he said to Lorimer that he felt himself a Catholic, but could not take the plunge of joining the Church—why, he did not say.

He did not write much of the War, but shared fully in the anxieties of that time. It came closest to him through the refugees and exiled servicemen he knew. He wrote a longish poem "The Refugees", of which only an amended version of part of the final chorus is included in the *Collected Poems*. Its failure as a whole was not due to any lack of feeling. He had private worries too. His wife took a long time to recover from her nearly fatal illness; he was at times unwell himself; and his son was going through a difficult time, suffering from deafness which was a special handicap to one who showed great promise as a musician. His serenity had not been easily attained, and was never secure nor complacent.

His inner life during this time must be approached mainly through the poems, but there are some interesting passages in letters to Stephen Spender. In March 1944 he wrote to him: "I've been going through all sorts of crises myself, which have been unpleasant and good for me, and have taken me uncomfortably near the kind of rejection of life for eternal ends which some people call religion. I'm glad I've got over it, but glad I've seen it and realised that I don't like it or want it at all, and would not have it at any price." This is rather surprising; I can see no sign in poems or letters or any where else of his being drawn in these years towards a life-rejecting kind of religion. Something must have happened within him to which he gave no expression but this rejection.

Later the same month he wrote again to Spender:

> I was much struck by what you say about death and the fortuituous snuffing out of life. [Something Spender must have seen during his work in the Fire Service in London]. I can't feel or think so clearly about it, for though I've lived so much longer I have never come in contact with it. It is the most horrible thing in the world, probably: I don't know. I shall stick to my belief in immortality, I feel that it is involved with so many of our instinctive feelings, especially the feeling that we have free will, which is simply, I think, the feeling that, in spite of the fact that all our actions and thoughts are obviously determined by all the things around us, and by our position in time, we are not completely contained by these things, therefore there is something else in us not dictated to by time. This may appear unconvincing to you: perhaps it is only convincing if one believes in immortality as I do. And at any rate it is several removes from the experiences you have been having: therefore less real, less immediate, and of no use to you.
>
> The problems are terrifying, as you say. The religions exist, I suppose, to provide an explanation of them. I can't accept any religious explanation that I know of, any more than you. I would rather have the problems themselves, for from

an awareness of them and their vastness I get some sort of
living experience, some sense even of communion, of being in
the whole in some way, whereas from the explanations I should
only get comfort and reassurance and a sense of safety which I
know is not genuine. I don't know why, this being so, my
religious experience is not without hope: I do not think it is
because of my belief in immortality: I still hold it, but for
some reason it doesn't mean so much to me as it used to do:
whether this is a bad sign or a good I really don't know. And
I don't know where I stand regarding tragedy. But may not
tragedy affect us so much because it is directly concerned with
these enormous and terrifying problems, without providing a
solution: the beauty may be incidental. And if the dignity
seems false to you, I feel all the same that it is something we
should claim, no matter who it is who is blasted out of life in
some horrible casual way, in a minute. Perhaps the dignity
could be expressed in a different way, in which it would be
more true for you.

For me too love is the supreme quality and more closely
connected with immortality than any other, immortality either
as you or I conceive it. And in a way I feel it is more important
than immortality. If I could really love all creatures and all
things I should not trouble about immortality. I should not
trouble about that because I should not trouble about myself.
(But that is far distant.) I've been greatly moved by a life of
Tolstoy I've been reading (by Derrick Leon), and though I
don't agree with him that the soul alone matters, and the flesh
not at all, what a wonderful human being he was, and what a
struggle he made for his idea of human love. I feel that most
of the things I'm saying will seem irrelevant or theoretical to
you: don't pay too much attention to them. . . .

I'm still writing a poem occasionally, but am not much
pleased with my latest ones.

Later the same month he wrote again to Spender, after the
latter had been up to Edinburgh for a lecture: "I was sorry I
was feeling rather low when you were here, and dispirited;
that is over now and I am looking forward very much to seeing
you in London in the beginning of July. I have quite unexpectedly written a few poems recently, which has made me
feel better. I have been reading the Bowra book on symbolism
and been much stimulated tho' I don't think it is quite as good

as it has been called." In a postscript he added: "Since writing this I've seen a doctor about my heart, after long hesitation. He told me, to my surprise and delight, that it is practically recovered. What has been bothering me is anaemia; I have only 70% of the blood I should have, so he says; and he is dosing me with iron. I am much cheered." Soon afterwards he wrote: "An absurd thing I realised after reading Bowra's book was that I had been writing symbolist poetry very frequently for years without knowing it. He's inspired me to write one deliberately, which I enclose. I think it isn't really bad: but I shouldn't have written it quite like that but for his book. I'm writing another just now, on a more ambitious scale, some of which I like, some not." I am not sure which the poems referred to are. Perhaps the shorter one is "The Rider Victory", and the longer "The Voyage".

XI

Poetry 1938-1945

I

RENEWED self-discovery and renewed vividness of response to the outer world in the years 1938 to 1941, combined with increased skill with words and metres, enabled Muir to write poetry with a new depth, range and simplicity; but the fruit was mainly gathered later. While his deeper self was going into the autobiography he did not write many poems, and in the first two years of the War he was mostly too tired and preoccupied to work at the ideas that came to him. In the summer of 1940 he wrote to Spender: "I've been able to write very little during the last two or three months, only a little poetry, and, very surprisingly, mostly in Scots—I expect that the present time is drawing us all back to our bases, a good thing in one way, I think." These poems he must have considered failures. He did publish several poems on Scottish themes at this time, but none in Scots; evidently he found that the Scottish language was not really his base. English was by now, I think, the natural and habitual language of his feelings as well as of his thoughts, and it was probably more suitable than Scots for his reflective kind of poetry. Soon afterwards he sent to Spender a poem, "In a Time of Mortal Shocks", which, he said, "came simply out of distress of mind which I tried to deal with". It begins and ends:

> Live on through these and learn what is this life,
> Pure spirit indwelling . . .
> Be at the root
> No fear can find, the foot.
> There stay secure.
> There is your only place of safety. Stay
> There in your house and keep your day.

He was not satisfied with this poem because it is too monitory, and he never published it. Another poem sent to Spender he thought good in its way, since "it came out of contemplation and not out of distress". One of the reasons he has been underrated is that many people now seem to prefer the poetry of "distress", of the fragmentary emotions of the moment, to the poetry of "contemplation", in which the wholeness and objectivity of art are attained.

In the same letter he went on:

> My mind is being teased by fragmentary intimations of poems more than it has been for some time, without anything further happening, lines like
> We were a tribe, a family, a people,
> King Lear was our father, ["Scotland 1941" and "The
> Ring"]
> and
> The doors yawned open in Ulysses' house, ["The Return
> of Odysseus"]
> (which has turned into a poem)
> and
> He who has not been yet will be some day,
> The gatherer gathered, the finder found, ["The Question"]
> (which has come to nothing).[1]

He was not able to do much during the terribly busy winter of 1940-41, though "The Wayside Station" was written then. During his illness in 1941 the few short poems sent to Aitken came; and by the middle of 1942 he had enough for a volume.

The poems written between 1937 and 1942, mostly towards the end of that time, were collected in *The Narrow Place*, published by Faber early in 1943. Dent having largely abandoned the publication of poetry during the War, T. S. Eliot was able to secure Muir for Faber, and was to prove a most helpful and courteous publisher to him. (Muir was handed on by one author-publisher to another. After his first two volumes of poetry had been published by Leonard and Virginia Woolf his next two were accepted by Dent thanks to the good offices of Richard Church.) This volume shows an advance on what had gone before both in skill and in range. There is a greater mastery of a variety of metrical forms and of rhythmical effects. A large proportion of the poems in

[1] E. M. to Spender, 2 Aug. 1940.

Journeys and Places, as in *First Poems*, are made up of quatrains, mostly of eight-syllable lines. In *The Narrow Place* no one metrical form is predominant, but in each poem he makes the form suit the content. In an unobtrusive way he shows great skill in handling difficult forms. "The Day" consists of one long, perfectly clear and logical sentence, fitted without apparent strain into sixteen lines of rhyming decasyllabic verse; and "The Question" is a single sentence of eight similar lines. The long sentences help to convey a sense of wholeness, of apparently discordant things being brought into relationship. In "The Ring" the difficult *terza rima* form is used, the binding together of each group of three lines with the group before and the group after well suggesting the idea contained in the title. "The Confirmation" is his first sonnet—a form of which he was to become a master. The language has, more consistently than before, the Wordsworthian simplicity and directness which one associates with his mature work.

There is a greater variety of subject than before. That he had found the place of safety within himself did not mean that he was going to retreat into complacent self-contemplation, but rather that he was now able to look out more. Only two poems return to childhood memories; a few others deal directly with more recent experiences of his own. But in most of the poems he looks outside himself—at Scottish history, the War, or some philosophical or religious theme. He is no longer so obsessed with the problem of time. His ability to bring together ideas and the description of an actual or imagined scene, to achieve fusion of image and theme, is more consistently displayed than before.

In *Journeys and Places* most of the places were mythical or dream-like, symbolical of mental states. Now they are more often actual places, in which meaning is seen. "The Wayside Station" brings a scene vividly before us. It dates, as he said in a broadcast, "from the first years of the War, at a time when I was working in the Food Office in Dundee and travelling every day from St Andrews. I had to change trains every morning at Leuchars, and in the winter mornings particularly there was generally a long wait in that cold and bleak station. In midwinter the dawn had still hardly come as I stamped up and down to keep warm; and over everything hung the thought of war."[2]   In the poem he is concerned not with himself, but with what he sees (the only "I" in the poem is in "I watch") and with the coming of this war-time dawn not just to himself but to the ploughboy and others and even to the animals:

> Here at the wayside station, as many a morning,
> I watch the smoke torn from the fumy engine,
> Crawling across the field in serpent sorrow.
> Flat in the east, held down by stolid clouds,
> The struggling day is born, and shines already
> On its warm hearth far off.   Yet something here
> Glimmers along the ground to show the seagulls
> White on the furrows' black unturning waves.

The light broadens as he watches a farmstead on a little hill, and thinks of the cattle, the ploughboy and the farmer waking, and of lovers parting; the branches of the trees are lit to dark silver, and

> The lonely stream
> That rode through darkness leaps the gap of light,
> Its voice grown loud, and starts its winding journey
> Through the day and time and war and history.

The horizon is widened in the last line, and the small things are seen in a large context of space and time.   There is more sense than in the earlier poems of the presence of concrete, particular things, though rather less than usual is done to show their significance for him.

"The Little General" also is based upon an actual scene, this time remembered from childhood, when General Burroughs used to come across to Wyre to shoot,

> The white smoke curling from the silver gun,
> The feather curling in the hunter's cap. . . .

Here more is done to make the details meaningful.   The feather in the hunter's cap corresponding to the falling feathers of the dead birds bring the two together.   Hunter and quarry

---

[2] B.B.C. "Chapbook", 3 Aug. 1952.

and the remnant of an ancient tower on the hill, which has looked out on many such scenes, together form a

Perennial emblem painted on a shield.

In another poem, "To J.F.H.", an actual scene in the present revives the past. Muir wrote to Professor Raymond Tschumi: "One day [in 1941], after an illness, I was walking out in the little town of St Andrews in Scotland, when I saw a young soldier, so like my dead friend that he could easily have been mistaken for him, dashing by on a motor cycle—he too had been in uniform the first time I met him. I was in one of the curious moods which sometimes come with convalescence: at any rate I did not know for a moment where I was; the worlds of life and death seemed to fuse for an instant."[3] This moment seemed to give him a deeper understanding of Holms, a closer sharing of his experience. For a moment he was in a state which, he thought, Holms had been in constantly. The latter throughout his life had remained "half wrapped still in eternity", had looked continually through a hole in space into a world beyond; and so had dashed full tilt through life, feeling always "the eating itch/To be elsewhere, nowhere". The poem stands appropriately at the beginning of this volume, in which the poems are arranged in a rough sequence, passing from emphasis on life in time as a narrow place, a maze, a stifling grove which must be gone through on the way to the high place, to emphasis on the value of the journey itself.

In such poems as "The Return of Odysseus" and "The City" scenes from the distant past rather than from the poet's experience are evoked. In "The City" pilgrims come, after great dangers, near their goal, and find to their surprise that some have settled tranquilly near not in the holy city. They go on, and find "a dead land . . . and crowds of angry men . . . with . . . raging rubicund faces", and see

The streets of the holy city running with blood,
And centuries of fear and power and awe. . . .

I suppose the idea is that the attempt to make the holy city on earth (Calvin's Geneva, John Knox's Scotland) leads to

[3] E. M. to Tschumi, 10 Jun. 1949.

o

the use of force, to strife and anger, that we must be content
with an imperfect and human order. In these poems actuality
and suggestion are well combined.

In the philosophical poems Muir is now able to give more
precise answers to the questions he raises. Earlier he had been
able to say only that man has intuitions both of necessity and
freedom; now he is able to go some way towards explaining
the paradox—though without removing the sense of mystery—,
and towards showing why the intuition of freedom is justified.
One can see this by comparing "The Solitary Place" in *Journeys
and Places* and the ideas behind it explained in the letter to
Spender quoted earlier with the more dramatic and effective
treatment of the same theme in "Robert the Bruce". As he
thinks of his murder of Comyn the dying Bruce sees that in the
order of fate he can never be released from that act. If there
is nothing but an endless chain of cause and effect, no action
is either good or bad; the past need not be regretted, and
cannot be redeemed; there can be no forgiveness:

> But that Christ hung upon the Cross,
>   Comyn would rot until time's end
> And bury my sin in boundless dust,
>   For there is no amend
>
> In order; yet in order run
>   All things by unreturning ways.
> If Christ live not, nothing is here
>   For sorrow or for praise.

The assurance that the order of history is not all is no longer
merely a personal intuition based upon the experience of art,
but proceeds from an event which is both within and beyond
history. If Christ hung upon the Cross and still lives, then one
can believe that man does not belong solely within the order
of fate, of history; there is something within him not dictated
to by time; the past can be redeemed.

The note of hope is more confidently sounded in these
poems than before, but there is no complacency. Evil as well
as good is now seen with increased sharpness of vision. Within
himself, beneath the deceptively "untroubled oval" of his face,

he is conscious of evil and destructive passions; beneath "the smiling summer sea".

The sun- and star-shaped killers gorge and play.[4]

In "The Refugees" he deals with the ultimately self-destructive indifference with which men contemplate the sufferings of others. In "Scotland 1941" he writes with unusual bitterness of the forces which have divided the Scottish nation and corrupted her culture. Scotland was once a family, a people, but has become a broken kingdom because of inner divisions as well as attacks from without. The broken kingdom of Scotland is related to the broken kingdom of humanity since the Fall and to the inwardly-divided person. Scotland too is on one level the "narrow place", whose parsimonious ground will bear but a few thin blades

> so proud and niggardly
> And envious, it will trust
> Only one little wild half-leafless tree
> To straggle from the dust.

Yet this vision of things is shown to be partial and therefore ultimately false:

> It is your murdering eyes that make
> The sterile hill, the standing lake,
> And the leaf-breaking wind.

The best poems in the volume are perhaps those, such as "The Narrow Place" and "The Human Fold", in which the littleness and confusion as well as the greatness of the human situation, the anti-vision seen by the "murdering eyes" as well as the vision seen by the imagination are contained. But the ones which I find most moving of all are those at the end—the love poems and the five written during his illness. It is remarkable, though characteristic of him, that his first love poems (I do not count the jejune verses in *The New Age*) should have been written at over fifty and after more than twenty years of marriage. Harvest fields were his favourite sight, and he was the poet of things ripened by time, yet exempt from time. In love he experienced a triumph over time, but one

----

[4] "The Face", in *C. P.*, p. 106.

which could happen only in time; love was born "Here in a time and place". In love soul and body act together

> To make us each for each
> And in our spirit whole.[5]

As a result of this experience he was able to see more clearly than before the meaning and value of the journey as well as of the goal. So the volume, which opened with the picture of Holms dashing impatiently through the narrow place, desiring extinction, "athirst for the ease of ash", ends, in "The Day", with the poet's prayer that he may have clarity and love to walk in the way destined for him. The way is in a sense predetermined, yet strangely there is still point in praying about it, still a possibility of freedom. It lies through the day, through time, though written in eternity. The perceptions of freedom and necessity, of mortality and immortality, which in the early poems had been laid side by side, are here brought together in a single vision, in a single sentence.

II

The Voyage, published early in 1946, contains most of the work of the Edinburgh years. The title poem is based upon a story told to him by Eric Linklater, who writes:

> It was during the war, and I had been spending a few days with soldiers and sailors training for combined operations some-where on the west coast of Scotland. On the way back I was talking to an oldish man who had gone to sea in stick-and-string days, and rejoined (Merchant Service) for war-time duty. He told me of a voyage to Australia on which, because of per-sistent bad weather (fog and storm) they had, for week after week, got no sight of the sun nor spoken another vessel. And presently a fo'c'sle rumour began to spread: Perhaps the world had come to an end, and they alone were left alive? The whisper went about at night, from one to another of the watch on deck: 'Is it true? D'you think it's true?' There was no panic, or anything of that sort, but an ever-growing fear and foreboding. And when at last, after a voyage that seemed interminable, they saw land, there was no rejoicing, but a sort of dismay, and foreboding of another sort.

---

[5] "The Annunciation", in *C. P.*, p. 117.

So far as I remember, that was the substance of the story, and Edwin at once asked me, 'Are you going to use it yourself, or can I have it?'

He shaped it, of course, to suit his own purpose: his poem is his own invention, his own creation—but my story was the yard from which he launched it.[6]

The poem started from a story, not from an idea; and the first thing in reading it is to respond to the re-created experience of the sailors rather than to think about metaphysical meanings. The regular, gently insistent rhythm well suggests the rolling of a sailing ship at sea. Some stanzas have a magical quality, reminiscent of "The Ancient Mariner", but not imitative of it. The sailors feel as if they have passed beyond the ordinary world of time, almost as if they were in eternity. The experience is similar to that expressed in a more concentrated way in the later poem "Orpheus' Dream". The sailors have travelled "Safe past the Fate and the Accident"; images from the ordinary world come to them, and seem both familiar and strange:

> The soft sea-sounds beguiled our ear.
> We thought we walked by mountain rills
> Or listened half a night to hear
> The spring wind hunting on the hills. . .
>
> The words we knew like our right hand,
> Mountain and valley, meadow and grove,
> Composed a legendary land
> Rich with the broken tombs of love.

In the end they come to land; they must leave the state of timelessness in which they have been voyaging, and know the familiar pain of ordinary life. In the first version there was a final stanza which contained the line

> In hope and dread we drove to birth

which suggests that the voyagers are souls entering the world of time from eternity. I think it was right to cut this out. In the final version the poem can be read simply as a re-creation

[6] Eric Linklater to P. H. B., 6 Aug. 1963.

of the sailors' experience and, more generally, of the not
uncommon one of seeing life for a moment timelessly and in a
new light. The story given him by Linklater enabled Muir to
embody a theme which was a common one with him in an
unusually vivid and particular way.

In a broadcast many years later he recalled the origin of
one of his own favourites among his poems, "In Love for Long";
"I was up at Swanston in the Pentlands one Saturday morning
during the War. It was in late summer; a dull, cloudy,
windless day, quite warm. I was sitting in the grass, looking
at the thatched cottages and the hills, when I realised that I
was fond of them, suddenly and without reason, and for
themselves, not because the cottages were quaint or the hills
romantic. I had an unmistakable warm feeling for the ground
I was sitting on, as if I were in love with the earth itself, and
the clouds, and the soft subdued light. I had felt these things
before, but that afternoon they seemed to crystallise, and the
poem came out of them."[7] There is nothing in the poem about
the particular scene. Muir, as poet, was not so much interested
in the circumstances which generated the emotion on that day
as in the emotion itself which recurred to him in various places.
It was a particular emotion, but it would be limiting it too
much to treat it as just an emotion about a particular place.
Richard Wilbur, the poet, remembers him reading this poem
at Harvard: "I recall his asking his audience to imagine or
remember the sort of experience men sometimes have—the
experience of sitting, perhaps, on a hillside in the country and
feeling oneself swept by a deep and sudden love for no particular
thing. This was by way of preface to his poem 'In Love for
Long', and during that preface I saw heads everywhere begin
to nod, Ivor Richards' among them; it was as if he were
telling a happy secret about us all which had never been told
before."[8] The two accounts may at first seem at variance, but
I do not think they really are so. The feeling must arise in
some particular context, and will include a fondness for the
things around one—for the thatched cottages and the hills, the
ground one is sitting on. At first it may seem to be just that;

[7] B.B.C. "Chapbook", 3 Sep. 1952.
[8] Richard Wilbur to P. H. B., 8 Aug. 1964.

but on reflexion it shows itself to be more than that, "a deep and sudden love" not tied to any particular thing.

This poem comes at the end of the volume, and at the end of a series of poems on transmutation in which the meditation, begun in *The Narrow Place*, on what may be built in time in time's despite is continued and extended.   In lasting love ("Time held in time's despite"), in being true to oneself ("For Ann Scott-Moncrieff "), in response to natural beauty ("A Birthday"), in artistic creation ("All We") something permanent is created out of the transitory or is seen in it.   An escape from time is no longer sought, nor an escape from the present into future or past; and he is no longer dependent upon dreams to revive a kind of perception lost in waking life. He writes of the present, of himself and his wife, of a friend whose honesty, naturalness and courage he had admired, of two lovers seen in the street.   The poetry is more directly human and personal, less concerned with problems than before, though without losing the sense of a larger context which gives particular things meaning.   Self-knowledge has led to a release from self and from inner tensions, and so to a new feeling of at-oneness with the world outside.   The distinction of the poems, of course, consists not in the thought which may sound quite commonplace as summarised, but in the sense of wonder and delighted discovery which they convey by their very simple words.   The rhetoric (in a bad sense), the declamation found sometimes in *First Poems* and *Chorus of the Newly Dead*, are gone. The danger now, nearly but not quite always avoided, is flatness.

A feature of this volume, in contrast to the one before and the one after, is the predominance of poems written in short lines—of eight or six or fewer syllables.   This was, perhaps, a symptom of his wish to cut out the inessential.   One may be tempted to fill up a long line with an unnecessary adjective. Sometimes he succeeded with these short lines ("A Birthday", "In Love for Long"), but in general I think he was better when he allowed himself more space.   In *The Labyrinth* and *One Foot in Eden* he returned to the decasyllabic line as his norm, using octosyllabics quite often too, but very seldom shorter lines.

XII

Prague and Rome

I

As early as September 1944 Muir was writing to Spender that he would like to get to Europe as soon as the War was over. When peace came he applied to the Council to send him to Czechoslovokia; the Czechs were eager to have him, and he was appointed Director of the British Institute in Prague. His time there was to be very different from his happy carefree visit twenty-four years before, but equally fructifying for him as a poet. Any one who believes, as he had come to, that "the rightness of human life has a deeper reality . . . than the evil, as being more truly native to man", needs to have this faith constantly challenged if it is not to seem too easy. In Prague he was to encounter the wrongness in more naked and powerful forms than he had ever done.

In the *Autobiography* he gives a vivid description of his journey out to Prague by car in the late summer of 1945, telling in a characteristic passage of seeing in Cologne among the roofless houses, the crumbling pavements and the sour stench of corpses buried under the ruins the people out as usual for their Sunday walk in their Sunday best. "The peaceful crowds in that vast graveyard were like the forerunners of a multitide risen in a private resurrection day to an unimaginable new life. It was moving to see a simple courteous inclination of the heart so calmly surviving, upheld by nothing but its own virtue after the destruction of all that had nourished it."[1]

Here the destruction was in the past; there was a prospect of things getting better, and it was not too difficult to believe in a resurrection to new life. And so it was at the beginning

[1] *A.*, p. 252.

in Prague. Though the immediate past had been dreadful and the present was uncomfortable, things were improving. During the first winter the people seemed poor and depressed. There was not much food, fuel was strictly rationed, memories of Gestapo atrocities were close, and the new occupying power, Russia, was feared and disliked. Stories of Gestapo cruelties, told him by people who had suffered themselves and through their families, brought Muir closer than ever before to extreme deliberate evil. But the Gestapo were gone. Before Christmas the Russian army left. In the spring the food situation improved, and an almost normal life established itself.

In the mean time the British Council people were working in difficult conditions, and at Charles University Muir was lecturing from memory on English literature to students who had hardly any books. In the absence of a restaurant the overcrowded office became a picnic-ground with saucepans and chipped crockery on the newspaper-covered desks. Constantly on top of one another and subject to many frustrations in their work, most became edgy; but Muir remained gently humorous amid the hurly-burly, and impressed every one by his quiet sense of purpose. Something was being achieved. The British were popular, and the Council, as a non-political body, was able to attract people from all political Parties. The students at the University were very keen, and Muir was much liked by them, being more informal and approachable than is common among continental professors. Material conditions improved in the spring of 1946 when the Council offices and the Institute moved to the Kaunitzky Palace and more books became available. The numbers coming to the Institute and to Muir's classes at the University continually increased. Britain held the position which France had had before the War of being the chief representative for the Czechs of Western civilisation.

Some idea of the scope of Muir's work and how he did it can be obtained from his report to the Council of his personal work in 1947. He lectured twice a week on English literature to a class of about seventy students at the University. At the beginning he found that they were accustomed to regard facts as of the first, almost of the only importance, and he set himself to change this, to lead them to enjoy and understand the literature and to express conflicting opinions about it with freedom. "What I have always in mind in lecturing on English literature is its great human value, for our literature seems to me above all a humanising force, perhaps the greatest in modern times. By bringing this out I think it is possible to convey a sense of the largeness of the English spirit at its best, and so help to efface the conventional image of the frigid, narrow-minded Englishman which is still current in many places." Also at the University he held a weekly two-hour seminar with a smaller group of students, at which one of the group read an essay and there was free discussion. "At first I found them somewhat bashful and inarticulate: but now I can scarcely get them to stop, and they tell me they still go on discussing the subject hours after I have left and the seminar is over."

At his home he ran a small poetry circle, consisting of young Czech writers who came to discuss contemporary English poetry. "I find", he reported, "there is more interest in English literature among young writers than among the middle-aged and old people, who are still under the influence of French culture which was so strong during the Masaryk republic. I think this is a group which will do considerable service for us, not because of any incitement from me, but because they wish it and have it at heart." He went to the monthly meetings of the Prague PEN Club, and went with the Czech delegation to the International PEN Conference at Zurich. At the invitation of the Council Representative there he visited Austria, lecturing on contemporary English literature in the Universities of Innsbruck, Vienna and Graz. Literary work relevant to the Council's activities included an article on English literature during the War for the University quarterly; an essay on Kafka for a collection of essays on him by Czech writers; an introduction to an anthology of English poetry in Czech translation; and the collection of material for a Scottish number of a literary monthly.

These, with his entertainment of distinguished visitors such as Stephen Spender and Herbert Read, were the activities listed in his report. They do not include the routine work of running the Institute and the arranging of classes in English for the large number of people who came to it, the social events, the sometimes irksome internal politics within the Council. It was hard work, and there were inconveniences such as the disappearance by theft of the Muirs' entire ration of coal when the thermometer was at forty degrees below freezing; but it was work which he did well and, except the politics, enjoyed. He was loved, as well as respected, by most of his colleagues, one of whom writes: "He was affectionate—like a very lovable child. . . . When I met him I felt as though I'd known him for years." She remembers him at parties very gay and full of laughter, standing hand in hand with his wife singing Scottish ballads, playing complicated games and trying not to shine too much if there was any one present who might be abashed. There were also pleasant holidays—at Mariánské Lažné, and at the Palace of Dobřiš some twenty miles from Prague, which had been given to the Czech Writers Guild as a holiday and working place for writers. "Dobřiš was an elegant Baroque palace, its walls a faded terracotta, modelled on a miniature scale on Versailles. Behind the palace was an Italian garden in which classical gods and heroes motionlessly walked on their pedestals, and Hercules went on strangling the lion for century after century. Behind the garden shielded an 'English' park, with a little lake where carp sullenly swam about. There were quiet corners where a writer could be quite alone with his work. The place was well-run and admirably fulfilled its purpose."[2] There he began his poem "The Labyrinth", and probably wrote several other poems.

The admiration with which Muir was regarded in the University was expressed, on the occasion of his sixtieth birthday in 1947, by the conferment on him of his first honorary Doctorate of Letters.

Meantime rumblings of the trouble to come could already be heard. He was anxious to make contact with the Russians, and was at first inclined to discount Czech stories against them as the kind of thing always said by people suffering hardship against a foreign army stationed in their midst. Gradually he became increasingly aware of the deep divisions between East and West and between the different Parties in Czechoslovakia.

[2] MS., notes for *A*.

Some individual Russians showed a momentary wish to be friendly, but they would always withdraw soon in fear of compromising themselves. At a reception Muir sat next to a prominent Czech Communist who later was executed by the Communist Government: "That evening he appeared to be somewhat uneasy; as a Communist no doubt he felt that in coming to the opening of the Institute he was doing something which his friends would misunderstand or disapprove. I met him once or twice afterwards; he was a sensitive, intelligent man, interested in literature and painting; I was conscious, when I was with him, of a sympathy for the West, along with a withdrawal, a fear of committing himself."[3]

A small incident showed him how widely Party divisions operated. The Institute ran a Summer School at Mariánské Lažné and chose to house the students in the hotel which seemed the cleanest and best run. Without knowing it they had chosen a Communist hotel, and found they had slighted the Socialist, Social Democratic and People's Party hotels. Football, he discovered, was political too, the great sporting event of the year in Prague being the encounter between two teams supported by the Socialist and Communist Parties. By early 1948 the great success of the Institute as the representative of Western civilisation was beginning to attract the open hostility of the Communists, who would gather at the door when people were coming for evening lectures and try to keep them from entering.

In spite of these warnings the putsch, when it came in February 1948, was unexpected. The Government was a coalition, including a minority of Communists. Elections were due in May, and the Communists knew that their vote would decline sharply. The Communist Minister of the Interior was packing the police with supporters of his Party; in protest against this the non-Communist Ministers resigned so as to force President Beneš to appoint a new Government. This gave the Communists who were left in office the chance to seize power with the aid of the police, the radio and the press. Beneš, ill and afraid of civil war and of Russian intervention, failed to act decisively, and was prevented from speaking to

[3] MS. notes for *A*.

the people. The battle was over before most people knew it had begun. A people whom Muir had seen forgetting the fears bred by the German Occupation were once again engulfed in an atmosphere of terror and mutual suspicion. Telephones were tapped; people would no longer speak freely to one another or criticise the Government; the press and radio became organs of propaganda; people were forced against their consciences to join the Communist Party in order that their families might live. At the University he could no longer make contact with his students; the class once eager to discuss everything was silent, and two Communist observers were there to take everything down. There were arbitrary and capricious arrests, and a feeling that justice had ceased to exist.

The atmosphere of hostility and fear was shattering to him. Many of his friends fled the country; others were imprisoned; for those that remained and were at large he could do nothing since contact with him would be dangerous to them. One friend used to come to see the Muirs sometimes at night; they would leave the flat door ajar so that he could come and go quietly without attracting attention. Disharmonies within the Council, which were not at all his fault, made the nervous strain worse. He could do nothing effective by staying, so he asked to be transferred, and at the end of July he and his wife left the country. At the frontier the train stopped for two hours. "People here and there were ejected, and luggage flung out of windows."[4]

Two incidents before this had slightly relieved the gloom. At Easter after the coup they went for a short holiday to a small town in the country. Going into a church they saw peasant women "kneeling before images of their Lord; one of them, just in front of me, with a worn, kind, handsome face, knelt motionless, and my eyes came back again and again to the worn and patched soles of her boots, a battered image of her own constancy and humble faith. I did not feel that this ancient humanity could ever be destroyed by the new order."[5] The other, slighter, incident was when officials came to check their baggage to see that they were not carrying any Czech

[4] *A.*, p. 273.   [5] *A.*, p. 272.

property out of the country. The officials noticed a quotation from the Czech poet Jan Neruda inscribed on a glass. This led to a discussion of Czech poetry. The baggage was cleared without further question. Writers, especially foreign writers who knew Czech poetry, were to be respected. It was a final, curious instance of the popular esteem for creative people which had struck him long ago on his first visit to Prague.

II

Most, probably all, of the poems in *The Labyrinth* were written in Czechoslovakia. It is remarkable that he managed to do so much during such a busy time. In July 1946 he wrote to Joseph Chiari, a friend he had made in Edinburgh, that he had written only one poem since he had been there. He had ideas for about half-a-dozen others, but had "never hit the mood in which I could write them: my life is too distracted. I shall not be able to write unless I succeed in putting my affairs in order during the next year." The one poem was "The Child Dying". Sending it to Chiari, he wrote: "I've been trying for some time to write poetry that was both simple and unexpected; and if this poem is good—I can hardly tell whether it is or not—I think I have succeeded. But where it came from I simply can't tell." I think in this poem he did succeed in being both simple and unexpected. He did not usually project himself so far as into the mind of a dying child. The poem came complete from a source deeper than conscious thought, and the words seem inevitably right as well as surprising.

Later that year he went to the Czech Writers' House at Dobříš, and there "The Labyrinth" was written, or at least begun, and probably several other poems. The following summer he went for a holiday and afterwards was able to tell Chiari that he had almost a volume of poems ready:

> I have been away for a month's holiday in Mariánské Lázné (once Marienbad), and I spent my time writing poetry there mainly; I had had a number of poems dammed up in me for some months, with no chance of coming out; and there by good luck I found the means and the right moment for them. I have almost a volume, but not quite, by this time; I intend to call the poems "Symbols", or something of that kind, for

they all deal with symbolical human situations and types; and I hope this will give the volume a sort of unity, and at the same time that it won't cause the contents to be monotonous. To get these poems out was a great satisfaction to me, but I was disappointed that I didn't get out all the poems I wanted. On the other hand new ones appeared, which was gratifying, and so I found myself partly in a state of poetic resolution and partly in a state of flux. The holiday hasn't given me as much rest as I really should have had, but instead excitement partly pleasant and partly painful.

The rest of the poems were presumably completed before he left Czechoslovakia and his subsequent breakdown; for he did nothing during the breakdown, and the volume had been accepted by Faber by the beginning of September 1948. So practically the whole volume was written in two years—an unusually rapid rate of composition for him. During these years he was most of the time busy, seeing a lot of people and many exciting, some distressing, things, but was occasionally able to withdraw into the peace of the countryside at Dobřiš and Mariánské. I imagine such an alternation is propitious for the writing of poetry. *The Labyrinth* contains some of his greatest poems, and is, I think, his most consistently excellent volume. "I really think it is the best I have done yet", he wrote to Chiari, characteristically adding "but that is a hard question to answer, for one is partial to what one has just been doing". It is the only volume which is printed entire in the final collection. At sixty he was reaching his peak at a time when quicker starters of his own, and even of the next, generation were faltering.

A feature of this volume is the inclusion of a number of longer poems in blank verse in which he tried to treat his ideas on time and human life more completely than before. The first of these, the title poem, "started itself", as he put it, at the Writers' House at Dobřiš. "Thinking there of the old story of the labyrinth of Cnossos and the journey of Theseus through it and out of it, I felt that this was an image of human life with its errors and ignorance and endless intricacy. In the poem I made the labyrinth stand for all this. But I wanted also to give an image of the life of the gods, to whom all that is confusion down here is clear and harmonious as seen eternally. The poem begins with a very long sentence, deliberately labyrinthine, to give the mood."[6] As usual when using a myth Muir modifies it to suit his purpose and gives it his own meaning. It is not necessary to know anything about the myth to appreciate the poem. In the original story Theseus was one of a party of seven youths and seven maidens paid as tribute by Athens to Crete to be fed to the Minotaur, half man half beast, who lived in the centre of the labyrinth. Theseus slew the Minotaur and escaped from the labyrinth by the help of a ball of thread given him by Ariadne. Most of this is irrelevant to the poem. The beast is simply "the bull"; the protagonist is alone, and there is no mention of the ball of thread nor of Ariadne. The change in title from "Theseus" in manuscript to "The Labyrinth" suggests that Muir realised that he was telling his own story, or Everyman's, rather than that of Theseus. Read autobiographically—too limiting an interpretation, but part of the whole—the poem deals with Muir's state of alienation in his Glasgow years, his escape from it and his later efforts to reconcile two apparently contradictory conceptions of human life. In the maze the speaker was in a state of inward division (he feared to meet himself "returning at some smooth corner"; he was like a spirit seeking his body) and of alienation from the ordinary world which he could not reach. The maze suggests among other things the self, in which the neurotic person—and in some degree all of us at some times—feels imprisoned. Inner division forcing the attention inwards goes along with alienation from the outside world. Escape from this state does not come, as in the case of Theseus, by conscious effort and contrivance, but just seems to happen:

> the maze itself
> Revolved around me on its hidden axis
> And swept me smoothly to its enemy,
> The lovely world.

This corresponds in Muir's life to the time of his marriage and the recovery of a sense of vivid contact with nature on the

---

[6] B.B.C. "Chapbook", 3 Sep. 1952.

Continent afterwards. At first the protagonist "stared in wonder at the young and old", at the ordinary world of time, outside which he had strayed. But later the feeling of being in the maze returns; and now the maze is not any particular place, but the whole world appears to be a labyrinth of deceiving paths which seem to be going somewhere but which lead to no end. In very simple words and images Muir conveys here very effectively a Kafkaesque nightmare feeling of intricacy and frustration and meaninglessness. This is one way of looking at the world of time; but there's another. Using an actual dream of his own he presents a vision of the gods "each sitting on the top of his mountain-isle", while below the ordinary life of men goes on, "all permissible, all acceptable." The gods

> Conversed across the sounds in tranquil voices . . .
> And their eternal dialogue was peace
> Where all these things were woven, and this our life
> Was as a chord deep in that dialogue,
> As easy utterance of harmonious words,
> Spontaneous syllables bodying forth a world.

This is the real world, one in which time is contained within eternity rather than being opposed to it. He is not here seeking an escape from time, but only from the illusion of being imprisoned in a maze of roads "that run and run and never reach an end." The labyrinth has sometimes been taken as a symbol of the world of time, and Muir himself may seem to lend some countenance to this by saying that it is "an image of human life with its errors and ignorance and endless intricacy." But in the poem the maze is not properly speaking an image of human life, but only of a special way of looking at human life, which is specifically said at the end to be a lie, a "wild-wood waste of falsehood". And it is not really an image of time

> For in the maze time had not been with me;
> I had strayed, it seemed, past sun and season and change,
> Past rest and motion, for I could not tell
> At last if I moved or stayed . . .

In the maze a sort of timeless hell is experienced; whereas

P

within the vision of the gods all the changing events of life are contained. The maze is a lie, but it returns at the end:

> Oh these deceits are strong almost as life.
> Last night I dreamt I was in the labyrinth,
> And woke far on. I did not know the place.

The possible complacency of ending with the tranquil vision of the gods is avoided.

An even more impressive vision of people and things transformed, seen in a new light, is contained in "The Transfiguration", written some time later in Czechoslovakia. (It is curious that, when speaking of this poem only four years later in a broadcast, Muir should have said that it was written in Rome. By then Czechoslovakia had become associated in his mind with sad events and Rome with happier ones; so unconsciously this radiant poem was drawn in his memory into the Rome period.) Though he is bound to be impressed at once by its beauty a new reader may at first be perplexed by this poem, feeling that it is not really about the Transfiguration at all. In Matthew XVII. 2. we read that Christ "was transfigured before them: and his face did shine as the sun, and his raiment was white as the light". In the poem the disciples do not look at Christ, but their sight being cleansed they are able to see the whole world transfigured in His presence:

> So from the ground we felt that virtue branch
> Through all our veins till we were whole, our wrists
> As fresh and pure as water from a well,
> Our hands made new to handle holy things,
> The source of all our seeing rinsed and cleansed
> Till earth and light and water entering there
> Gave back to us the clear unfallen world.

The poem arose not so much from a reading of the Bible as from certain experiences of his own in which, both in waking life and in dreams, he had seen the world transformed. The scarlet suit worn in childhood that burned in his memory more brightly than anything he had seen since; the sight at Montrose of a robin with its unearthly radiance, pouring its light into the darkness; the feeling at Swanston of being in love with the earth; above all the May Day parade experience of spontaneous attraction to every human being, "as if all mankind were made of some incorruptible substance"—these had been in small ways instances of a cleansing of the sight which had given back to him momentarily in waking life the clear unfallen world. Two dreams were more direct sources of the poem. In one he saw a great crystal river in which multitudes of people of more than life size were bathing. He was momentarily disturbed by the thought that harlots were bathing higher up the river and that the water was infected; "but then I knew that these waters could easily wash away every impurity and still remain pure." The river seemed to him not less but more real than any actual one he had seen. Through the undulating country "flowed that great river of water, so living, so deep and pure, that an actual river would have appeared artificial beside it, as though it alone contained the original idea and essence of pure and cleansing and ever-flowing water".[7] In another dream he was woken by a robed figure who took him through moonlit streets into a field. On the way they met a shabby blood-stained man with rags bound round his feet so that he walked silently; the dreamer took him to be a murderer or robber, and was afraid until seeing his look of adoration for the robed man. A crowd of raggedly-dressed people they met all had this same look of adoration in their eyes. In the field all these and a host of animals joined in a solemn and mysterious act of worship. It was a dream of the Millennium. Much from these dreams went into the poem— the cleansing water, the sense of seeing a world more real than that of every day, the praying animals who "walked in peace, the wild and tame together,/As if, also for them, the day had come," and the murderers "with rags tied round their feet for silence" who "came/Out of themselves to us and were with us."

One is tempted to say that the poem, however beautiful, is not really about the Transfiguration, but, like the dream, about the Millennium. But this would be to reveal ignorance of Christian thought about the Transfiguration.[8] For the

---

[7] *A.*, p. 115.

[8] In what follows I am indebted to an article in *Sobornost*, series 4, no. 8, (Winter 1963), on "The Transfiguration of the Body" by Timothy Ware, and to conversation with the Rev. A. M. Allchin.

Transfiguration has been thought of by Christians, especially in the Eastern Orthodox Church, in much the same way as it is here presented, quite independently, by Muir. Christian thinking has always been opposed to the Platonic dualism by which the body is spoken of as the prison of the soul. The body is an essential and integral part of man, shall rise at the last day and share in the glory of Heaven. In the Transfiguration the true nature of the body, temporarily obscured, is revealed. It both looks back to the "clear unfallen world" and forward to the Parousia, to the last day and the general resurrection. "Transfigured to-day on Mount Thabor in His disciples' presence, Christ revealed the original beauty of the image, assuming man's substance into Himself . . . Transfigured, Thou hast made Adam's nature, which was grown dim, to shine once more as lightning."[9] Futhermore in the Transfiguration it was not only Christ's face that was transfigured but His clothes also. It is not only the human body, but the whole of the material creation which is to be restored to its true nature. "The created universe", writes Saint Paul, "waits with eager expectation for God's sons to be revealed. . . . The universe itself will be set free from bondage to corruption and will enter into the liberty and splendour of the children of God."[10] The full glory is to be revealed only at the Last Day, and was uniquely foreshadowed in the experience of the disciples who saw the Transfiguration of Christ. But lesser transfigurations have been not uncommon in the lives of the saints—of Saint Teresa of Avila, Saint Catherine of Bologna, Saint Catherine of Genoa and others. And they have happened not only in the distant past, but in quite ordinary surroundings and quite recently, as when a friend went to tea with Evelyn Underhill in Campden Hill Square in London in 1937: "Light simply streamed from her face illuminated with a radiant smile. . . . One could not but feel consciously there and then (not on subsequent recognition or reflection) that one was in the presence of the extension of the Mystery of our Lord's Transfiguration in one of the members of His Mystical Body".[11] These are instances of the divine light becoming manifest in

[9] Vespers for the Feast of the Transfiguration. [10] *Romans* viii. 19-21.
[11] *The Letters of Evelyn Underhill*, ed. Charles Williams, p. 37.

the bodies of people of special sanctity. Experiences of seeing material things transformed have been quite common among artists, and among ordinary people in response to art and nature. These experiences are given their true meaning when seen in relation to the Transfiguration.

When writing the poem Muir was quire unaware of all that had been written about the Transfiguration. It is remarkable that he should have arrived quite independently at insights which have been stated in more dogmatic terms by theologians—the connexion of the Transfiguration with the unfallen world and the Parousia, the oneness of soul and body, the eventual transfiguration of the whole cosmos. But he does not commit himself to belief. He makes the disciples (rather undramatically, perhaps) ask,

> Was it a vision? [In the original version "Was it
> delusion?"]
> Or did we see that day the unseeable
> One glory of the everlasting world
> Perpetually at work, though never seen
> Since Eden locked the gate that's everywhere
> And nowhere?

All the disciples are sure of is their experience:

> Reality or vision, this we have seen.

Shortly after the poem was first published Miss Maisie Spens, who has written much of the Transfiguration in her book *Receive the Joyfulness of your Glory*, wrote to Muir to thank him for it, and told him of its links with Orthodox Christianity. He answered:

What you say in your letter interests me very much. I know nothing of the literature of the Transfiguration, and in writing the poem probably did not see where it was leading me. On the other hand I have always had a particular feeling for that transmutation of life which is found occasionally in poetry, and in the literature of prophecy, and sometimes in one's own thoughts when they are still. This, I think, is one of the things which have always been with me, or more exactly, which have persistently recurred to me, and I suppose in this poem it has found a point of expression. But that is the total of my learning on the Transfiguration. I still remember how as a child it filled me with wonder. The idea of Judas going back into innocence has often been with me. But I seem to have blundered into something greater than I knew, though as it grew the poem became clearer and clearer in my mind. The ideas you mention move me very much; I hope to become more familiar with them. One lives and misses so much one does not know about.

Later in a broadcast he said:

I had always been deeply struck by the story of the Transfiguration in the Gospels, and I had felt that perhaps at the moment of Christ's Transfiguration everything was transfigured, mankind, and the animals, and the simplest natural objects. After the poem appeared I had a letter from a lady who had made a long study of the subject, and to my surprise I found that the idea which I had imagined in my own mind possessed a whole literature, and that in some of the Russian churches it was often represented pictorially. Perhaps in the imagination of mankind the Transfiguration has become a powerful symbol, standing for many things, and among them those transformations of reality which the imagination itself creates."[12]

Another longish poem, one of his greatest, "The Journey Back", distils perhaps more completely than other any his experience up to that time. In this, as in most of his earlier poems, he seeks the universal by deep penetration into himself. But in *The Labyrinth* more often and more effectively than before the approach is through what he had seen outside as well as through what he had found within. In the 'thirties and during the War he had been stirred by the great and tragic events of the time, and had wanted to write of them, but had seldom been able to do so in poetry. There was no abrupt transition, but putting it rather crudely one can say that between 1921 and 1941 his main imaginative effort went into self-discovery and into coming to terms with his own past and certain big problems arising from it. After 1941, his internal problems being less oppressive though not, of course, in any

---

[12] B.B.C. "Chapbook", 3 Sep. 1952.

neat way solved, he was ready to look out more. In Edinburgh he was rather remote from great events; so this change showed itself more in a turning outwards to people and things around him than to politics. Later his experience in Europe enabled him to write such poems as "The Interrogation", "The Good Town", "The Usurpers'" and "The Combat". Unusually he was to be in his sixties more specifically a contemporary poet than he had been in his forties. In this his evolution was opposite to that of many of the fashionable pre-war writers.

In the broadcast already quoted he told something of the origin of "The Good Town":

> A little after writing "The Labyrinth",—as I was walking one day in a park near our house in Prague—I had an idea for two poems about towns, one to be called "The Good Town", and the other "The Bad Town"; and I intended the towns to stand as symbols of two ways of life. But as things were then shaping in Prague, I saw that the only way to treat the theme was to describe a good town turning into a bad one. Yet the poem is not really about Prague or any other place, but about something that was happening in Europe. Stories of what was occurring in other countries to whole families, whole communities, became absorbed into the poem, which I tried to make into a symbolical picture of a vast change.

"The Good Town" is a poem, not history. The picture at the beginning of the good town where street was friend to street and house to house, the doors standing open and ivy growing across the prison door, might seem sentimental if taken as a description of any particular place. It gathers up memories of Orkney and perhaps of Prague in 1921, but is an evocation of an ideal. The later part is closer to history:

> And now you see our town, the fine new prison,
> The house-doors shut and barred, the frightened faces
> Peeping round corners, secret police, informers,
> And all afraid of all.

A European who knew nothing of Muir, hearing it read recently, said at once "The writer must have lived in a Communist country". But there is no mention of Communism in the poem; for Muir Communism as he saw it in Prague was only one manifestation of the contempt for human freedom which is the natural result of the reduction of the image of man. Unimaginative manipulators of men he found even in the Council itself and later at Newbattle.

At the end the old citizens ask themselves how the change came. It seemed to come from the outside, but sometimes they wonder whether it came also from within themselves. Was the restless evil really always present beneath the apparent peace, so that the seemingly secure place was betrayed from within as well as attacked from without? So this poem links up with earlier references, as in "The Castle", to a secure place betrayed; and the fall of the good town is linked to the Fall.

Another poem which grew out of Muir's experience in Prague is "The Usurpers", in which he tried to enter into the minds of those who committed atrocities. A large proportion of the poems in *The Labyrinth* are dramatic, in that they are spoken by some one other than the poet himself; but he never elsewhere chose speakers whose point of view is so distant from his own as in this poem. In the *Autobiography*[13] he tells of hearing from a young Czech writer of how her husband had been tortured by the Gestapo and of her receiving after his death his blood-stained shirt with scraps of torn skin on it. She showed him a photograph of the Gestapo men she thought had been responsible—young men "who stared out from the photograph with the confidence of the worthless who find power left in their hands like a tip by a frightened world." In manuscript notes for the *Autobiography* he speculated on how such things could happen, how children could grow up to be Gestapo men: "The idea of unlimited power, Hitler's idea, meant for his elect unlimited liberty, the free permission for example to experiment on the human body and to invent instruments specifically designed for the work. (I was shown some of them by young Frenchmen of the Resistance.) It encouraged young Germans to herd Jews into the gas chambers. These things seem incredible; the imagination cannot account for them. They are explicable only by an idea which has created a featureless vacuum round it, where the ordinary means of grace, it seemed, could not live: the idea of power". The

[13] *A.*, p. 260-1.

writings of Spengler had provided an excuse for anything the
young cared to do. He had exalted the barbarian who, until
recently "fettered and buried beneath the strict forms of a
high culture", was awakening "resolved to live otherwise than
under the oppression of piles of dead books and bookish ideals".
Muir comments: "The barbarian did arise, but it was not
joyous or healthy; the instinct of race became a pathological
obsession; the men who had 'the courage to see and deal with
things as they are', praised by Spengler, were the seedy, forlorn
young men in the photograph. For 'things as they are' to
Spengler and to them did not include the soul. When men
cease to believe in the existence of the soul it appears to die in
them, leaving a vacuum. When man ceases to be immortal,
there is no obligation to treat him with respect."

The speakers in "The Usurpers" can be imagined as being
the young Gestapo men in the photograph, given a self-
knowledge such people would not possess. They have been
able to "still the ancestral voices", all the traditional beliefs
and moral ideas of humanity, and have won a kind of freedom,
which is in fact illusory and at the opposite pole to the boundless
freedom and union of which Muir wrote elsewhere:

> We dare do all we think,
> Since there is no one to check us, here or elsewhere.

Not believing in the soul nor in immortality they live in a
vacuum:

> All round us stretches nothing; we move through nothing,
> Nothing but nothing world without end.

They live in light and darkness only, in the temporal only, not
seeking the place of vision where light and darkness meet, the
"place of images". Sometimes they are troubled by fancies
that "the mountains judge us, brooks tell tales about us", hear
"dark runes murmuring in the autumn wind"; but they
dismiss them:

> These are imaginations. We are free.

It is only by dismissing the imaginative intuitions which must
come even to them that the Gestapo men and other oppressers
are able to do the things they do, to treat men impersonally.

Closely associated with "The Usurpers" is "The Helmet", with its picture of a soldier or Gestapo man whom war has made into an impersonal instrument. Originally this poem was an appeal to the person behind the mask to take off the helmet and resume his proper nature; but the published version is more impressive in its honest, but compassionate, unsparingness:

> The helmet on his head
> Has melted flesh and bone
> And forged a mask instead
> That always is alone.

These poems are, in a broad sense, political; but they still do not have the kind of immediacy which some critics demand. The good town is not any particular place. In "The Usurpers" we hear nothing of the blood-stained shirt nor of the photograph of some unhappy young men from which, I think, the poem arose. To have thrown the blood-stained shirt in our faces would have won applause, but would not have been to Muir's purpose. It would have distracted from it. He wanted to get behind the particular event to its cause, behind the eyes in the photograph to the spiritual state. Poetry in his view should come out of "contemplation", not out of mere "distress". The wrong kind of immediacy may spoil a poem by arousing inappropriate expectations. Perhaps this happens to some extent in "The Good Town", which for that reason may be less effective as a poem than "The Combat".

The Labyrinth was well received. He wrote to Chiari: "*The Labyrinth* has brought out better reviews than I've ever had before. I didn't think that would please me so much; but it has. Perhaps people will begin to read me; or perhaps that's too much to expect."[14] Evidently a few more people did begin to read him; for a second impression was called for in the following year.

Essays on Literature and Society was published in 1949, the same year as *The Labyrinth*. It contains essays written over a long period, one as far back as 1931; and it covers a considerable range of subjects, authors and times. Yet a central theme

---

[14] E. M. to Chiari, 22 Aug. 1949.

can be seen running through it, as perhaps through all Muir's life and work, the search for wholeness. Henryson lived in an age in which "the life of man and of the beasts turns naturally into a story because it is part of a greater story about which there is general consent."[15] With the Renaissance agreement about the great story was broken; and so in *Lear* we find that Lear and his friends believe in relationship and natural pieties, but that in Goneril and Regan there is "a hiatus of memory, a breach in continuity; they seem to come from nowhere and to be on the way to nowhere; they have words and acts only to meet the momentary emergency, the momentary appetite."[16] But though the agreement about the great story was broken, most men continued to have a "feeling for a permanence above the permanence of one human existence", to believe "that the ceaseless flux of life passed against an unchangeable background. Men still felt this whether they were Christians or not. They felt also that there was a relation between the brief story of man and that unchangeable order; and this sentiment, in whatever terms it was held, was the final earnest of the completeness of their conception of life." Therefore the traditional novel was "a story of time against a permanent pattern". It could be given completeness, an ending. But now that the conception of life which prevails is a conception of life purely in time, no such completeness is possible. The endings of characteristic modern novels "are expressions of hope of completion, arrows shot into the irresponsive future". Though recognising the greatness of some of the writers who have worked in the new situation, he regards the change as altogether for the worse—from the point of view of artistic achievement as well as in a larger way. "A comprehensive and widely accepted conception of human life produces good imaginative art; a tentative and partially accepted conception of life, unsatisfactory imaginative art. . . . A story without an ending describes a mode of existence which has not been thought out and stops short of meaning."[17]

It is interesting to compare what he says here about the

---

[15] *E. L. S.*, p. 7; enlarged ed., p. 10.
[16] *E. L. S.*, p. 42; enlarged ed., pp. 43-4.
[17] *E. L. S.*, pp. 147-9; enlarged ed., pp. 146-7.

sense of incompleteness at the ends of modern novels with a dream which he described to Kathleen Raine: "The dream was a very simple one: it consisted of a semicolon. The meaning of this semicolon, as it revealed itself to the dreamer, was that the poet never knows all that he writes: he writes only, as it were, as far as the semicolon; beyond the statement is something more, that completes his meaning. We can never define it, for it is not finite in its nature, yet it is part of the poem, and part of what the poet communicates to the reader."[18] At first one may be inclined to ask why, if the poem should end with a semicolon, the novel may not end with an arrow shot into the future. But there is a difference. The silence that comes after the semicolon completes the circle. The something more is there, even though it cannot be defined; it is part of what the poet communicates; whereas in the kind of novel which Muir has in mind the future into which the arrow is shot is irresponsive, there is no completeness either stated or implied. The creative imagination "needs as a working hypothesis something more durable than the immediate subject matter on which it works."[19]

A complete conception of life involves the recognition of inner conflict as being a necessary consequence of man's situation, not an accident which can be eliminated by changing the environment. In the older conception the natural man could not become fully human until he put on the spiritual man, and this would necessarily involve struggle. In the last century and a half the idea has grown that man's life is a development rather than a conflict, and that this development can be controlled by altering the environment. "Consequently what has gradually been brought into prominence by the religion of development is the primacy of *things*, and it finds its fulfilment in the theory that men can be conditioned by things. Control things and you control mankind."[20]   Hence the reduction of the image of man in contemporary politics, the contempt for human life and human freedom. This reduction produces in life the treating of people impersonally, in art

[18] Hollander, *Bibliography*, p. 202.
[19] *E. L. S.*, p. 149; enlarged ed., p. 148.
[20] *E. L. S.*, p. 155; enlarged, ed. p. 154.

fragmentary and incomplete works. These changes in man's conception of himself as seen in literature and in life Muir examined with great penetration in "Natural Man and Political Man", which Mr John Lehmann described as "one of the most remarkable articles I ever published—in fact one of the most important published anywhere during the war."[21] Paradoxically Muir's quest for wholeness led to the recognition that it is not completely attainable in this life. Both the poem and man's earthly life stop at the semicolon.

III

On their return to England, wanting to be quiet and alone but not too far from London, the Muirs took rooms in a boarding house in Cambridge. She was ill, and he suffered a nervous breakdown, falling "plumb into a dead pocket of life which I had never guessed at before. It was hard to live there, simply because it was unimaginably uninteresting. . . . Memories of Prague now and then shivered the surface of my mind, but never sank deep into it. I wandered about the colleges, seeing but not feeling their beauty."[22] His normal openness had made him dangerously vulnerable to the atmosphere of fear and the dreadful stories that had been poured daily into his ears during the later days in Prague. The apathy that supervened was the result of a protective mechanism. This state lasted only for a few weeks. Early in September he wrote to Joseph Chiari:

> Do, do forgive me. For months now I have been suffering from both physical and nervous exhaustion, and to have them both put me in a curious blind dejection for days at a time—a thing I haven't suffered from since a bad time I had as a young man. The physical side is much better—I've been here a month, doing nothing but nothing; the nervous side I haven't yet quite got cured, though bits of almost cheerfulness are at last beginning to break in. I've stayed here in Cambridge not because I wanted to avoid Scotland—I have a keen longing for it, and strangely enough (for I was there only for three years) for Edinburgh in particular. But I felt I had to be in

---

[21] Lehmann, *I Am My Brother*, (London 1960), p. 176.   [22] *A.*, p. 274.

reach of London until the Council had come to some decision about me. They have been nice to me, and I think they are likely to find me a university post; I must not say where at the moment, for I do not definitely know yet. A post of that kind would give me a good deal of more leisure than I had in Prague, and I feel at present that I would like leagues and leagues of leisure, for as one gets older the questions that life asks seem to become vaster and vaster and stretch into endlessness. I have got some comfort in the last few weeks in the thought that there is forgiveness in the universe, that everything is not a mere play of forces and wills: I am beginning to understand faintly the Christian idea of forgiveness, very faintly, for it is surely one of the greatest of all ideas. I know so little about it that I shall say no more about it. That I can come to the point of writing at all is a sign that I have been helped to forgive myself at least, and to feel that in a far larger sense I am forgiven; so do you forgive me too, for I have been a sad burden on your patience and goodness.

He told Chiari that he had found comfort at this time in reading *Don Quixote*, "the sweetest, most universally kindly book I have ever read, almost a kind of human Bible."

Soon afterwards the Muirs went up to Edinburgh. He wanted to see Scotland before going abroad again, and to discuss with Chiari the poems in *The Labyrinth*. But he was not yet recovered. So many people wanted to see them that he got quite exhausted. They pretended to leave Edinburgh, but in fact settled in a quiet little hotel, where they had, he wrote to Miss Patricia Swayle, a colleague in Prague, "a large room with large windows looking out on trees and the Pentland Hills. It is one of those places where the meals are served in one's room; we have had to see literally no one but each other, a Polish man-servant and a Polish maid, and it has been really lovely. I think these misanthropical establishments should be encouraged."[23] In October they moved down to London, living until January with friends in Radcliffe Square and then for a few weeks in lodgings in Hampstead. Happy memories and present friends helped to make life "real, pleasurable and painful again".

[23] E. M. to Swayle, 16 Oct. 1948.

The British Council was paying him a salary, but his situation was disagreeably uncertain. They had offered him a post in Cairo, which he had refused. Then there had been a project of sending him to Padua, and then for several weeks he was almost sure it was to be Hamburg. By Christmas that too was off. He could not settle to sustained work in such a state of uncertainty, but was eager for something to do, and accepted an invitation to review books for the *Observer*. He was not certain of getting another job with the Council, and wrote to Chiari: "If the Council fails me, I shall make a living by reviewing, but I don't want to be reduced to that unless I get a steady weekly article to build upon."

Soon, however, he was appointed Director of the Institute in Rome, where he and his wife arrived late in January 1949. His predecessor as Director was still there; so until April he did not have a great deal to do and was able to settle down in a leisurely way. In March he wrote to Miss Swayle:

> We have got a sort of little pent-house on the top of a block overlooking the Tiber [Lungo Tevere Marzio 10], with a view of almost all Rome, and the hills surrounding it; on clear days we can see the Appenines. I feel we shall be very happy in this flat, which is rather small, in spite of having two terraces— rather like a gingerbread house suitable for Hansel and Gretel. . . I'm delighted with Rome, except for its noise, and the noise is relentless. . . The difficulty I foresee in taking over the directorship of the Institute is that my predecessor, Roger Hinks, is so much loved by the staff that I shall have to exert myself to compete with him. . . . However, I find everyone very friendly, and I do feel that things will go very well.

Things did go very well. After lecture tours to Naples and Palermo and to Florence, Bologna, Milan and Genoa he took over the Institute in April, and soon made himself as much loved by the staff as any predecessor could have been. His Italian secretary went on writing to the Muirs long after they had left. He could, she said, "make work a wonderful job, something you always looked forward to do, and for which every morning I thanked God for having given me the opportunity of working in such a marvellous atmosphere". A shy man himself he especially appreciated the way in which the people they knew in Rome "spoke from the heart, simply and naturally, without awkwardness, and put all of themselves, heart and soul, into what they said".[24] He had known fresh and natural speech among Orkney farmers, but not before among city dwellers. The warm climate of Rome made Mrs Muir well physically, and the friendliness and freedom of its people cured him of any depression still left from the later days in Prague. By December he was able to write to Chiari: "I've put a good deal into the work of the Institute, and the result is that it is going very well now, and attracting large audiences. But I shouldn't have said 'the result is', for it's not my doing or only partly; for I have a staff I should thank God for; it is great good luck that I have happened upon them." But he was tired, whether because of the climate or of age or of the varied work of teaching and administration at the Institute and of lecture tours all over Italy he was not sure. He had written very little poetry during the year, though he had gathered impressions which were to go into poetry later.

Many visitors came, and were entertained either on behalf of the Council or as personal friends. Among them were W. H. Auden, and Douglas Young ("From Douglas", he wrote to Chiari, "I got the feeling that the Lallans poets weren't doing as well as they expected. I have no ill-will towards them, but they never seemed to me to be very gifted, except for Grieve"), Graham Greene, V. S. Pritchett, Rex Warner and George Scott-Moncrieff. A pleasant little sketch of him is given by Paul Potts in his *Dante called you Beatrice*[25]: "I ran into him one day coming out of the Palazzo Quattro Fontane in Rome. I was on my way in to see him about getting some work, he was in charge of the British Council. He was leaving by car, driven by a chauffeur, as I was entering on foot. He got out of the car to speak to me, seemed very ashamed to be found in such splendour; after we had had our talk I had almost to give him permission to get back into the car again. He indeed was a truly gentle man. This is one of the most pleasant little incidents of my life."

Beneath the surface he was experiencing a deeper realisation

[24] *A.*, p. 275.   [25] Potts, *Dante Called you Beatrice*, (London 1960), p. 219.

of the Incarnation than he had ever had before. He wrote to Chiari:

> I'm much struck with Rome, and all its wealth of associations; you feel the gods (including the last and greatest of them) have all been here, and are still present in a sense in the places where they once were. It has brought very palpably to my mind the theme of Incarnation and I feel that probably I shall write a few poems about that high and difficult theme sometime: I hope so. Edinburgh I love, but in Edinburgh you never come upon anything that brings the thought of Incarnation to your mind, and here you do often, and quite unexpectedly. I'm rather afraid of writing on such a theme and though it occupies my mind whenever my mind is free from daily affairs, I feel nothing is ready yet to be written down. I haven't written much at all, a poem about the first seven days and one about day and night, and one with which I'm not very pleased, about the gods hanging round a ruined temple. But I hope things will emerge in time.[26]

One notices that he writes here of Incarnation rather than of *the* Incarnation. He had long been interested in this theme. When planning *The Marionette* he wrote notes on Hans's father: "His book is about the Incarnation. Student of comparative religions. His theme that incarnation is a symbol of the life of every man. Draws evidences too from the poetry of his own land. The Fall and the Incarnation are to him one and the same thing." Here the life of every man is an incarnation. This of course was long before he was a Christian. Now he had found in Christ the man who is

Image of man from whom all have diverged.

But he still did not want to formulate the mystery in a doctrine, to go beyond what he had directly experienced—a sense of divine immanence and of the splendour of Christendom as seen in the lives of his Italian friends and in art. Travelling on lecture tours through the cities of Tuscany and Umbria he and his wife were "astonished again and again by the prodigious energy which had created in a few centuries such a wealth of beautiful forms in painting and stone."[27] In his first draft he

---

[26] E. M. to Chiari, 20 Dec. 1949.   [27] *A.*, p. 278-9.

Q

went on: "They too [the Cities] had known violence and crime; but their beauty which had arisen from religious thought existed in a world of its own, untouched by the memory of such things. I had been unable to cast a single shadow of doubt on these lovely proclamations of a single life-giving faith, still young there." He revised this to: "They looked like new incarnations sprung from the inexhaustible source of metaphysical felicity, and though they had witnessed violence and crime, they rose from it into their own world and their own light. Christendom was still young there." The second formulation represents his position more accurately. The cities are "incarnations" rather than "proclamations of . . . faith"; the artists were able to create because they had access to a source rather than because they had beliefs.

To his old friend of his agnostic Glasgow days, Edward Scouller, he wrote: "Rome is supposed to give you a scunner at Catholicism, or a temptation to join. I haven't any scunner (except at some of the politics), or any temptation to join (I couldn't), but what a religion it is, how much it takes into itself, and how much more human Catholics are, at least in Italy, than Protestants anywhere. I'm immensely impressed with Romanism, on the whole I like it, and the carelessness of it, and all the imaginative ritual and richness; but I could no more join it than I could fly to the moon."[28] Why could he not? Because of a temperament which made him always dislike to be pinned down—seen, for instance, in his early reluctance to marry? Because of lingering prejudice, perhaps stronger in him than he realised? Perhaps partly; but mainly, I think, because of a feeling that

> If thought should thieve
> One word of the mystery
> All would be wrong.

Rome had been the perfect answer to Prague. Both intensified perceptions he already had. The differing conceptions of human life about which he had speculated in the 'twenties and 'thirties had crystallised before his eyes in action

[28] E. M. to Scouller, 19 May 1950.

and in people's lives. Both experiences helped him to embody his perceptions in more concrete froms.

In May 1950 the Muirs went on their last lecture tour, to Sicily, where Mrs Muir, as usual the quicker to master the language, lectured in Italian, he in English. "After Italy Sicily seemed to belong to an earlier world. . . . It was the third week of May and the hills were covered, mile after mile, with yellow grain, ready for harvesting. By the road we watched oxen trampling out the corn on a threshing floor in the middle of a field, while a group of peasants stood about, winnowing the chaff from the grain with huge, unwieldy flails. On the roads we met occasional carts glittering with painted scenes of medieval battles or religious scenes and drawn by horses with scarlet plumes and embossed trappings; the driver sometimes asleep in his seat."[29] They were taken for a drive up Mount Etna, seeing vines growing luxuriantly out of sooty earth, and deep sulphurous yellow flowers. These experiences produced the poem "The Island", and contributed to "The Desolations".

When they got back to Rome in June it was time to get ready to return to Scotland. The Institute was to be closed, and he had been appointed Warden of Newbattle Abbey College near Edinburgh. He wrote to Miss Swayle: "I am leaving the Council, with some sentimental regrets, for it grows upon you, but with very real relief. I have been offered the post of Warden of Newbattle Abbey, an adult education college which is to be opened in October, half an hour's journey from Edinburgh. . . . I think the post will be an interesting one, and not so worrying as the B. C." Though sorry to leave Rome they were pleased at the prospect of settling down and of living in a cooler climate.

IV

He had experienced much in Italy that was fructifying to him as a poet. Some of these new impressions had to wait until later for adequate embodiment, but he had already written a handful of fine poems—including "The Animals", "The Days",

[29] *MS.* notes for *A.*

"Day and Night", "The Island", "The Late Wasp", "The Son", "The Annunciation", "One Foot in Eden" and "The Other Story". "Adam's Dream" and "The Succession" were written by the autumn.

The main new experience which began to enter into the poetry during this time was his realisation of the Incarnation. This was to enable him to write with greater authority and confidence. In the 'thirties he had sought the fable mainly in his own story; now he could see it more clearly outside himself in the Christian story, in which more than in the life of any individual story and fable are one. But his treatment of the theme in "The Son" is, as he knew, inadequate to the subject. This poem is a fairly conventional meditation on the Incarnation. He needed a starting point in a particular experience of his own, whether in dream or in waking life, in order to write at his best; and this was provided when he came on a little plaque representing the Annunciation on a wall of a house in the Via degli Artisti: "An angel and a young girl, their bodies inclined towards each other, their knees bent as if they were overcome by love, 'tutto tremante', gazed upon each other like Dante's pair; and that representation of a human love so intense that it could not reach farther seemed the perfect earthly symbol of the love which passes understanding."[30] What struck him about the plaque was that it was a bold representation of a *human* love. The resulting poem, "The Annunciation", one of his best religious poems, treats the theme unconventionally in laying stress on the love between the angel and the girl. The idea of eternity in love with the productions of time is made vivid in a particular scene:

> See, they have come together, see,
> While the destroying minutes flow,
> Each reflects the other's face
> Till heaven in hers and earth in his
> Shine steady there. He's come to her
> From far beyond the farthest star,
> Feathered through time. Immediacy
> Of strangest strangeness is the bliss

---

[30] *A.*, p. 278.

> That from their limbs all movement takes.
> Yet the increasing rapture brings
> So great a wonder that it makes
> Each feather tremble on his wings.

The scene is clearly visualised. The angel is not just a messenger, but a living being capable of rapture. At the same time the event is in a way deliberately generalised by the reference simply to the angel and the girl rather than specifically to Gabriel and the Virgin Mary. Without denying the uniqueness of this particular event when the supernatural entered time in a special way Muir seems to suggest that any intense human love may be a kind of annunciation, any human birth a kind of incarnation.

"The Fall and the Incarnation are to him one and the same thing", he had written of Hans's father. Now his own fuller realisation of the Incarnation led to a more positive treatment of the other theme also. The emphasis now is on "the flowers in Eden never known" that bloom in the darkened fields of time. Adam in his dream of his descendants does not feel the horror that might be expected at the consequences of his sin:

> And he remembered all, Eden, the Fall,
> The Promise, and his place, and took their hands
> That were his hands, his and his children's hands,
> Cried out and was at peace . . .

Experience is accepted. We are to look, not back, but on to

> the passing of this fragmentary day
> Into the day where all are gathered together,
> Things and their names, in the storm's and the lightning's nest,
> The seventh great day and the clear eternal weather.

XIII

Newbattle

NEWBATTLE ABBEY stands in wooded grounds by the river Esk near Dalkeith some eight miles south of Edinburgh. Cistercian monks settled there in 1140 under the patronage of David I. At the Reformation the Abbey, much altered in the fourteenth century, was given to the last Abbot, Mark Kerr, and then passed to his son, the first Earl of Lothian. In 1544 most of the old building was destroyed by the English army, but the crypt, now the students' common room, and the warming room, now a chapel, remained. A fine new house was built on the old site, and was later much altered and added to by the Lothian family. In 1936 it was given by the eleventh Marquess of Lothian to be a residential adult education College, the only one of its kind in Scotland. Lord Lothian wanted to give to some who had not been to University the chance to get out of routine jobs for a time and to study and think and develop their latent talents in an atmosphere of peace and freedom without having to conform to any examination syllabus. He left furniture and books and pictures, and some curious objects with historical associations such as a saddle reputedly Robert the Bruce's, handing over a complete house not just a shell to be filled with institutional furniture. The College had hardly got going before war intervened. In the autumn of 1950 it was to re-open, and Muir was appointed in March to be its Warden.

In some ways he was the ideal man for the job, and the job the ideal one for him. In his twenties he had been just the kind of person for whom the College was intended; and he must have seen something of himself in the twenty or so students who arrived that first autumn. Most had left school at fourteen or not long after. One had worked for twenty years behind the counter of a Co-op store; there was a metal-turner, a general labourer, a journalist, a mine-worker, a short-hand typist, a Post Office engineer and several clerks. They were untrained intellectually and, some of them, rather brash, but eager to make full use of their opportunity. Muir was astonished by their intelligence and hard work, and enjoyed seeing their minds unfold. The non-vocational nature of the College and the absence of examinations were entirely in accordance with his ideas as to what education should be. He used to say that Newbattle was the best university in Scotland because its people were there only out of genuine interest, led by some inner light. At Newbattle the students were not prepared for any examination or occupation. They were guided in their choice of lectures, though in fact many of them went to them all, and were expected to write a weekly essay for their tutor, but were left free to follow up whatever interested them. Each was treated as an individual, and allowed to flower freely. They were adults, and were treated as such. Not only in work but in the general life of the College also discipline was made as slight and unobtrusive as possible.

It was a noble ideal, but one not easy of realisation in the modern world (if ever), and especially not in utilitarian-minded Scotland. The place must have been quite expensive to run. Besides the Warden there were three full-time tutors as well as occasional outside lecturers and clerical and domestic staff. Outgoings must have been substantially greater than the fees received from about twenty students. So the College was dependent on the support and goodwill of the Local Education Authorities and Trade Unions, who sent the students and paid, or helped with, their fees, and of the Scottish Education Department, who provided a grant. Such bodies like to see a tangible result for money. A person sent to a Training College or a University comes back with a sacred piece of paper, a diploma or degree; sent to some industrial course he comes back a more efficient tube-maker or Trade Union official. But what did a person sent to Newbattle come back with? Sometimes he obtained entry to a University and so a passport to the eventual useful piece of paper, and that could be understood as worth while. But more often he came back and said that he had had one of the happiest years of his life, that he had had his mental horizons widened; such gains were not easy to put into a balance sheet. So, though there were plenty of people who would have profited by going there, not all suitable applicants were able to get grants, and there were never, in Muir's time, much more than twenty-five students there—only about a third of the number the house could hold. This under-use of the facilities made the Scottish Education Department uneasy, and the continuance of their support from year to year was sometimes in doubt. The Governors, a large miscellaneous group, and the Executive Committee, the effective governing body with whom the Warden had to deal, had not been of one mind in appointing Muir, and as time went on a section of them became increasingly disappointed at his failure, as they saw it, to make the place successful in a way they could understand. Some of them wanted to fill the place with short-term courses lasting a week or a fortnight. Muir was firmly opposed to this as a piece of window-dressing, and to the idea of making the College more vocational. As often in such cases it was the supposedly unpractical idealist who was concerned with the real thing which the College was intended for, and the hard-headed realists who were out for something of no real substance—being able to say that the house was full irrespective of whether anything valuable was going on in it.

So during his latter years at Newbattle Muir had increasing difficulties with his Committee. This caused him great distress, though he did not show it, and probably shortened his life. Some members supported him stoutly; others disagreed with him on matters of policy, as they were entitled to do, in an open and honourable fashion; but there were also—so, at any rate, he believed—intrigue and underhand dealing which he found unbearable and which he could not cope with. To deal with the situation he would have had to be two things he was not—a showman and a politician. He was not able nor willing to stump the country "selling" Newbattle like a detergent; nor had he the guile which the successful committee-man needs. He was always perfectly courteous even to those who treated him with incivility, and few knew the strain he was suffering. He was also perfectly unbending when a matter of principle was involved, and Newbattle stayed the way he wanted it until the end of his time there. But he was not able to enjoy a fight, even a successful one. In December 1954 he wrote to Kathleen Raine that, though he liked the work with the students, the perpetual controversy "has spoilt everything; and I've got tired with fighting back (successfully so far); and I hate fighting. That is why I've been thinking for some time of throwing the whole thing up: the worry and dissension give me pains in the chest at the least occasion, and all sorts of other silly complications." After he left he wrote to one of his students, the poet George Brown: "I was sorry to leave Newbattle and my work there, but I had been fighting for three years against the committee to keep the college a long-term one: the influential section of the committee was trying to turn it into a short-term one: literature, history and philosophy and of course economics, in a week-end. I got a painful and embarrasing difficulty in breathing during the fight, and did not wish to shorten my life by hanging on."

He was disappointed in his hope that the post at Newbattle would be "less worrying than the B.C."; but one must not think of his five years there as dominated by "politics". Most of the time he was getting on quietly with his creative work as teacher and writer. While the other tutors dealt with history, economics, politics, philosophy and psychology, he lectured on English literature, and took students individually for tutorials, as well as being responsible for the whole running of the College. Mrs Muir did a great deal, unpaid, to help those who wanted to learn languages outside the normal curriculum. They would sometimes have small groups of students to their private flat for informal talk in the evenings; and sometimes a visiting speaker would be invited to lecture and join in discussion. Mrs Muir was a brilliant conversationalist, giving lively, often irreverent, descriptions, illustrated by superb mimicry, of people they had known. He would sit quietly enjoying her performance, and then add his milder, though penetrating, comments. Her outspokenness must sometimes have acted as a kind of safety-valve for him, expressing without inhibition some things which he must have felt but could seldom bring himself to give voice to in public. He did a great deal for those who sought his help, but never interfered in people's private lives unasked. His shyness and respect for others' privacy gave some the impression of remoteness; but his influence pervaded the College and gave it a tone recognised even by those who were not wholly in sympathy with him.

He was not a spectacular lecturer; he talked rather than orated, speaking in an unemphatic way which might at first seem flat. You had to work to get what was there; the plain words were deceptively simple. He was best with small groups rather than on formal occasions. Sometimes he would leave his prepared notes to go off on a chase after some elusive thought that had just struck him, often starting with a modest "I don't know," and in the end leading those who could follow to new light. Ernest Marwick gives a feeling of this in his poem

Lecture in the Crypt, Newbattle

Up to the window's edge the sand-hued stone
Sun-lanterned through the leaves, affirmative of the light.
. . . Shadows flickered his face, as the soft voice spoke on
To the room's chiaroscuro, half-day and tenebrous night.

Some chafed at those hesitant lips, impatient of pause,
Untutored to join that eye, illimitably seeing,
While the poet groped meekly for words to give hint of the cause
Which shone like light on the leaf, more light in his being.

The best way to give some impression of him at Newbattle is to quote some extracts from letters from former students

Muir, as warden, did give a very fine tone to life at Newbattle during the time I was there. Though he was a little aloof and certainly shy of too much personal contact, he did disseminate, if obliquely, a remarkable sense of culture, in the precise Arnoldian sense. There was a genuine feeling of sweetness and light in the air. . . .

During the time I was at Newbattle, I was going through a period of crisis in my life, and Dr. Muir's friendship and quiet happiness in my recovery made him very dear to me.

Edwin was never dogmatic, but always spoke quietly weighing carefully his judgments and views. Human beings and their ideas (and his students) held for him continual interest, but his interest was never merely analytic but a kind of feeling of involvement with all mankind. From behind his pale face and thoughtful eyes he looked out on the world with toleration, affection, humility and humour, and from him emanated what I can only describe as 'goodness'. One sensed at the same time a certain vulnerability and deep sensitivity which made one want somehow to protect him.

It was not long before I found myself going over my written work (which was never for his attention), ruthlessly striking out superfluous words, and striving for clarity and economy—all without a direct stricture from him. Edwin Muir never dictated, never pointed out directions; only made certain ones seem more attractive than others.

There were two factions in the College. One was pro-English Dept., and the other was anti. . . . For me Edwin Muir never appeared to have both feet firmly on the ground. His thoughts were always elsewhere.

It was his fellow poets among his students, men like Tom Scott, George Brown and Ernest Marwick, who were able to appreciate him most fully. George Brown wrote: "He was very pleased that his students were trying to write plays and poems and stories, for he believed that only the exercise of the supreme gift of imagination could save the world from slow decay or quick disaster. He discussed our crude productions with delicacy, kindness and understanding. . . . In his company all stir and fret died away. . . . The students who went to Newbattle knew and loved them both—'respect' is too mild and neutral a word for it."[1]

Muir gave something of incalculable value to those able to get on his wavelength; to others he was always kind and courteous, but seemed remote. Many of the students were more interested in politics than in literature; some held crude political and anti-religious views, and could not share his

[1] George Brown, "A Marvellous Singer", in *Scottish Library Association News* (November-December 1963), No. 61, and *The Orcadian*, 15 Jan. 1959.

perceptions; some were disappointed that their work did not lead to more tangible benefits than it did. But nearly all were strongly impressed by him, and gained from living in the atmosphere he created around him.

By this time he was a famous writer, and was constantly being asked for his advice. Correspondence would pile up on his desk unanswered, but in the end he would read everything and give a courteous and honest answer to all. He would give an adverse opinion quite firmly, but in such a way as to cause the minimum hurt, for instance: "I have read your poems: I think that they have probably given you considerable happiness in writing of them, and that it is good for you to write them. . . . But I am sorry to say that I do not think they would merit publication . . . and I can only advise you to continue writing until your technique is more equal to the emotion you wish to express."

To poets whose work he did admire, especially young ones, he was always anxious to give help and encouragement. He was in touch by correspondence with some of the young poets of the time, helped to get their work published, and was glad to meet writers when he went to London for meetings of the British Council Publications Committee or for some such purpose. George Fraser gives an impression of him:

> One hasn't got anecdotes about him, because in any setting, the most sedate or a wildish one, he retained the same kind of kindness and serenity, which had an odd effect, an almost magical one, on any company. I used to have regular gatherings of young poets, or would-be poets, in my flat in Chelsea on one Wednesday evening of every month. We drank a great deal too much—it was a sort of poetical bottle party—and the young poets, who divided up into gangs, tended to be savagely rude to each other, and especially to any older writer with more reputation than themselves. The night Edwin came, these wolf cubs were like lambs. He never raised his voice but was always listened to; it was a gentle, slow voice, with an odd little burr or catch in it, and little precisions of phrase and idiom which struck me not only as Scottish but as very precise old-fashioned refined Scottish-English. A kind of rhythm went through the sentences and a kind of little tune that seemed to

weave a net for people; yet he never seemed to be talking for
effect but to be following thoughts suggested by what someone
had said, and, because he could not help it, weaving his thoughts
into a design of art. . . . He seemed to me the least stagey
(indeed he was not stagey at all) of any poet I have met—most
poets act, at least in any strange company, the part of the poet
they think themselves, wonder if they can keep it up, and
either break down or over-act it; or act it sometimes too
professionally, too well. Edwin was quite obviously the poet
he was, but the person he was, like the poet he was—like the
prose-writer also—had a queer sort of transparency.

II

In spite of the distractions he wrote quite a lot during the
Newbattle years. He continued with his reviewing for *The
Observer*. It may seem strange that he did this at a time when
he did not absolutely need the money. But he had no capital
saved up for old age, and presumably felt that he must keep
his place in the world of literary journalism in case he should
again be dependent upon it. Reviewing was easy for him. He
would type his review at the last moment, always knowing
exactly what he wanted to say. More important work was
written in longhand, and much revised. His teaching led him
to rediscover, sometimes to discover for the first time, old books;
and his reviewing kept him in touch with the latest literature,
much of which saddened him because of its joylessness, though
he tried to be fair to it. He wrote to George Brown in May
1953: "The term is grinding on, and today I was talking about
James Joyce. A writer to be admired (and sometimes enjoyed)
but a sad chap altogether. I wish I was talking to the students
about poetry instead of prose. I only half believe in prose, it's
a sad fact. But the course made me read 'Clarissa', which was
a thrill I don't think I succeeded in conveying to any of the
students, not even you: you don't know what you missed."
George Brown was ill at the time, and Muir looked through
his shelves for books to send him: "I have been struck by the
number of dismal books which in my perverse pursuit of
'culture' I've managed to accumulate. Hardly one that would
even raise a horse-laugh. It's quite extraordinary. Have you

ever read Osbert Sitwell's 4 volume autobiography; now there's an exception. . . . And there's Alain Fournier's 'Grand Meaulnes', an interesting book that I think would be completely in your world. I love it. But so much of modern literature has come out of hatred, or disgruntlement, or what people call sophistication, which seems to me the most vulgar thing in the world."

His chief prose work during this time was the bringing of his autobiography up to date. *The Story and the Fable* had obtained high praise, though it had not sold very fast. By 1952 it was out of print; the publishers wanted it still to be available, and thought that a revision brought up to date would sell better than a mere reprint. Muir accepted this commission rather reluctantly. In 1938-9 it had been of real value to him to go back and recover something of his past and try to interpret it, but now he no longer needed to do this. The later part of his life was not easy to arrange into a pattern. In the earlier book the fable of Eden, the Fall and the journey back had revealed itself under the story of his life. But much of his later life was merely story—a succession of things that had happened to him or that he had seen; or, if he could discern the fable beneath, he now preferred to express that in poetry rather than in prose. The new parts of the autobiography were written rather hurriedly during the summer of 1953 and the following winter. In September he wrote to George Brown: "I have not much news except about this confounded autobiography, which is giving me a headache and which runs quite nicely for a little while, and then stops, and then runs again not so nicely, and then stops again, and doesn't seem to have much shape of any kind; I don't see how one can give any shape to one's life." He was not vain enough to think that a mere account of what he had done and seen would be valuable. He wanted to find a pattern so as to reveal something about human life in general not just about himself. In preliminary notes he asked himself: "What shall I put in? In a man's growing all is movement, and can be described in a sequence of episodes. In his maturity (or at least in mine, if this is maturity), there seems to be a relative absence of episodes, and when they do appear they are on a stationary plain, not moving forwards, not pointing to something still in front, but rather revealing what is already there. The advance, when there is advance, is an inward one." He then jotted down notes of incidents and people met since 1922, and then, realising that these would not do much to illustrate the inner advance he had made during the period, added "All this fairly external". If he had really wanted to make his inner life the centre of the new chapters he should have dealt more fully with the new religious insights that had come to him; but he was still reticent about these. The next words in the notebook suggest that he had thought of an idea which might give him a different, more external, theme. "Where to start? Perhaps in Prague" (i.e. in the second period in Prague). The theme was the increasing impersonality of the modern world. He wrote a much longer essay on this than the one we have in the first of the new chapters in the *Autobiography* (chapter seven), and incorporated in it stories of the inhumanity of the Gestapo and later of the Communists in Prague. He must then have decided that he would not be able to carry the work through in this thematic, non-chronological way; so he cut down the length of the preliminary essay and transferred the Prague material to its place in the story of his life. All this helps us to see what to him were the most important things in his experience of the last thirty years. On the one hand was his experience of Incarnation, of Transfiguration, of Grace; on the other his observation of that terrible impersonality which could treat people as if they were not human, and which is to be found everywhere, not only in Communist and Fascist countries. "The picture I am trying to present is of power growing more and more impersonal as it becomes more mechanically perfect, and of the greater part of mankind, its victims, who contrive, in the greater and greater stresses, to remain human. Omnipotent impersonality on the one side, fumbling and unequipped humanity on the other. The conflict between Communism and democracy seems small compared with this, and while we fight it out is perhaps already obsolete, as wars in the past so often have been."[2] The forces making for impersonality exist in the democracies; fumbling human

[2] *MS.* notes for *A*.

beings strive to remain human under any system. In this context his old belief in immortality was especially important. In *The Story and the Fable* the loss and the recovery of his belief in (or, better, experience of) immortality had been treated mainly as a part of his personal history. Now the loss of this experience in so many is seen as one of the things that have made possible the growth of impersonal power. His belief in imagination also gained increased significance in this context. For it is impossible to treat some one in a wholly impersonal way once one has begun to establish some communication with him. To enter into communication with a person one has to employ imagination. "All communication between man and man, except when it is functional, a matter of business, or compulsion, or direction of work or duty, or mass action, or propaganda, is an act of imagination."[3] Hence the importance of all means of strengthening the imagination, especially the arts. This was one of his constant themes at this time, and was developed at length in his broadcast talk, "The Decline of Imagination". In the light of this preoccupation all his work at this time can be seen as connected—his poetry, his criticism and broadcast talks, his stand at Newbattle for real education as against mere cramming.

It is interesting to find him, a year or so before this, writing to Chiari: "I've taken a great fancy for Gabriel Marcel, whom I almost adore." His position on many matters was close to Marcel's, in whose works he would find many of his insights formulated in a philosophical language which he could not command. He would have vibrated to such a passage as this in Marcel's *On the Ontological Mystery:* "A presence is a reality; it is a kind of influx; it depends upon us to be permeable to this influx, but not, to tell the truth, to call it forth. Creative fidelity consists in maintaining ourselves actively in a permeable state; and there is a mysterious interchange between this free act and the gift granted in response to it."[4] Much of Marcel's *Decline of Wisdom* might be read as an unconscious commentary on Muir's *Autobiography*, published in the same year. For

[3] *MS.* notes for *A*.

[4] Marcel, *On the Ontological Mystery*, in *The Philosophy of Existence* (London 1948), p. 24.

instance: "Everything seems to show that gratitude and admiration tend to lessen in the measure that creative power weakens. And let us add that as this power withdraws it is replaced by its toxic and deceptive substitute, the claim to innovate, and by the vanity that goes with it. The self styled innovator is centred upon himself, that is why he is so unwilling to admire or to be grateful; no doubt he feels that one way or another he risks being diminished or humiliated, whereas the creator as such does not think of himself, is not occupied with himself. You could say that the creative act is essentially ingenuous. . . ."[5] The connections between gratitude, grace, a sense of piety towards the past and continued creative power are analysed by Marcel and exemplified by Muir. In the latter we see the essentially "ingenuous" quality of the creative act and the maintaining of himself to the end "actively in a permeable state"; sadly many examples could be given of the vanity of the self styled innovator.

In spite of all his other activities Muir managed to produce poetry at Newbattle at about his usual rate. His reputation was rising, helped by the appearance of his *Collected Poems* in 1952. The story of how this volume came to be published is rather a curious one. Mr John Hall contributed an essay to *Penguin New Writing* No. 38 (1949)—as far as I know the first consideration of Muir's work in anything longer than a review. When sending this to Muir he suggested that the time had perhaps come for a collected edition. Muir did not answer for a year, and then wrote that he was too pre-occupied with other things to get together a collection. Thereupon Hall wrote to say that he would be only too pleased to do the editorial work if Muir would allow him. Rather to his surprise Muir readily agreed; so he made his selection, wrote an introduction, and went up to Newbattle to see him early in 1951. Muir accepted his selection without demur. As so often in his career he did nothing to push his own interests, but when some one turned up to help he was tremendously grateful. In all his correspondence with Eliot at Faber's about the volume his main interest was to try to get for Hall a larger fee out of royalties than the payment of his modest expenses which was

[5] Marcel, *Decline of Wisdom*, (London 1954), p. 24.

R

all that Hall wanted. He was very pleased by the reception of the volume, writing to Eliot in August 1952: "I'm very grateful to you for bringing out my collected poems, and I've been very pleased and surprised by some of the reviews. In reviews of the separate volumes, I've always felt that even the critics who liked my work were faintly concerned about me and wondering if my health were improving, whereas now they seem to think I've passed the crisis: I hope to goodness it is so." The 1952 collection not only helped his reputation in Britain, but brought him to the attention of American poets and readers. Though his *First Poems* and nearly all his prose works were issued concurrently in America and London, none of his subsequent volumes of poetry were published in America until the Grove Press issued the *Collected Poems* there in 1953.

Nine new poems, written since *The Labyrinth*, were included in the 1952 collection. Most of these had been written in Italy, but one comparatively recent one, "Orpheus Dream", may be taken as representative of the work he was producing during the first year or so at Newbattle. The MS of this poem in the National Library of Scotland enables us to see how much hard work went into its making. Four MS sheets, all but the last heavily revised, contain four separate drafts. As always when reading Muir's mythological poems we must be careful to attend only to what the poem says. In the best known version of the story, in Virgil's fourth *Georgic*, Orpheus, having by his marvellous music brought Eurydice up from the underworld almost to the light, loses her by looking back too soon. In the story as told by Phaedrus in Plato's *Symposium* he does not even achieve this degree of success. "The gods sent Orpheus away from Hades empty-handed, and showed him the mere shadow of the woman he had come to seek; Eurydice herself they would not let him take." Muir may have taken a hint from Plato, but he reverses the situation; for in his poem the lovers are united and at the end it is only the "poor ghost" (in earlier states the "image", "phantom", "twin ghost") of Eurydice that is left in the underworld. The lovers have attained a state of at-oneness and security from which they are able to look back without danger. What they look back at is a state of aloneness, of being imprisoned in an underworld—

perhaps within the self, like those in the "labyrinth of their own loneliness" in "The Transfiguration". The inspiration of the poem is not literary. It uses myth and dream to convey a new sense of the meaning of ordinary human experience. The word "foundering" in the first stanza produces a sense of weight, of physical actuality. "Eurydice was there." The words in the next stanza about leaving "earth's frontier wood" are controlled by "as if". It is *as if* the lovers had passed beyond time and won "the lost original" (in earlier states "the true shape", "the archetype", "the simple lineaments", "the first original") of the soul. But the last three lines of the stanza are in the indicative:

> The moment gave us pure and whole
> Each back to each, and swept us on
> Past every choice to boundless good.

Whatever may be the explanation of it, whatever may have produced it, the lovers' experience of what love can give is a fact. The fact is distinguished with careful honesty from the doctrine.

For all his preoccupation with the state which he calls Eden and which he associates with childhood Muir was nothing of a Peter Pan. Unlike some other writers, such as Forrest Reid, who have vividly reconstructed a childhood or boyhood world, he was a poet of maturity, able to be so mainly because of his experience of mature and lasting love. In "Orpheus Dream" the lovers do not look back to Eden, but in the present experience a moment of wholeness which has the quality of Eden, and are then swept *forwards* "to boundless good". From the opening words the poem conveys powerfully a sense of quiet wonder. The stanza form, in which the first line rhymes with the sixth, the second with the fifth round a central couplet, helps to give a sense of completeness, of finality.

In the summers of 1951 and 1952 the Muirs went up to Orkney (in 1951 to Shetland as well) for their holidays, and it was there that a considerable proportion of the poems belonging to these years were written. Poems which had been knocking on the door at Newbattle could be completed in peace. It was in Orkney that a letter from T. S. Eliot reached him in

July 1952 asking whether he could provide a poem of from twenty to sixty lines to be brought out in pamphlet form at Christmas the next year as one of Faber's series of Ariel poems. Though the poem which he sent, "Prometheus", has not quite the force of his very best poems, the correspondence with Eliot about it is of some interest. Muir answered that he had no poem ready at the moment, "but one is in the course of formation; this is why I have not answered your letter before; I hoped that it might have completed itself. But it is still unfinished, and I shall have to wait until I can see my way through it." About a month later he sent "Prometheus": "I outstayed my time, and still have produced nothing that seems satisfactory. I send the result, but am not pleased with it, and can scarcely think it adequate or suitable. Dante said more in a casual line which has been running in my mind

> Le gente antiche nell' antico errore.

I am sorry this is the best I can offer at the moment." A little later he sent a slightly revised version, and at the end of September Eliot wrote to express his delight in the poem and to make, very courteously, one or two suggestions:

> My other query is still more tentative, and may be due to a misunderstanding. In the last paragraph, Prometheus says: "a god came down long since". It is a little unexpected to find Prometheus surviving into our own epoch, since one has started with the usual assumption that one is being taken back to the era of early Greece. I don't ask you to change this, but I wonder whether a line or so could prepare the reader for this continuity of the agony of Prometheus up to date. Do forgive these comments if they seem impertinent to you.

It is rather typical of Muir that he should not have foreseen any difficulty for the reader in imagining Prometheus as still living on in the Christian era. In response to Eliot's suggestion he added the paragraph beginning "The shrines are emptying . . ." This inserted paragraph contains some fine writing; it enriches the poem and makes it in some ways easier to understand. But there was also, perhaps, some loss in separating the questions asked in the paragraph before it from the answer suggested in the final lines of the poem. When the story of

mankind is over and the clamorous races that have lived upon
the earth lie silent in the ground, the heedless gods may,
Prometheus thinks, raise their eyes and bid him come again
among them. If so, what shall he say to them? Will they be
interested in his story of the world's pain? And what answer
will they give? The implication is that the old gods will
neither be interested to hear nor will be able to give any
answer to make the earth's dark story meaningful, that there
was no real connection between the eternal and temporal as
understood in the old religion. The gods are heedless; the
earth's story is but gossip to them. This leads on directly to
the final paragraph. Prometheus has heard of a god who,
unlike the Olympians, really entered into the temporal order,
and, unlike Prometheus himself, came down

> Not in rebellion but in pity and love

returning to heaven "with all the spoils of time" so that

> time itself is there a world of marvels.
> If I could find that god, he would hear and answer.

He would hear because really concerned in the earth's story,
and in answering show the meaning of that story.

Two other poems, "Telemachos Remembers" and "Song
for a Hypothetical Age", written at about the same time, also
make use of a story from Greece. He had for long been
fascinated by the story of Penelope, "the great image of love
and constancy", and had used it in "The return of Odysseus".
He now thinks of Penelope as also an artist who, if she had
finished the web, "would have achieved the supreme work of
art, but in doing so would have renounced her humanity".
The theme is hinted at in "Telemachos Remembers" and more
explicitly stated in the second poem, which is "a fanciful statement of the claims of life and art, and describes the desolation
which would follow if they were quite divorced from each other,
as fortunately for us they cannot be."[6] "Telemachos
Remembers" is richer than "The Return of Odysseus" not
only in adding this extra meaning, but also in paralleling
Penelope at her treadle with Odysseus far away on "the

---

[6] B.B.C. "Scottish Life and Letters", 23 May 1954.

treadmill of the turning road". (To a friend who objected to this image as inappropriately un-nautical Muir wrote: "I was not trying to give a correct account of what Odysseus was doing, but conveying the anxiety and bewilderment of Telemachos and his mother, and I think the picture of someone wandering about in a circle gives a better impression of frustration over a long stretch of years than any nautical image could possibly give. At least that is how I see it. I think I have read the Odyssey about twenty times, so that I was not floundering about at random.") It was an improvement too to give the story to Telemachos instead of, as in the earlier poem, letting Penelope make large claims for herself. "Telemachos" is more effective than the "Song" in conveying its meaning by story and image without the need for abstract statement.

Quite a number of poems must have been written between coming to Newbattle and early in 1953; for very little was done during the next year. Early in 1953 he was not well, his ailments being brought on, or at any rate worsened, by worry about the College. He suffered also from eye-strain, writing in April to Kathleen Raine: "I've been having trouble with my eyes—so acute at one time that I had a shrinking from reading that curiously gave me a feeling that books would sting me, a recoil as from nettles or thistles." He was better by the summer, when he started on the extension of his autobiography. When working on this he found, as usual when writing prose which came from the depths rather than just the surface of his mind, that he could not write any poetry.

The early part of 1954 was overshadowed by worry over his wife. In June he wrote to Chiari:

> I've been very worried for a long time about Willa's health, and last February she at last agreed to go into a hospital in Edinburgh. There the surgeon operated upon her, but found that he had to make two operations instead of one; an older growth behind the one shown by the X-ray. Two days later internal bleeding was still going on, and another operation had to be made to stop it. For some days she hovered between life and death, but then gradually began to recover. Then pleurisy set in, throwing her back again, but at last she began

to come back to life. She has been back home now for several
weeks, steadily improving, but still not able to make much
effort. All this is the last phase of a long illness, which has cast
anxiety over her and me. Now that the operation has been
successful, I think she will be better in health than she has
been for years. I feel as if we were beginning to emerge out of
a long dark fog of anxiety into light again. I hope this will help
to explain and excuse my long silence. And in addition there
have been worries about this college too. I haven't written
more than two poems this year—28 lines in all.

I think the two poems referred to are the sonnets, "Milton"
and "The Great House". Those who spoke of his serenity
seldom realised the strains and anxieties he was suffering. A
friend at Newbattle who was close enough to him to realise
what he was undergoing saw him one day looking much better;
Muir explained to him that the sense of strain could be lifted
by acceptance and prayer.

In December he wrote to Kathleen Raine:

Thank you for your letter and thank you for your review [of
the *Autobiography*], in which you were far too kind to me. No,
my struggle hasn't been heroic, as you said there; it's only that
there has been something stubborn in me, perhaps peasant. . . .
But you know the life that I knew as a boy and still know, and
it will come back to you again, perhaps quite unexpectedly: I
feel this from my own experience. We all feel that we shall
never write another poem, and feel it sometimes for long
stretches: I think it is a common experience, and very painful,
and very unpleasant, until the gates open again. I know how
unpleasant the world is growing. I can feel it here as you feel
it in London, though not so thickly, for I'm not in that
dense atmosphere and not meeting intellectuals. The three
poems in the New Statesman are affected by it—a little infusion
of poison in them except for the third, which comes from an
old memory. I have a few more satisfactory poems in my mind,
but not written all these weeks because I'm so occupied here.
It's taken me quite a long time to recover from the thought
that Willa might die (she was very near it), and I'm still very
tentatively, and slightly fearfully, attempting poetry. But
something will come.

The three poems mentioned are the first, third and fifth of "Effigies", the first two of which indeed have a for him unusual asperity of tone. The first is the most unsparing portrait of an evil man that he ever drew. I do not suppose that it is intended as a picture of any particular person, but his recent experience on committees had introduced him to some successful manipulators of men and so contributed to this portrayal of the man of power for whom people are pawns to be moved on a board. For all his gentleness, his judgments on people were now shrewd and by no means over-indulgent. His ultimately optimistic view of man's essential nature was not based on any illusion as to what they now actually are. The few more satisfactory poems in his mind probably included the wonderful "The Horses".

By the end of 1954 he was thinking of leaving Newbattle. He was feeling his age. It was about this time that his friends began to think of him as rather frail and old. Worry and controversy made him ill, and might, he thought, shorten his life; and he wanted to write more poetry. He would have to make his living by writing, and for this purpose was thinking of going to live in or near London. Fortunately, at just the right moment, the offer came to him of the Charles Eliot Norton Professorship at Harvard. This involved going to live at Harvard for an academic year and giving a series of six lectures; he would get a salary of 17,000 dollars. So now, near the end as at the beginning of his writing career, it was from America that effectual and timely help came. The offer was welcome not only as being financially profitable and as providing a graceful exit from Newbattle, but also in itself. He had warm feelings towards America, and was glad of the prospect of meeting American writers.

In the mean time he must have managed to get out some at least of the more satisfactory poems that had been in his mind; for early in 1955 he sent a collection of forty-eight poems to Eliot at Faber. They were at once accepted, and he corrected the proofs before leaving for America in the summer. Letters show that he at one time wanted to change the title of this collection from *One Foot in Eden* to *The Succession*. Eliot managed to dissuade him on the ground that the former is much the more striking and memorable title. In this he was surely right, but it is worth asking why Muir wanted to make the change. "The Succession" deals with the wanderer Abraham and his sons, and with ourselves who

> through the generations came
> Here by a road we do not know . . .
> And still the road is scarce begun.

The poems in this volume are mostly about the road with all its dangers, about the gains as well as the losses resulting from the fated departure from Eden. The tone is not nostalgic, not backward-looking except in the emphasis on the need to remember what we were in order to become what we essentially are. Furthermore, though informed by personal feeling, most of the poems are in a sense impersonal, deal with the experience of the race; only about one sixth speak directly in the first person singular. These are, I think, the reasons why he wanted to transfer attention from "One Foot in Eden", an "I" poem in which the poet appears as seer, to "The Succession", a "we" poem in which he appears as one among many pilgrims.

The volume is divided into sections. In the first the "fable" is approached more directly, through the Bible and through myths; in the second, more indirectly, through "story". In the first the poems are arranged in a definite sequence, the Bible providing the great story which can give meaning to particular stories. But the poems, except a few which are inadequate to their themes, are still based securely on what Muir had experienced and seen, not on doctrine. Some of them will seem to Christians to be true in ways in which they will not to others. But Eden, the Fall, Hell, Annunciation, Incarnation, as he writes of them, are *at least* ways of describing human experience. Thus "The Annunciation" conveys a sense of wonder at once at the entrance of the supernatural into time and at the possibilities of human love now; and "The Incarnate One" deals both with the betrayal of *the* Incarnation by our "race" (whether Scottish or human) and of incarnation, in all men, by those who would

> Build their cold empire on the abstract man.

In the second section there is no such definite sequence as in the first, though there is a progression from the bitterness of "Effigies" to the acceptance of "Song". The poems are more personal and occasional, and deal with specific situations in the passage through the "difficult land" of time rather than with the over-all vision, though that is always in the background. Here are the tyrants and the victims (though the tyrants are victims too)—the manipulators of men in "Effigies", the man in Czechoslovakia whose human face is hidden behind a "blindfold mask". Men, once "young princes", are now exiled from their proper natures and assailed by "doubt that kills courtesy and gratitude"; living "dull discourteous lives", they are nevertheless still dimly conscious of what they are. But "they" is wrong; Muir says "we". All, himself included, fail fully to realise their true natures—and not just because of external conditions.

> There's nothing here to keep me from my own.

The "confident roads" run wrong, but he is not really deceived by them. He is *willingly* duped, because

> even at my dearest cost I'd save me
> From the true knowledge and the real power.

This poem, "My Own", shows a new depth of self-knowledge. Usually before he had imaged himself as a pilgrim genuinely seeking a goal amidst bewildering roads. Now a closer approach to the truth had shown that it is frightening in its demands; that we do not find it partly because we do not want to.

Taken as a whole *One Foot in Eden* presents a profound and comprehensive view of human life. Though gathered round a common centre, the poems are not monotonous. As in Kafka, the universal situation is entered from many points. Related to the timeless themes are specifically contemporary ones. Muir's involvement in the world of the fifties is shown in his preoccupation with fears of atomic war, which enter into one of his finest poems, "The Horses". This, like many of his later poems, takes up old interests and intuitions and sets them in a new context. He had long had a special feeling for animals—real animals, not just heraldic ones. In the Orkney of his childhood something of the ancient companionship of men and animals had still existed. He had been repelled and frightened as well as delighted by the animals on his father's farm, but had always felt close to them, felt that he shared a common life with them. In and near Glasgow he had been appalled by the famished fields and blackened trees, and had found in modern industrial life a sense of alienation—of men from the earth and the animals as well as from each other. Now he saw possible atomic war as the final fruit of man's misuse of nature. In "The Horses" a seven days' war has "put the world to sleep"—seven days of destruction corresponding to the Biblical seven days of creation. A remote community has survived. Their situation is vividly imagined; the radios stand silent in the rooms; a warship passes, its decks piled high with dead; an aeroplane plunges overhead into the sea. The people return to pre-industrial conditions, except that the relics of industrialism lie around them; the tractors rust in the fields.

> And then, that evening
> Late in the summer the strange horses came.
> We heard a distant tapping on the road,
> A deepening drumming; it stopped, went on again
> And at the corner changed to hollow thunder.
> We saw the heads
> Like a wild wave charging and were afraid.

The horses have come as if under command to find again "that long-lost archaic companionship "with men. Among them are colts, born since the war,

> Dropped in some wilderness of the broken world,
> Yet new as if they had come from their own Eden.

Life is renewing itself in them. At first the men look with wonder at the horses, not thinking of them as "creatures to be owned and used"; but they enter into their "free servitude" to men again; their coming was a new beginning. The poem is both simple and strange. It can be read as a myth about the recovery of lost innocence, of a lost Eden; at the same time there is nothing in it that might not happen just as described, and every detail is clearly imagined. To the men the horses seem strange

> As fabulous steeds set on an ancient shield . . .

but they are ordinary horses and behave in a quite credible way. To a student who sent him an essay on the poem in 1958 Muir wrote:

> I think you have gone wrong in thinking of the horses as wild horses, or as stampeding. It is less than a year since the seven days' war happened. So the horses are good plough-horses and still have a memory of the world before the war. I try to suggest that they are looking for their old human companionship. As for the 'tapping': have you ever listened, on a still evening, to horses trotting in the distance? the sound is really a pretty tapping. The drumming sound indicated that they were drawing nearer: the hollow thunder when they turned the corner meant that they saw the village or farmstead and found their home. I think I am right in the choice of verbs here. And the apparent contradiction between the lines you quote afterwards is not a real one. For the horses are seeking the long lost archaic companionship, accepted in former times by men as an obvious right, so that it never occurred to them that there was anything surprising in using and owning horses. It is the surprise of the return that makes them realise the beauty of that free servitude.

This shows Muir's care to get the words right—not just right so as to suggest some symbolic meaning, but literally right to convey sound and sight. There has been a tendency to over-stress the symbolic and fabulous elements in his poems at the expense of their actuality. For instance, Mr C. B. Cox in a sensitive article[7] on this poem says: "We have left the normal reality for the world of fable. . . . The landscape and the incidents are symbolic, depicting a rebirth of innocence." He writes of "the coming of the divine horses". I think the symbolic meanings seen by Mr Cox are there. But primarily the horses are, as Muir says, "good plough horses". He does not so much leave normal reality for the world of fable as perceive the fable beneath the surface of normal reality.

[7] *Critical Survey*, vol. 1, no. 1 (Autumn 1962), pp. 19-21.

One can compare this poem with a passage from a war-time diary:

> As the train lay at the country station I sat watching a tractor in a field and two horses in a plough. Then really too glorious, really too much, four horses abreast dragging something that looked like a great harrow. They looked wild and legendary, as if they had just risen full-grown from the mould. As I watched their necks arching and leaping, like four waves overtopping one another, I felt that these creatures had been fed in fields of inalienable strangeness, in quite another world from the world we know. I reflected a little while afterwards that this was really so; that this statement was strictly accurate, the horse's world being a different world from ours. But we centre everything in ourselves so almost automatically that we hardly ever realise it.[8]

Again these are actual horses, seen in quite ordinary surroundings, not symbolic nor heraldic horses. They do not live in the human world; we cannot enter into their experience; but they live on the solid earth. Muir was perceiving the strangeness of the actual world, not drifting into a world of fantasy. The perception of the wildness and strangeness of the horses, expressed here and elsewhere, contributes to produce the sense of wonder in the poem that they should willingly enter into their free servitude to men.

During the early summer of 1955 Muir was preparing *One Foot in Eden* for the press, and getting ready to go off to America. He was both glad and sorry to leave Newbattle. He had enjoyed the teaching and the relationships with his staff and students. Looking back a year later he wrote to his faithful collaborator there, Kenneth Wood: "I often think of Newbattle, and of the happy time we had there, in spite of committees; I think that, with occasional little rubs, we were a more friendly and harmonious staff than could be found in many residential colleges. I am very happy, looking back on everything, and we did very good work. I regret nothing, either being there with Donald [Gordon] and you for five years, or leaving when I did." He was excited by the prospect that freedom from administration would give him more time to

[8] *The New Alliance*, (September-October 1943), pp. 6-7.

write, though friends warned him that he would not be able
to write much poetry in America.   In August he wrote to
Kathleen Raine:

> A few weeks ago I got the idea for a long poem, after re-reading
> a miscarried attempt long since published, a "Chorus of the
> Dead", and realising that I could do it better now and in quite
> a different way.   It has made lines and passages come more
> readily than I have known them to come in the past years.   Do
> you remember that you told me I would not write any poetry
> in America?   Herbert Read told me the same.   I don't know
> whether it was a cunning trick of my peasant unconscious that
> gave me beforehand something that would occupy my mind in
> America, or whether it was a real movement of my imagination,
> but I hope the last;   really I think it is, for such things don't
> make themselves known except at their time.   Forgive me for
> speaking of these large plans, but they have excited me, and
> everything is still in movement.   But I am glad, remembering
> what you said, to have the idea to take with me to Harvard.

He seems never to have made much progress with the new
"Chorus".   Among his papers are some fragments of dialogue
between Philosopher and Chorus;   that is all.

Some friends in Edinburgh arranged a dinner for him at
the Scottish Arts Club.   They had a gay evening, though with
an underlying feeling of sadness because he was leaving.   Some
one came to say his car was ready;   they all rose;   he went
round the table, simply and naturally like a child going to bed
kissed each one and left in silence.   They were all very much
moved.

XIV

The Reviewer

FOR almost the whole of his literary life Muir worked as a reviewer. From 1924 to 1928 he reviewed regularly for *The Nation and The Athenaeum*, dealing mainly with fiction, sometimes with as many as ten books at a time in less than a thousand words. From 1933 to 1945 he was the chief fiction reviewer of *The Listener*, writing about once a fortnight usually of three books in about fifteen hundred words; and for most of this time he was contributing also to *The Scotsman* about once a month. Later he reviewed fairly regularly for *The Observer*, and less often for *The New Statesman*. He contributed occasional reviews to many other periodicals. Altogether he must have written about a thousand reviews, dealing with more than twice that number of books, usually at the rate of about one a fortnight, in the years 1935 to 1939 about one a week.

All this work was less irksome to him than one might expect. In the early days he did complain, in a letter to Sydney Schiff, of the impossibility of doing a proper job of criticism within the limits imposed. "One can only give a caricature of one's raw impressions". Even in a two-thousand word article "one is forced to be either grotesquely one-sided and convey an unjust impression of one's author, or . . . say nothing about him at all except what everybody knows. The métier is grotesquely impossible. . . ."[1] But later he complained remarkably little about the reviewing. He was bored at times by having to read so many mediocre books; but the actual work of reviewing came easy to him. He was able to make up his mind about a book with great speed and sureness, and to express a balanced opinion in few words. His own later work is the best disproof of his contention that in a short review or article it is necessary to be one-sided or banal. Except when too hard pressed he

[1] E. M. to Schiff, 18 Aug. 1924.

was able to combine criticism with creation. What did dry him up as a creator was worry. In London in 1948, too unsettled to do any creative work but wanting something to occupy his mind, he was positively glad when asked to review for *The Observer*, though he did not urgently need the money at the time. Later he was sorry that absence in America had temporarily lost him his regular niche in that paper. So perhaps one need be less sorry for him about the reviewing than one is at first inclined to be. It was work which he did for a living, and was modestly content to do. It was a sad waste that he did not have more time for his poetry and for critical works on a larger scale; but it is better to salute his achievements than to indulge regrets. He served the readers and writers of his generation well, and some of his reviews are well worth preserving. Sometimes he gave a better balanced assessment of a writer in a review of a single early work than some later critics have done when surveying that writer's whole oeuvre.

The best way to give an idea of the quality of his reviews is to quote a substantial part of one of them rather than just to select snippets. In the first week of March 1939 he had a batch of fiction to review for *The Listener*—a routine weekly task, performed at a time of private (his wife's illness) and public anxiety. One of the books was by an established author, one of his favourites, and he might well have been forgiven if he had concentrated mainly on it. But there was also a first novel by a completely unknown writer, whose quality, even in this immature work, he immediately recognised. He wrote:

> There are two ways of portraying life: from the outside and from the inside. In the first case the writer produces a surface or a crystallisation, something that can be surveyed or seized. In the second he follows a process, or flows watchfully with a flux, coming to the surface now and then when the process relaxes or when it becomes so urgent that it shoots him up for a moment of terrified relief. Miss I. Compton-Burnett's latest novel, *A Family and a Fortune*, is an admirable example of the first kind, and *Happy Valley*, by Patrick White, of the second. *Happy Valley* is a first novel, and a remarkable one; it deals at length and sometimes brilliantly with a province which Miss

Compton-Burnett touches only in an indirect way; and it has a vivid, troubled surface produced by innumerable bright points, moments of relief caught from the flux. Where it is behind Miss Compton-Burnett's novel is simply in differentiation. A writer determined to show us the inside of life finds himself presently wandering in one vast, uncharted Inside which belongs to none of his characters in particular but to them all generally; this happened to D. H. Lawrence and it has happened in a lesser degree to Mr Joyce. Appearance is differentiation; character is differentiation; and a surface is necessary for the portrayal of character, as it is necessary for the mere matter of existing. When a writer concentrates on the inside of life, thinking that the final reality is there, he throws away one half of reality, or rather discards the condition which makes real things possible at all: their embodiment in individual and unique forms. This is to put the case too strongly. There are characters, that is to say individuals, in *Happy Valley*, but the more securely Mr White gets inside them, the more they tend to become one character; whereas Miss Compton-Burnett's characters become more definitely themselves the longer we know them. And in the end, without deserting the surface, we know most of what is happening inside them.

After a long paragraph on *A Family and a Fortune* he returns to Mr White:

Happy Valley deals with the life of a small Australian town, and contains a great number of characters, all of whom are seen from the inside. The great merit of the book is its closeness to the hidden, instinctive life of the characters; its weakness is its too obvious derivation from Lawrence and Mr Joyce. It moves on two levels; one of genuine powerful imagination, and the other of impromptu fancy. At its best the writing is very good indeed. . . . But at other times it can be full of echoes:

> Hilda Halliday was almost forty. Oliver was thirty-four. But they were happy, she said. Sitting on the seat in the Botanical Gardens, in the warm smell of Moreton Bay figs, he said he would write a poem. She was wearing a yellow hat that made her look slightly pale. And of course Rodney was pale, he took after her, not Oliver, and it was not anaemia as everyone said.

To get a meaning into thought-associations—and Mr White

s

deals at length with thought-associations—one has to impose a pattern upon them, and the pattern is always artificial, an aesthetic design, convincing merely as an arrangement. That day in the Botanical Gardens when Dr Halliday said he was going to write a poem is an integral part of his wife's thought-association pattern, and for most of the other characters there is a corresponding motif, which has to recur so that the pattern may exist. The result is a kind of mechanical spontaneity reached by an enormous simplification. This applies, however, only to Mr White's method, which weighs heavily on the book. He is clearly a writer of unusual imagination, with a substantial grasp of things, and a sense of pity which goes far beyond conventional pity. Only one or two of the characters are really individualised; they are felt than rather outlined, but they are felt with intensity. There are touches quite beyond the usual, as when a wretched school-teacher's life seems to be typified as he sits miserably tapping a bad egg with his spoon. This touch is far better than the murder scene which follows, and it is in such crystallisations of misery that Mr White shows he is an original writer.

Muir shows here his ability to respond at once to new merit without being blinded by it, to give a balanced assessment, and to combine general reflections about literature and life with detailed, though not niggling, criticism. His criticism was well balanced, but he did not hedge. About Mr White's next book, *The Living and the Dead*, he committed himself unreservedly: "To read it is an experience resembling one's first experience of the work of Joyce and Lawrence; it is of the same order; it has the same unexpectedness; and one feels that it may turn out to be even more significant. . . . He creates independent characters and keeps intact the balance between them."[2] This was in 1941, long before Mr White's stature was widely acknowledged.

His taste was unusually catholic. Writing of T. S. Eliot's early criticism he said that it was the best of his generation (a compliment which Eliot later returned), but that it would be better still "if it were compatible with an appreciation of the importance of Milton as well as of Marlowe, of Wordsworth as well as of Dryden, in the English poetic tradition. Until it is,

[2] *Listener*, 31 Jul. 1941.

it will have a faint but damaging, and altogether misleading, resemblance to the criticism of a school."[3] Muir's criticism was never that of a school. At the same time it was not just amiably eclectic. He could write with witty asperity, especially about fashionable writers he thought overrated.

What he looked for above all was evidence of imaginative vision, of ability to see life whole and in proper proportion. In L. H. Myers' *Pool of Vishnu* he praised the "consistent effort to see life completely. This is not the same thing as to see it in detail, though detail is the subject-matter of every pattern; it is rather to be aware of the factors that make up human life and to give to each its due importance; for a complete picture of life depends finally on a just evaluation of the things which constitute life, not on observation however miscellaneous."[4] Writing of Neil Gunn's *The Serpent* he traced the typical development of a writer of true imagination. "At the beginning we find vivid flashes of insight into this or that province of experience." Later a semblance of indecisiveness may appear, produced "by the writer's struggle to use in one book all the potentialities of imagination which he has employed in different books at different times." Finally the writer may achieve maturity. "The effect of imaginative maturity is to make you feel that everything you are shown is in its proper place and on its true scale."[5] The mature imaginative writer is the true realist in that he is able to see life whole and to see things in their proper proportion in a way that the superficial "realist" who sees only details cannot do. To see life whole it is necessary to experience it fully, and then to distance it, to achieve a certain objectivity. "Distance is, I think, the condition of all art."[6] "In every act of creation personality is transcended."[7] Ivy Compton-Burnett was close to "life", and remote from "events".[8]

"The test of a good novel is the extent to which the imaginative element interpenetrates everything",[9] he wrote. He had a strong sense of form, judging always from within, not by

[3] *Calendar of Modern Letters*, May 1925.   [4] *Listener*, 1 Aug. 1940.
[5] *Scots Magazine*, August 1943.   [6] E. M. to Schiff, 14 Jan. 1925.
[7] *New Age*, 8 Mar. 1923.   [8] *Listener*, 10 Feb. 1944.
[9] *Listener*, 29 Jul. 1943.

narrow pre-conceived notions. He was always sympathetic to writers seeking new forms to express a genuine vision, but was not deceived by modish innovators.

In contrast to works of imagination are propaganda ("propagandist poetry is essentially rhetoric, and rhetoric is an instrument of the will, not of the imagination"[10]), confession, and works made up merely of detached observations or informed by a narrow vision of life ("to see life as sensation is to see it with a long and steady first glance".[11]) In Hemingway's *For Whom the Bell Tolls:*

> The love scenes are minutely described, but they are all on the level of naturalism, and very little can be said about love on the level of naturalism, where love is merely sensation. "Every time Robert Jordan looked at her he could feel a thickness in his throat". This is one way of expressing emotion, but Romeo and Antony would not have thought of saying that they felt a thickness in their throats; they had so much more to say. The thickness in the throat is a cousin of the lump in the throat; and if the lover remains at this point, he has to fill the ensuing silence with some sort of sentimentality. The great fault of Mr Hemingway's description of love, thoroughgoing as it is in its sensuality, is sentimentality and prettiness.[12]

But, though Hemingway's characters live only on the plane of sensation and instinct, they do have this limited amount of life, and Hemingway tries to tell the truth as far as he sees it. In his mature criticism Muir's greatest asperity is reserved not for the shallow "realists", but for those who seemed to him pretentious, those whose supposed imaginative vision seemed to him false. Of Charles Morgan's *Sparkenbroke* he wrote: "A genuine belief in immortality cannot be expressed in such an accent of petulant superiority". The three chief characters are presented "in a smoothly oiled style which is securely padded against the impact of experience".[13] Yet he tried to be fair even to this, one of his least favourite writers, and reviewed *The Voyage* and *The Empty Room* rather more favourably.

His fairness is seen in his treatment of best-selling writers

[10] *New Statesman*, 21 Dec. 1940.   [11] *Listener*, 18 Nov. 1936.
[12] *Listener*, 27 Mar. 1941.   [13] *Listener*, 29 Apr. 1936.

whom high-brow critics are apt to regard with sneering superiority. For instance he did not think Hugh Walpole's novels successful as wholes, finding them amorphous; but he saw a "strange subterranean imagination" in Walpole's ability to evoke Cornelius' hidden world in *John Cornelius*,[14] an undeniable insight into evil in *The Sea Tower*,[15] and in *The Blind Man's House*[16] "flashes of genius, as there are in almost all his books when he writes of innocence or evil, children or curious vice".

It is the business of the critic to discriminate, and Muir distinguishes clearly between the greater and the lesser; but he did not think that critical rigour demands that those who come short of greatness should be treated with reprobation. For instance, reviewing the first of C. P. Snow's series of novels *Strangers and Brothers*, he gave a more balanced account of Snow than some have given who have had the whole series to judge by. It "lacks the final grace of imagination, intimacy, but it is the work of a man of wide intelligence and sympathy, and on a level of its own . . . displays the remaining qualities of imagination with freedom and skill. . . ." The whole work "will diagnose the historical wounds of the last two decades without perhaps touching the wound of life itself, which possesses the imagination of Mr. Joyce. . . . He enters sympathetically into these young hopes, as Bennett did, but with a disillusioned pity which Bennett did not know."[17] Of another author who has often been written about in an intemperate manner by both detractors and admirers, Edith Sitwell, Muir wrote always in a well balanced way, finding in her *I Live Under a Black Sun* both "exact and powerful imagination" and "loose and idiosyncratic fancy".[18]

When dealing with fashionable writers he sometimes saw merits quite other than those which were being currently praised. In the mid 'fifties when Mr Empson was regarded as the forerunner of the "Movement" poets and was praised for his intellectual control, Muir reviewed an anthology of recent poetry. "One begins to suspect," he wrote, "that most

---

[14] *Listener*, 22 Sep. 1937.   [15] *Listener*, 12 Oct. 1939.
[16] *Listener*, 2 Oct. 1941.   [17] *Listener*, 26 Dec. 1940.
[18] *Listener*, 29 Sep. 1937.

of the younger poets are content to do the lesser thing neatly rather than attempt the greater thing clumsily." But Empson he found quite different. He "moves one by the spectacle of a shocking struggle for control. In his followers the control is almost complete."[19] Empson wrote to him: "I was really grateful today for what you wrote about me in *The Observer* because it seems true to me and is so unlike what everybody else says. I keep getting caught in some bar and scolded as the ancestral pedant who made all the modern boys as dry as the bones in the valley."

Near the end of his life a young American writer wrote to Muir to thank him for being one of the very few people who "have been willing to take the trouble to see what my stories are about." In his criticism he did much more than that of course; but it is enough to distinguish him from most reviewers to say that he always did at least that—took the trouble to see what the author was trying to do and then told his readers about the work rather than crowing about himself. He had the intimate understanding of literature of a creator combined with unusual detachment. Creators have been the greatest critics, but some have been biased—by need to shake off influences that might be harmful to them, or by special attachment to writers from whom they could learn, or by their own practice. As Muir wrote: "James deduced his canons of prose fiction from his own practice as a novelist, Coleridge his canons of poetry from his immense knowledge of, and profound sympathy for, poetry in general."[20] Muir had his favourites, and was sometimes over-indulgent to young writers in whom he saw promise. But I can think of no important writer of his time of whom he wrote, whom he failed to treat with sympathetic understanding—however far the writer's practice and beliefs were from his own. T. S. Eliot was surely right in thinking Muir's criticism of the best of our time.

[19] *Observer*, 14 Oct. 1956.   [20] *Scotsman*, 29 Apr. 1935.

XV

Last Years

I

AFTER a few days in London the Muirs crossed to New York by sea, and were established early in September in the Hotel Continental, Cambridge, Massachusetts, which was to be their base throughout their stay in America. Their happy expectations were in some ways more than fulfilled. They found the hospitality warm, considerate and not too insistent. They made friends, and enjoyed much good talk and laughter. America "has great merits and obvious ones", he wrote, "more charity, I think, than we have, hope that fills me with astonishment, with alarm, and faith—there I get quite lost."[1] And yet he felt it to be a very strange place—one that he could not understand nor feel quite at home in. Increasingly he felt a longing to get back to Europe, especially to Orkney.

His impressions are best given in his own words in letters to friends. In September he wrote to Kenneth Wood:

> Here all is still strange and rich, rich and strange. Everyone is kind . . . I found the New Yorkers abrupt and sardonic (at least they looked sardonic), but in Cambridge, and I should say in Boston, they are more urbane and leisurely, though the streams of cars, I'm sorry to say, roar through the rustic looking streets: what a charming place it must have been fifty years ago.

He had met the poets, Donald Hall and Richard Wilbur, and commented on how much America does for its young poets. In December he wrote to George Brown:

> We like this place and we like the people. We met Robert Frost the other night; he is 82 and makes one feel quite young: I felt he was a great and wise man—I don't think I have met any one else who ever gave me so clearly that feeling. His mother was of Orkney stock, and he is interested in Orkney.

---

[1] E. M. to Raine, 28 Feb. 1956.

When they met at parties Frost would take him by the arm and talk of "we Orkneymen".

By the following spring his sense both of the kindness of the people and of the strangeness, the to him alien nature of the country, had increased. He wrote to George Brown:

> The Cambridge people, the Harvard professors, are almost the kindest lot, I think, I have ever met. . . . There is great urbanity of manners, great insistence on custom; when you are invited out for supper the table is always lit by candles (I found that very pleasant), and when supper is over the ladies retire, and the men sit over their wine a while longer. Not what I expected at all, but we are told that Harvard and Cambridge are not like the rest of America. . . . In spite of all the kindness, and lots of good conversation, I would not live in this country for good; it is not my atmosphere, and Willa feels the same. But why it remains so strange to us I cannot tell.

He went some way towards explaining the strangeness in a letter to Kathleen Raine:

> I know I have been writing some very queer poetry since I came, with a good deal of new horror in it; why, Heaven alone knows, for every one here has been extraordinarily kind, and considerate at the same time. But I am not at home here . . . I was far more at home in Italy. You say that for poetry Cambridge [England] is a spiritual desert, but I want the landscape, the soil . . ., things shaped by generations with affection and made into a human scene. I shall try to get up to Orkney this summer if it can be managed at all. I suppose what is wrong with me here is that I am hungry. Horrible thought: I don't know whether Eden was ever here.

He had not taken his Shakespeare to America, but found that he could not bear to be without it, and bought another copy—a symptom of his need to keep in touch with his roots in the past and in Europe.

His duties as Norton Professor were confined to giving six lectures, three in December and three in March; they were warmly received. He twice visited New York, where he saw Djuna Barnes and advised her about the revision of her play, *The Antiphon*. (He was a great admirer of her novel *Nightwood* and of *The Antiphon*—as was T. S. Eliot, who told me that having published her work was one of the things he was most proud of in his career as a publisher. Eliot quoted Muir's appreciation of these as an example of his genius for seeing merit in unusual work which some people were inclined to deride.) He travelled a good deal to give lectures and readings of his poems—to Washington more than once, to Bryn Mawr, to Chicago and to colleges in Connecticut. He was not altogether at ease on the public platform, having a small, though pleasing, voice, and being incapable of self-dramatisation. But even those who heard only his public lectures and readings were impressed by his sincerity and modesty. It was on smaller and more intimate occasions that he came into his own. In spite of his shyness he was able to convert acquaintanceship into friendship with unusual speed. Several of those who met him in America remember him as one of the best and most remarkable men they have ever known.

While in America he wrote, apart from the lectures, a few reviews and critical articles for *The Observer* and other periodicals and about as much poetry as he usually did in the time. In February 1956 he told Kathleen Raine that he had written eight or nine poems, "mostly from lines that came when I was wakening in the morning. There is no knowing when such things will come, or where." He had just got her *Collected Poems* for review. "What strikes me again is the absoluteness of vision in them; I don't know of any one else who has it, or maintains it in its purity. I depend myself too much on invention, which is a weakness." I suppose he means here that, though the initial inspiration for a poem "came" to him, he then had to work at it with the conscious mind, to invent, more than he imagined she had to. Sometimes poems did come to him almost complete and without difficulty, but this was evidently not so with these American ones, with which he was not on the whole very pleased, speaking of them as dull.

Poems certainly arising from experiences in America include "The Church", "Salem, Massachusetts" and "The Poet". The last of these "started from something a Harvard student said. She had attended a lecture of Ivor Richards, and he had set off on one of those wonderful inspired passages of his, so

that the poor girl was left, as she told me, and as she told him,
'in bewilderment'. And his reply to her struck me as very fine,
and seems to have struck her too: 'That's splendid. That's
where one should start!' But the poem is not at all equal to
that."[2] He was not satisfied with this poem, and it was not
published in his lifetime. He thought it too abstract, "only a
note for what might turn into a poem, as I see it now. I think
if I found an 'objective correlative', it would come to life; and
I think I have found one, the poet Hölderlin in his half-mad
prophetic phase. There is something in Plato's idea of 'divine
madness', in Shakespeare's too, and Hölderlin is the great
modern representative figure. But the poem, if it comes off,
will be a different poem."[3] He did not live to write this
"different poem", but the one we have is a moving final
statement in verse of his beliefs about poetry. The poet tells
more than he knows; the true poem incarnates—in a tiny
way paralleling the Incarnation—meanings which cannot be
fully stated.

"After a Hypothetical War" was probably written in
America. It paints a much less hopeful picture than the
earlier "Horses" of the possible state of humanity after an
atomic war. Instead of a reconciliation between the survivors
and the animals and the earth, there is a loss of all order. The
purblind peasant squats, elbows out

> To nudge his neighbour from his inch of ground

and

> Soil and air breed crookedly here, and men
> Are dumb and twisted as the envious scrub
> That spreads in silent malice on the fields.

This poem was followed in his few remaining years by others
expressing vividly a sense of horror at the dangers confronting
humanity. The greater prominence of this note of horror in
the poems of his last years may have something to do with his
stay in America, where there are both a greater sense of faith
and hope in the future than in Britain and a greater sense of

---

[2] E. M. to Janet Adam Smith, 22 Sep. 1956.
[3] E. M. to Adam Smith, 26 Sep. 1956.

danger. The pressure of the machine and of mass society on the individual is more keenly felt. Living in America would naturally turn one's thoughts towards the future.

Muir's Harvard lectures were published, as *The Estate of Poetry*, in 1962. He spent some time during his last years revising them, but was never satisfied with them. He was a tired man. The style has not the wit nor the brilliance of his earlier prose. Nevertheless the lectures are moving because of their very simplicity, because of his evident desire to express his central convictions about poetry without any parade of cleverness or learning. Poetry was once a general possession, not just for the few; and so it should be. For imagination is a faculty which belongs to us all, in however fragmentary a degree; it is "that power by which we apprehend living beings and living creatures in their individuality, as they live and move, and not as ideas or categories". Imagination "makes us understand human life vividly and intimately in ourselves because we have felt it in others".[4] The gulf which has opened between the poet and ordinary people is bad for both. Imagination decays, and the poet's scope is narrowed. "For it is clear that the more wide-reaching the imaginative world of poetry is, the greater will be the audience it wins"; and, conversely, "the smaller and more select the audience for poetry, the more the poet will be confined." He writes in a vacuum, "through which no warmth from the great world outside penetrates, whereas in happier ages the sustaining warmth, the atmosphere of expectation, was there".[5] The divorce between poet and public is evidenced, and worsened, by a kind of criticism which gives the impression that a poem is something to be analysed and not to be enjoyed. Wordsworth did something to bridge the gap by returning to sources, to incidents and situations of common life and to the earth itself, and Yeats by making himself into a public man and a public poet. Perhaps the audience will increase if poets will attempt greater themes; "for great themes have to be stated clearly".[6] Poets must resist the temptation to turn inwards, "to lock themselves into a hygienic prison where they speak only to one another, and to the critic, their stern warder. In the end a poet must create

---

[4] *E. P.*, p. 81.   [5] *E. P.*, pp. 23, 24.   [6] *E. P.*, p. 93.

his audience, and to do that he must turn outward".[7] This does not, of course, mean that he must seek popularity by compromise. His responsibility is "to preserve a true image of life. If the image is true, poetry fulfills its end. Anything that distorts the image, any tendency to oversimplify or soften it so that it may be more acceptable to a greater number of people, falsifies it, degrades those for whom it is intended, and cannot set us free".[8] Poetry, if it were to resume its natural estate, could help to set us free, to keep us human, to communicate as persons.

Muir himself felt keenly his isolation as a poet during most of his writing career; and he welcomed the sustaining warmth that came to him in his last years from even the limited amount of appreciation that he received. He did not, like Yeats, seek to become a public man and a public poet; nor did he, like Wordsworth, often treat of incidents and situations of common life. He had to write the kind of poetry that he could. But he did write of great themes, clearly and in plain language, without over-simplification and without pretentious obscurity. "Poetry," he had written long before, "is concerned in my mind with great themes, and is the response of the individual mind to those at the few moments when it is raised above itself."[9] His conception of poetry, and his practice as a poet, were influenced by his affection for the ballads. One of his last, as several of his first, poems was a ballad; but it was not in the direct imitations that the influence of the ballads was most fruitful. Though more reflective and less dramatic than the ballads his poetry has something in common with them—in its timelessness, its combination of passion and impersonality, its use of simple language and metre and of archetypal characters, its spareness. It preserves a true image of life by keeping things in due proportion; and it appeals, more than that of most modern poets, beyond the narrow circle of those who are interested in poetry as such.

II

During his last months in America, Muir was longing to get back to Europe, and especially to that place where for him

[7] *E. P.*, p. 109.   [8] *E. P.*, p. 108.   [9] E. M. to Schiff, 6 Oct. 1924.

Eden had been. Before leaving Scotland he had discussed with Robin Richardson of the B.B.C. the idea of revisiting Orkney and writing a script on it. He wrote to Richardson in April: "I would love to drink the Orkney air this summer, and refresh myself with the old life and the old scenes: I have never felt this desire so strongly before. If it could be in mid-summer, with the unending light, it would be a wonderful comfort." He would have liked to have gone straight on to Orkney on arrival in England at the end of May, but the business of finding a house had first to be attended to. With the help of friends a suitable house was found quickly—at Swaffham Prior near Cambridge; and the Muirs flew to Orkney at the end of June, and stayed there three weeks. After the vastness of America the smallness, homeliness and security of Orkney and the leisured tempo of life were more than ever welcome. There had been many changes since his boyhood. The land was far more productive, the people more prosperous; on the other hand mass communications had to some extent reduced the distinctiveness of the speech and of the local culture in general. He did not indulge any sentimental regrets over change, but in his script for the B.B.C. stressed the positive achievements of the past fifty years and his renewed delight in the unchanging things—in the beauty of the islands themselves and of the light, in the faces of the people and their musical, unassertive voices. He spent much time just sitting on a bench in the main street of Kirkwall watching people as they passed. "These faces still look as if they were fashioned from an archetypal racial mould, the high cheek-bones, the eyes widely set and as if they were looking into great distances —perhaps the horizon which always draws one's eyes in Orkney: the expression is one of extraordinary purity, the purity of sight itself. You find it in the eyes of women both old and young; it gazes out of quite young faces and more startlingly out of the concentric wrinkles of the old, the eyes apparently quite unchanged by age, or perhaps grown still clearer by looking for so long at distant horizons." The voices, he wrote, have a kinship with those of the Western Highlands and the Hebrides, "an intonation that seems to be asking an implicit question and making a statement while inviting an answer: not voices for laying down a dogma or clinching an argument to bring conversation to an uncomfortable end. These are the voices which in the dark Orkney winters, for century after century, kept talk and stories going for hours at a stretch while the family and the neighbours sat round the ingle. . . . It is a kind of voice that can take its time". He went to Wyre and saw his old home, The Bu. Above all he enjoyed evenings of talk and music in farm kitchens, where he would prompt his hosts to repeat old stories and to sing the old ballads. On one such evening he tried to recapture his skill on the accordion, but ruefully had to admit that he had lost the knack. He was able, however, to sing from memory verses from the ballad, "Sir James the Rose". Memories were revived of earlier occasions when the talk had gone on through the night.

> I remember years ago being taken to a farm-house one evening about ten o'clock. My wife and I were led into a roomy kitchen where there seemed to be a great many people sitting in a ring. There were the farmer and his wife, a beautiful woman, and their grown-up sons and daughters, and young people from the neighbouring farms. My wife and I were taken into the ring with many welcomes to Orkney. Then after a while we saw a big bowl filled with home-brewed ale coming towards us from hand to hand. We drank and passed it on. Then another bowl of the black ale heaved up. It passed, and a third came and went by: three black moons calmly revolving. We talked, accepted and passed on the dark bowl; the light slowly faded but still lingered; time went past and yet seemed to stand still; and when at last we broke up morning was there. . . . There was no drunkenness that evening, no raised tipsy voices, but only talk and pleasant companionship.

He was not sure whether such nights were still spent in Orkney, and in any case was not fit for such sustained, even if moderate, drinking, and returned to Kirkwall by the light of the setting rather than the rising sun. His friend and Newbattle pupil Ernest Marwick remembers driving home with him on one evening of extraordinary beauty. Great shadows lay on Rousay; the gold light of the setting sun fell on the hills of the

West Mainland and glinted on the sea in a track that led from the shore right over Wideford Hill. Visibly much moved he said: "Ernest, we are poets; but where have we words for that?"

In the autumn the Muirs settled in to their new home; it was in a sense their first, in that it was the first house which they owned. His good salary at Harvard had enabled him to save enough to buy it. This was not the end of the help he got from America; for he had been awarded by the Bollingen Foundation a grant of three thousand dollars a year for three years to enable him to work on a book on ballads.

Swaffham Prior is a very pleasant village, set in rich agricultural land about six miles from Cambridge. Priory Cottage is a charming small house, going back to the fifteenth century, with lots of old heavy gnarled beams, well and not conspicuously modernised. It is in the main street, and the village shop was next door. The houses run down one side of the road only; opposite, the ground slopes up to two knolls on which are two churches, both with partly ruined towers, one damaged by lightning long ago, the other by time. One is a Norman tower, the other a Perpendicular of the fifteenth century. "So," he wrote to Ernest Marwick, "nobody over-looks us but these two venerable presences. . . . I am looking at the two towers as I write; as I cannot have the Castle in Wyre to look at they must serve me instead. I have become very fond of them."[10] One of the churches, that of St Cyriac, has associations even older than the Norman Conquest; for the original church on the site had been given, he was told, to the Abbey of Ely by Byrhtnoth, Alderman of Essex, the hero of *The Battle of Maldon*. Behind the house is a small walled garden; so they could enjoy privacy as well as the advantages of living in a village among kind neighbours. Their first winter there was a mild one, and all his letters speak of his delight in bird song. He had a strong sense of the sacredness of common things, and delighted in the house, and in being able to give visitors to lunch vegetables grown in their own garden. One of the reasons he was not more strongly drawn to any Church was perhaps that he had a sense of ritual in

[10] E. M. to Marwick, 10 Dec. 1956.

ordinary life, of any meal taken together being an affirming of
life together:

> This that I give and take,
> This that I keep and break,
> Is and is not my own
> But lives in itself alone,
> Yet is between us two,
> Mine only in the breaking,
> It all in the remaking,
> Doing what I undo.

It was a pleasant retreat, and their pleasure in it was
marred only by ill health. He suffered from pains in the chest,
caused, a Harvard doctor had told him, by false angina. "The
angina may be false, but the pains are real", he wrote. ' She
was rather crippled by arthritis, and he was worried by the
fact that she had to do the cooking—there was no room for a
maid, even if they could have got one. In an article[11] Mr
Bernard Gill has given an impression of how the newcomers
looked to their neighbours—"a pale delicate-looking, unassum-
ing man with silvery hair, and his wife, also white-haired but
of a ruddy complexion, who walked slowly, bent over a stick.
When she sat down her stoop vanished and she looked ten
years younger." They seldom went further than the garden,
but their son could be seen striding over the fen droves or the
lanes that go over the chalk ridge to Newmarket Heath.
(Deafness prevented his early promise as a musician being
realised, and he has used his other talent, in mathematics, for
scientific work.) Their apparent ingenuousness over the every-
day affairs of life aroused the protective instincts of neighbours,
who began to run errands for them, do odd jobs in the house
and garden and give seedlings and cuttings for the garden. At
Christmas the Gills had a small party to which the Muirs came.
Her frailty was only of the body. She was still a brilliant
raconteur, delighting the company by the vividness of her
stories of people they had known. He was content to be quiet,
expanding mainly on his childhood days. Talk turned to song,
and "Willa, with flushed face and tousled hair (she had
rumpled it in mimicking the oddities of a well-known writer

[11] *Western Humanities Review*, vol. xiv, no. 3 (Summer 1960).

and dramatist) began to sing Victorian music-hall songs. 'Oh, Flo, why do you go Riding about in your motor car?', 'Jolly good luck to the lass that loves a sailor', 'It's the soldiers of the Queen me lad', and 'Ta, ra, ra, ra, *boom* de-ay'." Edwin contributed "in a voice soft, gentle and low, 'After the ball was over'. How like his verse-forms," Gill thought, "is his voice!—muted, yet compelling."

Friends, especially John Holloway and Kathleen Raine, came sometimes from Cambridge; and old Newbattle students and others came occasionally from further afield. But they had less social life than in the past, and were content that it should be so. To one visitor he spoke of one of his earliest love poems to his wife, "The Confirmation", which he seemed to regard with special affection. Years had added further confirmation to what he had said in it.

Honours came—in 1957 the Russell Loines award for Poetry from the American Academy of Arts and Letters, and in 1958 an Honorary Doctorate of Letters from Cambridge to add to those already awarded by Prague, Edinburgh and Rennes. Reviews, articles and letters from admirers showed that his poems were now more justly and widely appreciated on both sides of the Atlantic than before. Honours sat lightly upon him, but with true modesty he acknowledged to Bernard Gill that the greater appreciation of his work gave him immense satisfaction. I remember myself the warmth of his response to a few stumbling words of admiration I said to him about *One Foot in Eden* when he came to Edinburgh; I was moved that a famous man should seem to value a few words from a stranger of no special importance.

But he had no wish merely to bask in his pleasant retreat in the glow of honours obtained by past work; nor was he in a position to do so. His savings had all gone into the house, and he had had to ask for an advance from one of his publishers in order to furnish it. The Bollingen award would last only for three years (as far as he knew, that is; in fact it was transferred after his death to Mrs Muir, who has written the book on the ballads, which he was not able to do). He still had to think of making a living and saving for old age. For the first time since 1942 he was without any work other than writing,

T

and was, as he wrote to T. S. Eliot, rather daunted by this. "I confess that sometimes I have a slightly sinking feeling, knowing that now I have nothing to do but write, and must depend upon it. But I feel that it will be all right."[12] He started to collect ideas for his ballad book, but his health was not strong enough for the sustained effort required for a long work. He left nothing in writing, and the book which Mrs Muir has written is entirely hers. He continued nearly to the end to review, at the rate of about one review a fortnight, for *The Observer* and *The New Statesman*, and to write and plan poems. Those late reviews have not quite the verve and the wit of his earlier prose, but show his keen sensitivity, his fairness and integrity as plainly as ever. Until late in 1958 he reviewed poetry for *The New Statesman*, and then wrote to his friend Janet Adam Smith, the literary editor: "I am beginning to acquire qualms about reviewing poetry; I feel it difficult, I feel I do not do it well, and finally I feel that my criticisms are of no use to the young poets and are of no guidance to those who may wish to read their work. I am out of touch and sympathy with nine-tenths of the new poetry, and obviously I am not the man for the job."[13] Yet he had shown considerable sympathy for the younger poets, and ability to appreciate them. Earlier he had written to Janet Adam Smith about an anthology of modern poetry which he was not looking forward to reviewing; he had found little to inspire him in it, "yet," he went on, "I feel a certain sympathy for these young people, though they are so cautious and, so it seems to me, so sad, and so careful not to hope.   strange generation; I wonder sometimes if something unique may come out of it yet".[14] He regretted the absence of joy, of a sense of glory from the new poetry, but was not inclined to blame the poets. He was quick to respond when he did find the qualities he most admired, and to praise merit even in work he did not much like. When he could find nothing to praise he preferred to remain silent. In *The Observer* he reviewed criticism and miscellaneous prose, and occasionally fiction. He could still write sharply, especially about established writers. After reading

[12] E. M. to Eliot, 17 Oct. 1956.   [13] E. M. to Adam Smith, 24 Oct. 1958.
[14] E. M. to Adam Smith, 26 Sep. 1956.

Faulkner's *The Tower* he wondered "how a writer so super-latively good as Mr Faulkner can be so catastrophically bad." Much of the academic criticism he found wearisome since the writers in expounding ideas tended to ignore the poetry. Appropriately one of his very last reviews was of a new edition of Thomas Traherne. Of the third and greatest of the *Centuries of Meditation*, which describes the recovery of innocence, he wrote: "Traherne returned with the knowledge, gained by experience, that his happiness could not be complete until he became aware of it, as a child cannot; until he knew that the beauty of the world, revealed in his first years, should be shared with all mankind, and realised that this is the will of God, who made the world for our entertainment and pleasure." He himself too had had to lose his early vision in order that, in recovering it, he might be able to share it.

For deeper insight into his mind during his last years we must turn, as always, to the poetry. In view of the inner serenity he had attained it is surprising, and admirable, that his late poems should contain so much darkness. The conflicts are now not in himself, but observed in others and in the world in general. Unusually he was able to experience the latter as vividly as he had the former. He remained open to the dark-ness as to the light—to the horror of present tyranny and of possible atomic war; could enter the nightmare state of those without knowledge of Eden, for whom the world is empty, meaningless and soulless; could look into hell—not a super-natural hell, but

> The secret universe of the blind

a state in which we are

> Shut from ourselves even in our mind.

Two very powerful poems "After 1984" and "The Strange Return" deal with this state and the possibility of a way out from it—not into a supernatural heaven, but into the strangely familiar world of ordinary life. The alternatives are immediate, are *here*—an ordinary, good, *human* order, and a state of alienation for the individual and of tyranny in society. The enemies are not only the wielders of pitiless power, but also the cynical nihilists, those who

> Crack a dry witticism on sin,

those who degrade the image of man, the purveyors of "murdering lies".

A small notebook, marked "Dreams and Diary Items" shows the origin of some poems. In November 1957 he wrote in his note-book:

> Dreams in the last few weeks. Dream of the watchers in a dark place (coming on the words somewhere, "The Well of Life", I have associated them with that, though the words came later, in some poem or other in a book). Except for the watchers, all was deep darkness, and I could see only their faces, which were lighted by a brilliant beam of light: a horizontal beam which lighted the heads only, all else above them and below in complete darkness. It seemed to be an underworld, and how the beam of light came, and from what source I did not know. The faces strongly radiant, serene, almost indifferent, hard to describe: "indifferent" a too cruel word for them, for there was a sort of hidden tenderness. No, I cannot catch the expression, very beautiful. Radiance above all, unearthly.
>
> Sometime later, another dream. Of a woman, or muse, or sibyl, speaking, it seemed, of human life, but in a dark and very spacious place. The story she told was great and elevated, uttered with solemnity. I thought of her as very tall, her voice of more than human volume, yet easy and full. On wakening I could not remember what she said, but thought it told of our life from birth to death, a great story, with nothing small or mean. I have associated it since with the Well of Life dream, and fancied to myself that this was how she would have begun her story, and that the rest of it would have been told in the same spirit, exalted and mysterious, to the end. Perhaps this is contrivance, but it might help. I've reflected since that, seen in this way, humour and irony are mere devices to hide the real nature of our life, which is infinitely serious and real, and a great event.

He at one time meant to use these dreams for a poem on

Lazarus. In notes for the poem he wrote: "Lazarus, in his return to life, as it were has second birth, remembers being with the guardians of the Well of Life. The child does not see them though they are there, his eyes being shut." The poem would have gone on to convey Lazarus' feelings on his return to ordinary life. He would have had something of the freshness of a child's vision combined with the knowledge of maturity. But the poem was never written, and the dreams were used instead for the final section of one of his last great poems, "The Last War". In the first three sections of this poem he gives a frightening imaginative impression of what it might feel like to be involved in an atomic war. One thing which will distinguish such a war from all previous ones is that fear of total annihilation will take away the hope, which all earlier generations have had, of life continuing into some possibly better future. If all are to die there will be no possibility of bravery and self-sacrifice, and no meaning in the deaths which are to be the seed of no future. He then turns to the present, and finds in it reason for both hope and fear. In "all that is full-grown/In nature, and all that is with hands well made" he sees "the harmony/By which we know our own and the world's health". He sees also sickness, both in natural things when neglected and in people:

> A tree thin sick and pale by a north wall,
> A smile splintering a face—
> I saw them today, suddenly made aware
> That ordinary sights appal. . . .

If we could translate the harmony and fruitfulness seen in a harvest field and in art into terms of our social life, atomic war would be prevented; but so far we have not, have not had "time to call on pity/For all that is sick, and heal and remake our city". What gives distinction to this part of the poem is the sharpness of the vision of the ordinary sights which are given an appalling significance in the context in which they are placed. The vision in the last section of the watchers at the well of life past whom "loaded with fear and crowned with every hope" the born stream past into life gives an extra dimension. It does not give easy consolation nor any answer to the question whether war will come, but conveys an enhanced sense of the mystery and greatness of human life even under the appalling threat.

Another dream, recorded in November 1957, was "about F. G. [Scott] my old friend, who has lately relapsed into senile decay, though a wonderful creature. I dreamed I met him, and that he was handsome and young, younger than when I first met him, a handsome and radiant young man in his twenties. At the same time I thought that my hair had grown quite white and very neatly barbered (it seemed to suit me)." This dream was not transformed into poetry, but a similar one was the origin of his poem, "The Brothers", about which he wrote to Kathleen Raine in January 1957:

> I'm trying to write one now about a dream I had recently about my two brothers, Willie and Johnny, dead fifty years ago. I watched them playing in a field, racing about in some game, and it was not a game which either of them was trying to win (there was no winning in it), and because of that they were infinitely happy in making each other happy, and all that was left in their hearts and their bodies was grace. It is very difficult to convey this in a poem. I had not thought of them for a long time. And when I did know them (I was little more than a boy then) there was affection, but also little grouses and jealousies, assertions of the will, a cloud of petty disagreements and passions which hid their true shape from me and from themselves. In the dream it seemed to me the cloud was dispelled and I saw them as they were. I'm sure Blake could have told me everything about it.

This was one of his own favourites among his poems.

Memory took him back to his parents too. In May 1958 he recorded:

> Suddenly thought of my father and mother to-day. Saw their goodness, their gentleness, their submission to their simple lot; thought that, if they had been known, they would have been called saints. How can I forget them for stretches of time, as if they had never been, and remember them only now and then. It is fifty years since my father died, and a few years

after my mother died too. How she must have suffered, living in that place, so strange to her. I realise this now, but I scarcely realised it then, I was too busy with my own discomforts in Glasgow. How cheerful she was, and how she sacrificed herself for us all. Human ingratitude is bottomless.

My father survived his coming to Glasgow only for a year. My mother had to suffer seeing Willie and Johnny dying, and it was Johnny's long and dreadfully cruel illness that brought on her own death. She was suffering herself from an inward pain, a tumour, but paid no attention to it, did not even tell of it, never complained but went on nursing her son. I remember one evening when Johnny threw his arms around her neck as she was bending over his bed—he had been complaining, driven mad with pain—and kissed her and asked her forgiveness. What things happen in life! Past imagination or invention or fantasy. And when Johnny was dead, and my mother went to see a doctor and was taken to hospital she died there in a few days. I remember still a day in Victoria Road, weeks after this, when I was walking back from my work in the evening catching sight of her on the pavement, and realising as I came nearer that it was not her, but a little woman somewhat like her, and becoming aware of the terrible difference between life and death: the finality of death. It is as if we cannot cherish those we love until we have lost them. We do not have enough humanity to be human. And how she would joke, so gently and light heartedly, and make up little rhymes to surprise and please us. And cook for us and look after us, she such a frail little woman. And I can forget her for weeks, for months, for years, as if she had never been. How hard the human heart is. I shall try to keep her in remembrance and make some recompense, after so long, and in remembering her simple and delicate humanity try to become more human myself. Perhaps I shall meet her again and have the infinite joy of her forgiveness. I do not know how to conceive immortality, though I still believe in it. If I meet her in another world, I know—and that is the infinite comfort—that I shall see her as she is, at last, the imperfections of mortality past, and that she will see me, and forgive me, for what I am. "And throughout all Eternity, I forgive you, you forgive me." What we desire above everything and what we can never find in this life. But remember, remember; we begin to die when we stop remembering.

Later he wrote in his poetry note-book ideas which might have been used for a poem:

About my father and mother
Realising long after their death their virtue and goodness.
How could they have been what they were but for Incarnation
The incarnation of a soul in a body
Simplicity, grace, infinite patience and kindness.

His thoughts went back too to his cousin Sutherland—no saint, but one whose failings were of the flesh rather than of the spirit; and he began to write a poem in which Sutherland soliloquises on wakening after death to find himself in heaven. This fine fragment brings vividly before us the Orkney sights and smells to which Sutherland wishes to get back out of an insubstantial heaven. The implication is perhaps that Sutherland is right to reject *this* heaven—different from Muir's Prometheus' conception of heaven as the home to which the god who was born of woman took back "all the spoils of time". Ideas for poems came to him on his solitary walks. 9 November 1957:

Towards evening went for my usual walk on the Station Road. Cold. While wandering along, I remembered the meeting between Penelope and Odysseus, and thought the only thing which identified him for her (after twenty years), was a brooch he described from memory, a brooch of beaten gold showing a dog and a fawn, the dog fastened to the fawn's throat, the fawn striking at him with its slender hoofs, the brooch lost now and the combat still going on, unchanged. She remembered it when he spoke of it. Then he spoke of the time when he was hunting in Parnassus and a wild boar gashed him on the thigh, far up. The scar was still there. The brooch and the scar, these were all that brought him back to her. For his hair was grey, his shoulders had shrunken, though his back was still straight, and his eyes were cold and pale, as if they had looked at things she would never know, or had been bleached in the snows of time. Were these enough to make her know in her heart he was Odysseus? A poem somewhere out of this.

The poem that grew out of this was "Penelope in Doubt", his final use of a story which had pre-occupied him for a long time.

Though he had used the story before this poem is quite new, dealing with the reunion of Penelope and Odysseus rather than the period of waiting, and treating more of the ordinary human feelings of Penelope, "near as a wife, and yet so far", rather than of emblematic meanings. I am not sure, however, that he managed to convey much in the poem which is not in the prose.

On his walks he was not always thinking of the past nor of themes from literature. He was keenly sensitive to what was immediately around him, though like Wordsworth he did not often make a present joy the matter of a song. One occasion when he did was after another walk "along the quiet road to the railway station. The evening extraordinarily still, bright clouds in the west, soft and suffused with all the colours of light flowing through them horizontally, yet lingering, reluctant to go. The trees along the road seemed conscious of this image of peace, and three horses in a field were subdued by it. Nothing which appeared to be unaware of it. Strange perfection of a common mood, sky and light and cloud and tree and the horses: I felt it too." This experience produced the poem "The Sunset"; in which more is added to what is already in the prose than in "Penelope in Doubt". In the poem we find "bush", not mentioned in the notebook, and much emphasis on fire as well as light. We are led to think of the burning bush in the Old Testament, and of the religious associations of fire. The personal experience is given the impersonality of art and wider significance.

Jottings in the poetry notebook show ideas which might have turned into poems if he had lived longer, for instance:

> Old Njal [The story of the burning of Njal and his family in their house appealed especially to him. Njal was a peacemaker. In his death he displayed "a kind of courage beyond the conception of the Vikings".[15]]
> Odin hanging from the tree, seven days and nights?
> Odysseus' meeting in Hades with his mother.
> David: That he should have seemed a man after God's heart.

---

[15] *Revisiting Orkney* [written for B.B.C., but never broadcast].

The dream: the traveller looking for a bed in Jerusalem at the Passover. Opens a door in a great inn; scene from a brothel. In haste tries another door; 13 men sitting at a table; something strange about them: they all look at him: he retreats. As he goes downstairs a man—one of the 13—stumbles past him and runs away.

He began to work out how this last subject might be treated: "Try to find an image or images for dense, sensual, sweaty misery of cities. Form—does not go with rhyme: an irregular measure?"

One is astonished at the freshness of some of these late poems of his. He was well aware of the temptation, that must come to all old men, merely to repeat himself. He wrote in April 1958 to Norman MacCaig:

I keep seeing poems by you everywhere, with friendly envy (if there is such a thing: I hope there is). How lovely to have the spring flowing freely . . . and not monotonously either, but with more variety than ever. I've been rather daunted in the last year or two by the fear that I am keeping on writing the same poem, and I fancy that it has inhibited (horrid word) the flow. I have written very few poems lately, but many parts of poems which ceased when they seemed to be taking the same old course. Some of the parts are quite good, I think, and perhaps the best thing I could do with them would be to integrate (another awful word) them in a longish poem: I don't know: that may be what they are best suited for.

MacCaig answered that, though the poems might exist in a circle round a common centre, they each pointed to that centre from a different angle. I think that some of the parts Muir mentions were "integrated" into "The Last War".

His last two poems were "The Day before the last Day" and "We have been taught . . .". The former reached the stage of being written out in typescript, but would probably have been further polished if he had had time. It originated from a re-reading of his own novel, *The Three Brothers*. In 1957 an American friend Joseph Summers sent him an article on his work,[16] in which he quoted a passage on one of David

---

[16] Later published in much reduced form in *The Massachusetts Review*, vol. II, no. 2 (Winter 1961).

Blackadder's dreams—the passage on the worm quoted above
p. 51. Muir wrote to him:

> I had forgotten that passage from 'The Three Brothers', and
> I was surprised to find that I wrote anything so good so long
> ago, in that very unequal story. I have not read the book for
> more than twenty years, and do not even have a copy of it now;
> my last remaining copy was lent to someone long ago. But the
> quotation does bring the past back very vividly, and not sadly;
> you were right—though how could you know?—that my main
> nausea was over at that time. I read the passage as if it were
> almost out of a book by someone else, and only gradually
> recognized it as my own: time plays strange tricks with us. I
> was glad to see it again.

He must have managed to get hold of a copy of the book, for
"The Day before the last Day" is based very closely on one of
David Blackadder's waking visions—that of the Last Judgment
near the end.

Lying in bed David thinks of how all things are eternally
present to God: "To Him, I thought, all is already finished,
and this present moment is not more visible to Him than the
Judgment Day and the accomplishment of all things." Then
there came to David himself a vision of the Last Day.

> I thought that I was standing naked on a vast plain covered by
> darkness. I stood without moving and I was alone; yet around
> me I was aware of a multitude without number which stretched
> from end to end of the earth; and each soul in that multitude
> was alone. Before me spread the ocean; yet how I knew this
> either I cannot tell; for darkness hid it; from end to end of it
> there was no sound nor motion; no wave lifted its head in it;
> and the stagnant water lay without advancing or retreating
> against the shore. And while we waited a dim light fell across
> our faces from the sky, and I saw the naked souls stretching
> from horizon to horizon, and they could not endure the light,
> but fell on their faces in wave after wave, and hid their faces
> on the ground. And I, too, fell on my face; yet I had no
> comfort of all that multitude, for each was alone. And as we
> lay the earth groaned and jarred, and behind me I heard the
> rending of wood, and the thundering of rocks, and the clanging
> of iron, as the graves and the caverns and the tombs burst open

to release those they had housed. And from the sea came sounds as of marine battle, and those who had been dead for a year or a thousand years came out with astonished eyes, and salt caking their beards, and strange sea creatures fastened like jewels or bright worms to their brows. And those living who had been at the point of death arose from their beds and came out and lay down again upon the earth. And women who had but then given birth came out with their newly born, and lay down, and laid their newly born babes beside them on the earth, and did not give them suck, but turned away from them. And lovers who had died in each other's arms walked out of their graves and lay down and looked not once at each other. And the souls who in life had been generous offered not to succour the rest, and those who had been greedy or feeble or deceivers craved not for succour. And the nice were not offended by their own or others' nakedness, and the proud complained not of their company. And the lecher did not lust after one woman among the many woman there, and the conqueror did not yearn to subdue his fellows, and seize universal empery over them, and the saint did not try to save them. For all thought but of themselves and the dawning of the Judgment Day.

And the sun rose over the sea, and I looked at it and thought: It has risen never to set again. And one by one the multitudes lifted themselves from the ground and stood and watched the sun moving up the heavens, and when it reached the zenith it stopped and moved no further. And when I saw it standing, it was as if a voice spoke within me: 'There shall be no more time, nor death, nor change, nor fear, nor hope, nor desire, nor secrecy, nor shame, nor need, nor endeavour, nor expectation.' And I thought that the voice spoke within everyone there, within the aged and the young, within those who had been dying and those who had but then been born; and great numbers, when they heard it, fell on their faces and grovelled in the dust, and called upon the earth to cover them, and upon the sea to swallow them up, because they could not endure that never-ending day. But there were others who were transfigured, and from their faces and limbs broke out a splendour as infinite as that endless glory and as unchanging as that sun fixed in the centre of the sky. And I thought: These are they which have endured to the end. Yet I knew not whether I was of them, or of those who could not face that everlasting brightness. And a voice spoke to me, "This is the heaven of the saved, built for them before the foundation of the world, but for the others it is a furnace seven times heated, where they will wander for ever and not once find rest or hope." And the voice said, "Choose! Choose!" but I stood, and my soul was filled with joy at the sight of the eternal day breaking, and with despair at the great sun standing in the sky, and I could not choose. And I thought of those who were neither hot nor cold, but were spued out of His mouth; and methought he whom I seemed to be cried out: "No, no! I am not of them!" And he turned to the ranks of the blessed—but then my thoughts failed and I could see no more.

I know not what it means, but this vision has brought me great comfort.[17]

It is interesting to see how this vision is used and modified in the new context in the poem. Thinking of David's vision Muir thought of the likenesses and differences between the situation of mankind awaiting the Last Judgment and of mankind awaiting the extermination which they might bring upon themselves by poisoning the atmosphere in an atomic war.

> If it could come to pass, and all kill all

then the end would be a

> Mechanical parody of the Judgment Day
> That does not judge but only deals damnation.

The end would be brought about not by God, but by man himself as a result of his own mastery of, or submission to, the machine. All would die; there would be no judgment, as between those who responded to the light and were transfigured and those who hid from the light. In the poem those awaiting death only dream that the sea gives up its dead. David's sense that at the point of death each was alone though in a multitude is taken up and given a new meaning. Mankind has not had pity on all that was sick nor healed and remade the city; and that is why they have come to this end. In the early vision David was aware—and believed all others to be so—of a voice within him proclaiming the end of time and death and change;

[17] *T. B.*, pp. 333-7.

and there was a choice open whether to respond to the endless
glory of the light or to reject it.   But in the later situation there
is no great voice crying, and there is no room for choice.   Silent
the dying think

> "Choose!   Choose again, you who have chosen this!
> Too late!   Too late!"

Mankind has chosen this end, and it is too late to undo the
consequences of their choice.   So the second vision, unlike the
first, brings no comfort.   But it should be remembered that
this is the day *before* the last day.   There is no implication that
the *last* day and God's judgment are not still to come.

It is fitting that this, his one from last poem, should show
him to the end honestly facing the worst; fitting too that his
very last one, "I have been taught . . .", should be an expression of gratitude and faith.   This is written at the end of his
last poetry notebook, and it is clear that a good deal more work
would have been done on it.   The published text, as revised in
the second edition of *Collected Poems*, is the best that can be
made of a difficult manuscript, and must be regarded as in
some places conjectural.   There is a special appropriateness in
this, his last word in poetry, being in this way unfinished; for
earlier he had written

> do not hope to find a sentence
> To tell what you have seen.   Stop at the colon:
> And set a silence after to speak the word
> That you will always seek and never find,
> Perhaps, if found, the good and beautiful end.
> You will not find that place.   So leave the hiatus
> There in the broken sentence.[18]

This last poem is a single broken sentence (I doubt whether full
stops should be printed at the ends of any of the stanzas except
the last).   There is a hiatus in it—after the first two lines (the
MS. shows that "And got" was intended to start a new stanza;
the poem should be six four-line stanzas).   The one long
sentence containing so many ideas within a whole suggests the
singleness and comprehensiveness of his vision; the brokenness

---

[18] "Images", in *C. P.*, p. 260.

suggests, albeit accidentally, the impossibility of ever fully embodying the vision in words. Like the final sentence of the *Autobiography* this final sentence of his poetry is an expression of gratitude—for what he has learned from dreams and fantasies, from ancestors and friends, especially his parents, from the founts, never spent, of traditional wisdom which have kept his feet

> from straying
> To the deadly path

> That leads into the sultry labyrinth
> Where all is bright and the flare
> Consumes and shrivels
> The moist fruit.

One cannot pin down exactly what is meant by the sultry labyrinth here. One thinks of the various labyrinths of fear in which he had at times believed himself to be imprisoned—of his childhood sense of guilt and isolation, of the loneliness and alienation of his time in Glasgow, of the more objective fears, for the world more than for himself, of his later years. At one stage the MS. read "where all is bright and false". Part of the meaning is that in the spiritual life the moist fruit is shrivelled by seemingly illuminating, but ultimately false, restrictive and unimaginative conceptions of life. To the dweller in the labyrinth time seems to be all and a prison. To the man of imaginative vision it is not all, nor is it a prison to be escaped from. Time, though it was growing shorter for him, is no longer thought of as an enemy. The version of the first line of the one from last stanza printed in the second edition of *Collected Poems* ("Have drawn at last from time which takes away") is somewhat conjectural, but is certainly nearer to his intention than that previously printed. What he wrote first was "But most I have learned from time which gives and takes away". He has learned from dreams and fantasies, from ancestors and friends, from the founts, but most from time itself, which he now sees as an image of eternity.

These poems have taken us near to the time of his death, and we must return to record briefly some of the events of his last two years. The mild winter of 1956-7 was spent quietly at

Swaffham Prior. At the end of May he went up to Edinburgh for a week to consult people in connexion with his ballad book; spent a memorable evening with some of his old Newbattle pupils, and gave a reading of his poems to the Poetry Reading Association. Back in Swaffham Prior he was troubled by chest pains and difficult breathing, but was able to work at a variety of literary projects—regular reviews, occasional poems, revising his script on Orkney for the B.B.C., editing a volume of poems by poets who had not been published in book form, helping and advising young friends.

Early in 1958 he went to Bristol for a month as visiting Professor under the Churchill Foundation. He gave two courses of four lectures each, to the students in the English department on Eliot and Yeats and to a larger audience on "The need for literature". In these latter lectures he developed themes he had touched on in his Harvard lectures, but they were not mere restatements. Summarising to Professor L. C. Knights, then Professor of English at Bristol, what he wanted to say he wrote:

> It is my belief that imagination is the main faculty by which we comprehend life, however imperfectly, and are able to know the people we know, including ourselves. It is employed at every level from the lowest to the highest, by people who never read a book, and by the greatest novelists and poets. The knowledge that it gives is not practical knowledge; yet as it is purely human it includes that too, and in the individual who possesses it, has an effect on practice.[19]

What impressed these his final audiences was the man himself even more than what he said—a man who was completely himself, without any disguise even on a formal occasion. Professor Knights writes:

> When I try to describe him I find I most want to say two things. One is that I have perhaps never known anyone who so combined gentleness and strength—the gentleness showing itself in a complete openness to the present experience and the present person; the strength in an unruffled acceptance of what had to be said and done, so that you would never imagine

---

[19] E. M. to Knights, 27 Dec. 1957.

him complaining—not even about the ties of regular reviewing
for money when there were other things he wanted to be at.
The second is that in his presence other people became more
completely themselves; quite unconsciously they dropped their
masks. I wish I could back this up with instances that would
recreate the impression. But all that remains is vivid memories
of things trivial in themselves, but carrying a sense of happy
ease and underlying gaiety. I remember the evening when,
before a dinner party given in his honour by the Vice-Chancellor,
Sir Philip Morris, he came to rest for an hour in our house, and
got absorbed in talk with two students from my wife's training
college who had come to 'sit' with our young children; when
we came into the room with our outdoor things on he looked up
in surprise and put the mildest of questions—'Are you going
out?'. I remember Edwin on his knees in an untidy kitchen
before a shapeless female guinea-pig crooning its name,
'Jennie, Jennie': my son had requested a poem on his pet and
Edwin was obviously wooing the Muses. . . . But none of this
could very well convey to others the quality of these moments.
I suppose what I am trying to convey is the elusive fragrance of
a rare integrity.

Early in June he was in Cambridge to get his honorary
Doctorate of Letters. "I was partnered with Hammerskjold in
the procession. . . . He is very nice and has a wide knowledge
of literature, though the only time he has left for it is in bed
each night before he goes to sleep. He complained that he has
no private life left".[20] This was, I think, his last journey
beyond the immediate neighbourhood of Swaffham Prior.
Later that month he was giving a talk on poetry in the nearby
village of Bottisham. Towards the end he was obviously in
distress, hardly able to summon up breath for speech. He was
found to have water on the lung. He was treated for this, and
by August was telling T. S. Eliot that he was breathing freely
again; he "had not realised for quite a while that breathing
could be such a pleasure". (Eliot wrote that he was deeply
moved by this last remark. Occasional human touches in the
rather formal and very courteous correspondence between
these two, mainly on publishing business, show them coming
closer together. They had always admired each other's

[20] E. M. to Marwick, 24 Jun. 1958.

U

criticism, but had taken different paths as poets. In a broadcast
Eliot admitted that, intent on his own development, he had
given little heed in early days to Muir's poetry. "But when I
came to study the volume of his *Collected Poems*, before publication, I was struck, as I had not been before, by the power of
his early work. Yet on the other hand it is still his late work
which seems to me the most remarkable." He thought that
Muir had been less concerned about technique than himself.
"But under the pressure of emotional intensity, and possessed
by his vision, he found almost unconsciously the right, the
inevitable way of saying what he wanted to say."[21] Muir too
felt at the end of his life that he had earlier not properly
appreciated the other's work, that he had read into his poetry
things which were not there and failed to see things which
were. He now thought of him as "the greatest poet and the
greatest critic of my time".[22] It is pleasant to watch the
convergence of these two great men, who were very different,
but who both had to an unusual degree the quality of integrity.)
By the autumn Muir was cheerfully reporting himself
"dehydrated". But he was iller than he knew. His wife tried
to get him to do nothing but rest, eat and sleep. But he had
several projects on hand. He was looking over his past work
for a new collected edition of his poems. John Hall's collection
of 1952 had really been a large selection. It was now proposed
that there should be a collection of all the poems up to 1956
which he wanted to preserve. Poems written since 1956 were
not to be included because he hoped soon to have enough for
a new small volume. Rather typically the work was delayed
by the fact that he did not have copies of all his own books;
but it was finished by the end of September. He was sorry
that nothing could be done about "that stiff language" in his
earlier work; but "was comforted in reading on to see that my
language began to reform itself." He added some twenty
poems left out by Mr Hall and all of *One Foot in Eden* except
five poems. These five include four which are perhaps his
most specifically Christian poems—in the sense of expressing
Christian beliefs as well as Christian attitudes. These omissions

[21] *The Listener*, 28 May 1964.
[22] MS. notes for a never-completed essay.

should not be taken to mean that he wanted to repudiate what he had tried to say in them; for he wrote to Eliot: "I have decided to leave out four of the religious poems, which seem to me now to be quite inadequate." Inadequacy to the subject is a sufficient reason for rejection in every case except perhaps "The Lord", which is quite powerful. It passionately, almost angrily, repudiates those

> Who say that lord is dead; when I can hear
> Daily his dying whisper in my ear.

Probably he did not like this poem because it is too declamatory, and because he had departed in it from his normal humble reticence about his inner religious life.

He was looking again at some of his early prose too. There was a project for a new and expanded version of *Essays on Literature and Society*, to include some new essays and perhaps some early ones which were out of print. He was held up here too by the lack of a copy of *Latitudes*. When one was obtained for him, he was dismayed by what he now thought the foolishness of most of it, but thought that a few of the essays might be worth reprinting in revised forms. He was never able to complete the revision.

While working as much as he could on his own literary projects, he seems to have been more excited about other people's publications than his own. He was pleased when the Hogarth Press on his recommendation accepted Bettina Linn's *A Letter to Elizabeth*, and even more so when they agreed to publish a volume of poems by his young Orkney friend George Mackay Brown. He took a keen interest in the latter, and gave detailed, though unassertive, advice as to which poems should be included.

In October he wrote cheerfully: "I think in a few months I shall be in better health than I have been for years." But in fact he was failing. He was easily tired, and was not able to do much work. His heart gave trouble again, and he had to take to bed. He needed constant attention, and his neighbour Bernard Gill sometimes took a turn at sitting with him: "Not much was said at these vigils—Edwin was too weak to talk—but much was communicated. In his presence was

U 2

tranquillity, the aura of a man modest, considerate, religious, utterly sincere, a personality 'rooted and grounded in love'." By Christmas the end was near, and two days later he was taken to Addenbrooks Hospital in Cambridge, where he died on the 3rd of January 1959. "Shortly before he was taken off to hospital," Mrs Muir records, "he said to me, with great urgency: 'There are no absolutes, no absolutes'. He was then in a confused state, but he said it with such force that it was poignant. I said: 'No, darling, there are no absolutes at all,' and he was comforted. I don't know myself what to make of it, unless he meant that even death was not an absolute; but there it is."[23]

He was buried in the churchyard at Swaffham Prior under the two towers he had loved to look out at. On his tombstone are inscribed words from his poem "Milton":

> his unblinded eyes
> Saw far and near the fields of Paradise.

About a year later a friend dreamed that she was walking with him in the country. At first she seemed to be leading, but after a time she realised that it was he who was leading. They went into a house, and upstairs into a high, dimly-lit room. He went up to a wall, touched it and seemed to vanish suddenly through it into a sunlit world beyond. After a little she too found herself out of the dimness in a realm of splendour full of light and the song of birds. In life by being what he was as well as by his words and after death by his poems he led and will lead many, unobtrusively, to share his vision.

[33] Michael Hamburger, "Edwin Muir", in *Encounter*, December 1960, p. 52.

Bibliography

I. WORKS BY EDWIN MUIR

Those who require full bibliographical details of Muir's published works may consult R. Hollander's *Textual and Bibliographical Study of the Poems of Edwin Muir*, and E. W. Mellown's *Bibliography of the Writings of Edwin Muir*, both listed below, § II. 1.

1. PUBLISHED IN MUIR'S OWN WORKS

(a) Verse

First Poems. London (Hogarth) 1925; New York (Huebsch) 1925.
Chorus of the Newly Dead. London (Hogarth) 1926.
Six Poems. Limited edn, Warlingham (Samson Press) 1932. Repr. (except one poem) in *Journeys and Places*.
Variations on a Time Theme. London (Dent) 1934.
Journeys and Places. London (Dent) 1937.
The Narrow Place. London (Faber) 1943.
The Voyage and other Poems. London (Faber) 1946.
The Labyrinth. London (Faber) 1949.
Collected Poems 1921–1951. Ed. J. C. Hall. London (Faber) 1952; New York (Grove) 1953, 1957.
Prometheus. Illustr. John Piper. London (Faber) 1954. Repr. in *One Foot in Eden*.
One Foot in Eden. London (Faber) 1956; New York (Grove) 1956.
Collected Poems 1921–1958. London (Faber) 1960; second edn, with some minor corrections and the addition of one poem, London (Faber) 1963; with preface by T. S. Eliot, New York (Oxford U.P.) 1965.
Selected Poems. Ed. T. S. Eliot. London (Faber) 1965.

(b) Prose

We Moderns. Under the pseudonym "Edward Moore". London (Allen & Unwin) 1918; New York (Knopf) 1920.
Latitudes. London (Melrose) 1924; New York (Heubsch) 1924.
Transition. London (Hogarth) 1926; New York (Viking) 1926.
The Marionette. London (Hogarth) 1927; New York (Viking) 1927.
The Structure of the Novel. London (Hogarth) 1928; New York (Harcourt, Brace) 1929.

John Knox—Portrait of a Calvinist. London (Cape) 1929; New York (Viking) 1929.

The Three Brothers. London (Heinemann) 1931; New York (Doubleday) 1931.

Poor Tom. London (Dent) 1932.

Scottish Journey. London (Heinemann) 1935.

Social Credit and the Labour Party. A pamphlet. London (Nott) 1935.

Scott and Scotland. London (Routledge) 1936; New York (Speller) 1938.

The Present Age, from 1914. (*Introductions to English Literature* Vol. v.) London (Cresset) 1939; New York (McBride) 1940.

The Story and the Fable. London (Harrap) 1940.

The Scots and their Country. A pamphlet. London (British Council: Longmans) 1946.

The Politics of King Lear. Glasgow (Jackson) 1947. Repr. in *Essays on Literature and Society.*

Essays on Literature and Society. London (Hogarth) 1949. Second edn, revised and with the addition of six previously uncollected essays, London (Hogarth) 1965; Cambridge (Harvard U.P.) 1965.

An Autobiography. A reprint of *The Story and the Fable,* with some revisions, and seven new chapters. London (Hogarth) 1954; New York (Sloane) 1954. Second edn, London (Methuen) 1965.

The Estate of Poetry. London (Hogarth) 1962; Cambridge (Harvard U.P.) 1962.

2. PUBLISHED IN OTHER BOOKS

"Introductory Notes", in the Muirs' translations of Kafka, *The Castle* (London 1930), and *The Great Wall of China* (London 1933), both listed below, § I. 4.

"Introductory Essay", in Robert Frost, *Selected Poems.* London (Cape) 1936.

"Franz Kafka", in *A Franz Kafka Miscellany.* New York (Twice a Year) 1940.

Text in A. Zyw, *Poles in Uniform: Sketches of the Polish Army, Navy and Air Force.* Edinburgh (Nelson) 1943.

"Poznámka k Franzi Kafkovi", in *Franza Kafka in Praha* (Prague 1947). Repr. in *Essays on Literature and Society.*

"A Tribute", in *T. S. Eliot, A Symposium.* Edd. R. Marsh and Tambimuttu. London (Editions Poetry London) 1948.

"Preface", in George Mackay Brown, *The Storm and Other Poems,* Kirkwall (Orkney) 1954.

"Preface", in *Annals of Scotland.* Edinburgh (B.B.C.) 1956.

"Translating from the German", in *On Translation.* Ed. Reuben A. Brower. (Harvard U.P.) 1959.

"Preface", in *New Poets 1959.* Ed. Edwin Muir. London (Eyre & Spottiswoode) 1959.

3. PUBLISHED IN PERIODICALS & NEWSPAPERS

In this connection, see especially E. W. Mellown's *Bibliography of the Writings of Edwin Muir*, listed below, § II. 1.

(a) Poems

Most of Muir's poems appeared originally in periodicals. When they were collected into volume form amendments were sometimes made. For the variants and for those poems which have never been collected see Hollander's *Bibliography*, listed below, § II. 1. One unimportant item, "Utopia" (*New Age* 16 Apr. 1914), is not in Hollander.

(b) Reviews

Mellown lists about 850, not including those unsigned early reviews which cannot be identified with certainty. The great majority are in *New Age* (1920–4), *Freeman* (1922–4), *Athenaeum* (1920–1; anon, but identified by Mellown from marked copies), *Nation and Athenaeum* (1924–9), *Listener* (1933–57, practically all by 1945), *Scotsman* (1934–45), *London Mercury* (1935–9), *New Statesman* (1933–58, mostly 1956–8), *Observer* (1948–58).

(c) Articles, etc.

Most of the best were collected in *Latitudes*, *Transition*, and *Essays on Literature and Society*. The following is a selection of uncollected ones:

"New Values". Under the pseudonym "Edward Moore". In the *New Age*, xxv (1919), pp. 345–6, 409–10, and xxvi (1919) pp. 39–40.

"Our Generation". Under the pseudonym "Edward Moore". In the *New Age* from xxviii (11 Nov. 1920) to xxxi (28 Sep. 1922) every issue except those for 27 Oct. 1921, 9 Feb. 1922 and 9 Mar. 1922, contains "Our Generation".

"At Salzburg", in the *New Age*, xxxiii (1923), pp. 231–2.

"Hugo von Hofmannsthal", in the *Freeman*, viii (1923), pp. 152–4.

"Sehnsucht in German Poetry", in the *Freeman*, viii (1923), pp. 178–80.

"The Meaning of Romanticism", in the *Freeman*, viii (1923–4) pp. 368–70, 416–8, 443–4.

"Arnold Bennett", in the *Calendar of Modern Letters*, i (1925), pp. 290–6. Repr. in *Scrutinies* (1928), ed. Edgell Rickword, pp. 16–27.

"Parallels", in the *Modern Scot*, i (1930), pp. 6–10.

"Reynard the Fox", in the *New Statesman*, xxxvi (1930), pp. 112–3.

"A Note on Hans Carossa", in the *Bookman* (New York), lxxii (1930). pp. 404–8.

"Virginia Woolf", in the *Bookman* (New York) lxxiv (1931), pp. 362–7.

"Hermann Broch", in the *Modern Scot*, iii (1932), pp. 103–10.

"Bolshevism and Calvinism", in the *European Quarterly*, i (1934), pp. 3–11.

"Contemporary Scottish Poetry", in the *Bookman* (London), LXXXVI (1934). pp. 282–3.

"An Enquiry". Six answers to questions on poetry, in *New Verse*, 11 (1934), p. 17.

"Yesterday's Mirror: Afterthoughts to an Autobiography", in the *Scots Magazine* (New Series), XXXIII (1940), pp. 404–10.

"The Decline of Imagination", a broadcast talk, in *The Listener*, XLV (1951), pp. 753–4.

"Toys and Abstractions", in the *Saltire Review*, IV (1957), pp. 36–7.

4. TRANSLATIONS BY EDWIN & WILLA MUIR

All items marked † were translated by Mrs Muir alone.

ASCH, SHOLEM. *Three Cities*. London (Gollancz) 1933; New York (Putman) 1933.

——. *Salvation*. London (Gollancz) 1934; New York (Putman) 1934.

——. *Mottke the Thief*. London (Gollancz) 1935; New York (Putman) 1935.

——. *The Calf of Paper*. London (Gollancz) 1936; entitled *The War Goes On*, New York, (Putman) 1936.

BROCH, HERMANN. *The Sleepwalkers*. London (Secker) 1932; Boston (Little, Brown) 1932.

——. *The Unknown Quality*. London (Collins) 1935; New York (Viking) 1925.

——. † "A Passing Cloud", in the *Modern Scot*, IV 1934, pp. 304–12.

BURCKHARDT, CARL J. *Richelieu*. London (Allen and Unwin) 1940; New York (Oxford U.P.) 1940.

CAROSSA, HANS. † *A Roumanian Diary*, tr. "Agnes Neill Scott". London (Secker) 1929; New York (Knopf) 1930.

——. † *A Childhood*, tr. "Agnes Neill Scott". London (Secker) 1930; New York (Cape and Smith) 1932.

——. † *Boyhood and Youth*, tr. "Agnes Neill Scott". London (Secker) 1931; New York (Warren and Putman) 1932.

——. † *Doctor Gion*, tr. "Agnes Neill Scott". London (Secker) 1933; New York (Ballon) 1933.

FEUCHTWANGER, LION. *Jew Süss*. London (Secker) 1926; entitled *Power*, New York (Viking) 1926.

——. *The Ugly Duchess*. London (Secker) 1927; New York (Viking) 1928.

——. *Two Anglo-Saxon Plays: The Oil Islands* and *Warren Hastings*. New York (Viking) 1928; London (Secker) 1929.

——. *Success*. London (Secker) 1930; New York (Viking) 1930.

——. *Josephus*. London (Secker) 1932; New York (Viking) 1932.

——. *The Jew of Rome*. London (Hutchinson) 1935; New York (Viking) 1936.

——. *The False Nero*. London (Hutchinson) 1937; entitled *The Pretender*, New York (Viking) 1937.

In the American edition of Feuchtwanger's *Paris Gazette*, New York (Viking) 1940, the translation is attributed to the Muirs. Mrs Muir, however, says this was an error.

GLAESER, ERNST. *Class of 1902.* London (Secker) 1929; New York (Viking) 1929.

HARSÁNYI, ZSOLT DE. *Through a Woman's Eyes.* New York (Putnam) 1940; entitled *Through the Eyes of a Woman*, London (Routledge) 1941.

——. *Lover of Life.* New York (Putnam) 1942.

The Muirs' part in these translations was merely to polish the English.

HAUPTMANN, GERHART. *Dramatic Works* Vol. VII (contains *Indipohdi*, *The White Saviour*, and *A Winter Ballad*). London (Secker) 1925; New York (Huebsch) 1925.

——. *The Island of the Great Mother.* London (Secker) 1925; New York (Huebsch) 1925.

——. *Dramatic Works* Vol. IX (contains *Veland*, the translation of which is credited to Edwin Muir alone). London (Secker) 1929; New York (Huebsch) 1929.

HEUSER, KURT. *The Inner Journey.* London (Secker) 1932; entitled *The Journey Inward*, New York (Viking) 1932.

KAFKA, FRANZ. *The Castle.* London (Secker) 1930; New York (Knopf) 1930.

——. *The Great Wall of China.* London (Secker) 1933; New York (Schocken) 1946.

——. *The Trial.* London (Gollancz) 1937; New York (Knopf) 1937.

——. *America.* London (Routledge) 1938; Norfolk (New Directions) 1940.

——. *Parables in German and English.* New York (Schocken) 1947.

——. *In the Penal Settlement.* London (Secker) 1948; New York (Schocken) 1948.

——. "Aphorisms," in the *Modern Scot*, III (1932), pp. 202–8.

——. † "First Sorrow", in the *European Quarterly*, I (1934), pp. 46–9.

——. "From Kafka's Diaries: Excerpts", in the *New Statesman*, XXXI (1941), pp. 321–2.

——. † "Selections from Diaries and Notebooks of Franz Kafka", in *Orion*, I (1945), pp. 104–15.

KÜHNELT-LEDDIHN, ERIK MARIA VON. *Night over the East.* London (Sheed and Ward) 1936; New York (Oxford U.P.) 1936.

LOTHAR, ERNST. *Little Friend.* London (Secker) 1933; New York (Putnam) 1933.

——. *The Mills of God*, London (Secker) 1935; entitled *The Loom of Justice*, New York (Putnam) 1935.

MANN, HEINRICH. *The Hill of Lies.* London (Jarrolds) 1934; New York (Dutton) 1935.

NEUMANN, ROBERT. *The Queen's Doctor.* London (Gollancz) 1936; New York (Knopf) 1936.

——. *A Woman Screamed.* London (Cassell) 1938; New York (Dial) 1938.

PALÉOLOGUE, GEORGES M. *The Enigmatic Czar*. London (Hamish Hamilton) 1938; New York (Harper) 1938.

RENN, LUDWIG (pseudonym of Arnold Friedrich Vieth von Golssenau). *War*. London (Secker) 1929; New York (Dodd, Mead) 1929.

——. *After War*. London (Secker) 1931; New York (Dodd, Mead) 1931.

RHEINHARDT, E. A. *The Life of Eleonora Duse*. London (Secker) 1930.

WINSLOE, C. (Baroness Hatvany). † *The Child Manuela*, tr. "Agnes Neill Scott". New York (Farrar and Rinehart) 1933; London (Chapman and Hall) 1934.

——. † *Life Begins*, tr. "Agnes Neill Scott". London (Chapman and Hall) 1935; entitled *Girl Alone*, New York (Farrar and Rinehart) 1936.

II. WORKS ABOUT EDWIN MUIR

1. BIBLIOGRAPHIES

HOLLANDER, ROBERT. *A Textual and Bibliographical Study of the Poems of Edwin Muir*. Unpublished thesis available in the National Library of Scotland, Edinburgh University Library, and Columbia University Library.

MELLOWN, ELGIN W. *Bibliography of the Writings of Edwin Muir*. Alabama (University of Alabama) 1964; revised edn, London (Nicholas Vane) 1966.

2. BOOKS AND ARTICLES

For an extensive list of reviews and other writings about Muir see Hollander's *Bibliography*, listed above, § II. 1.

BLACKMUR, R. P. "Edwin Muir: Between the Tiger's Paws", in the *Kenyon Review*, XXI (1959), pp. 419–36.

BRUCE, GEORGE. "Edwin Muir: Poet", in the *Saltire Review*, VI (1959) pp. 12–6.

BUTTER, P. H. *Edwin Muir*. Edinburgh (Oliver & Boyd) 1962; New York (Grove) 1962.

COX, C. B. "Edwin Muir's 'The Horses' ", *Critical Survey*, I (1962), pp. 19–21.

ELIOT, T. S. "Mr. Edwin Muir", *The Times*, 7 Jan. 1959, p. 14.

——. "Introduction" to a series of broadcasts, in *The Listener*, 28 May 1964, p. 872.

GARDNER, HELEN. *Edwin Muir*. A lecture. Cardiff (University of Wales) 1961.

GILL, BERNARD. "Sunset Light: A Poet's Last Days" in the *Western Humanities Review*, XIV (1960), pp. 283–8.

GRICE, FRED. "The Poetry of Edwin Muir", in *Essays in Criticism*, V (1955), pp. 243–52.

GRIEVE, C. M. In *Contemporary Scottish Studies*, pp. 108–19. London (Parsons) 1926.

——. ("Hugh MacDiarmid"). "Introduction" in the *Golden Treasury of Scottish Poetry*, pp. xvi–xxxii. London (MacMillan) 1946.

HALL, J. C. *Edwin Muir*, in the series "Writers and their Work", No. 71. London (Longmans) 1956.

HAMBURGER, MICHAEL. "Edwin Muir", in *Encounter*, 87 (1960), pp. 46–53.

HOLLOWAY, JOHN. "The Poetry of Edwin Muir", in *The Hudson Review*, XIII (1960–1), pp. 550–67.

JENNINGS, ELIZABETH. "Edwin Muir as Poet and Allegorist", in the *London Magazine*, VII (1960), pp. 43–56.

MILLS, R. J. *"Edwin Muir: A Speech from Darkness Grown"*, in *Accent*, XIX (1959), pp. 50–70.

——. "Edwin Muir on Poetry", in *The Christian Scholar*, XLV (1962), pp. 238–48.

——. "Eden's Gate: The Later Poetry of Edwin Muir", in *The Personalist*, XLIV (1963), pp. 58–78.

MORGAN, EDWIN. "Edwin Muir", in *The Review*, 5 (1963) pp. 3–10.

O'CONNOR, PHILIP. In *The Lower View*, pp. 175–88. London (Faber) 1960. An account of an interview with Muir.

ORAGE, A. R. In *Selected Essays and Critical Writings*, pp. 165–72. London (Nott) 1935. A review of *We Moderns*.

RAINE, KATHLEEN. "Edwin Muir: An Appreciation", in the *Texas Quarterly*, IV (1961), pp. 233–45.

SUMMERS, JOSEPH. "The Achievement of Edwin Muir", in the *Massachusetts Review*, II (1961), pp. 240–60.

TSCHUMI, RAYMOND. In *Thought in Twentieth Century English Poetry*, pp. 74–118. London (Routledge and Kegan Paul) 1951.

WATSON, J. R. "Edwin Muir", in the *Critical Quarterly*, VI (1964) pp. 231–49.

III. OTHER BOOKS CITED IN THE TEXT

Autobiography of David. See RAYMOND, ERNEST.

GUGGENHEIM, PEGGY. *Out of this Century.* New York (Dial) 1946.

LEWIS, WYNDHAM. *Apes of God.* London (Arthur) 1930.

MARCEL, GABRIEL. "On the Ontological Mystery" in *The Philosophy of Existence*, tr. Manya Harari. London (Harvill) 1948.

——. *The Decline of Wisdom*, tr. Manya Harari. London (Harvill) 1954.

MARWICK, HUGH. *Orkney.* London (Robert Hale) 1951.

Modern Poet, The. See MURPHY GWENDOLEN.

MURPHY, GWENDOLEN. Editor, *The Modern Poet.* London (Sidgwick and Jackson) 1938.

NICOLL, MAURICE. *Dream Psychology.* London (Hodder and Stoughton) 1917.

NICOLL, MAURICE. *Psychological Commentaries on the Teaching of Gurdjieff and Ouspensky.* London (Vincent Stuart) 1952.

——. *Living Time.* London (Vincent Stuart) 1952.

NEITZSCHE, FRIEDRICH. *The Joyful Wisdom,* tr. T. Common. Edinburgh and London (Foulis) 1910.

——. *Thus Spoke Zarathustra,* tr. R. J. Hollingdale. Harmondsworth (Penguin) 1951.

POTTS, PAUL. *Dante Called you Beatrice.* London (Eyre and Spottiswood) 1960.

PROUST, MARCEL. *Remembrance of Things Past* Vol. XII, tr. Stephen Hudson. London (Chatto and Windus) 1931.

RAYMOND, ERNEST. Editor, *Autobiography of David.* London (Gollancz) 1946.

INDEX

I

WRITINGS OF EDWIN MUIR

II